GREENPEACE
CAPTAIN

Bizarre wanderings on the Rainbow Warrior

Peter Willcox
with Ronald B. Weiss

SANDSTONEPRESS
HIGHLAND | SCOTLAND

Published in Great Britain by
Sandstone Press Ltd
Dochcarty Road
Dingwall
Ross-shire
IV15 9UG
Scotland.

www.sandstonepress.com

All rights reserved.
No part of this publication may be reproduced,
stored or transmitted in any form without the express
written permission of the publisher.

Copyright © Peter Willcox 2016
All maps © Cameron Jones
Drawing of Pete Seeger © Leo Hartshon
Notepaper art before Chapter 17 courtesy of
Maggie Willcox and gratefully acknowledged

The moral right of Peter Willcox to be recognised as the
author of this work has been asserted in accordance with the
Copyright, Design and Patent Act, 1988.

Greenpeace Captain was first published in the United States of America
and Canada by Thomas Dunne Books, an imprint of St Martin's Press.

The publisher acknowledges support from
Creative Scotland towards publication of this volume.

ISBN: 978-1-910985-52-6
ISBNe: 978-1-910985-53-3

Cover design by Mark Swan
Picture layout by Raspberry Creative Type, Edinburgh
Typeset by Iolaire Typesetting, Newtonmore
Printed and bound by Totem, Poland

This book is dedicated to my father,
Roger Willcox, who passed along his love of sailing
and his belief in working for a better planet.

Contents

List of Illustrations

Cover image. The second Rainbow Warrior. © Greenpeace/Daniel Beltra

1. Me steering my family's 36' Alden Coastwise Cruiser *Luau*. I was probably imitating my paternal grandfather with the pipe.

2. At the helm of the good ship *Clearwater*, probably the late 1970's. Note the eagle's head carved into the end of the long wooden tiller. © Marty Gallanter (Clearwater)

3. Maggy Aston (her maiden name. We got married 35 years later.) and me in 1978, my third year as Captain of the *Clearwater*.

4. The Greenpeace version of a 'Seal Team', heading out to spray paint baby seals (to protect them from being hunted for their fur), with the *Rainbow Warrior* in the background surrounded by pack ice. © Greenpeace/Pierre Gleizes

5. The Soviet warship that chased *Rainbow Warrior* off the shores of Lorino after we engaged with the Soviet freighter *Tanwet*. © Rick Dawson

6. Jim Henry in an inflatable on his way to Nome, Alaska, carrying film evidence of the commercial scale whale hunting and mink farms. © Rick Dawson

7. *Rainbow Warrior* on her side in Auckland, New Zealand, after French commandos planted two bombs on her hull and sunk her, killing our photographer, Fernando Periera. © Greenpeace/John Miller

8. A New Zealand investigator standing in the hole caused by the first of the French bombs. © Gil Hanly

9. Fernando Pereira, probably in the Marshall Islands around the time of the evacuation of Rongelap. © Greenpeace

10. Many children on Rongelap had birth defects. It is impossible to say for sure if radiation caused this particular girl's deformities, but it seems highly likely. © Greenpeace/Fernando Pereira

11. Andy Biederman, our ship's doctor, and a deckhand (centre, wearing shorts) and Davey Edward, our chief engineer (right) assisting one of the Rongelapese. © Greenpeace/Fernando Pereira

12. Rongelapese children on the deck of *Rainbow Warrior*. © Greenpeace/Fernando Pereira

13. Me at the bow, a knife-edge, of the destroyer after it stopped, but before the crew aimed their firehoses at me. © Greenpeace

14. I'm sure the sailors on the bow were enjoying this much more than I was. After a while, someone else took my place and I was brought back to our ship, the *Moby Dick*, to warm up and rest. © Greenpeace

15. In October of 1993, we brought *Greenpeace* to the Sea of Japan to prove that the Russians were dumping nuclear waste. Here, Dima Litvinov and I are communicating with a Russian tanker. © Greenpeace/Hiroto Kiryu

16. Our activists got close to the radioactive tanker with a Geiger counter, which showed exceedingly high readings. © Greenpeace/Hiroto Kiryu

17. Crizel Jane Valencia, a six year old girl, and her family lived in one of the most polluted areas of Clark Air Force Base, Philippines. Crizel was dying from acute myeloid leukemia. © Jonathan Taylor

18. Although Crizel was terminally ill, this brave and creative little girl made some drawings that we used in our February 2000 toxics tour of Asia.

19. The forklift and container filled with toxic waste that I drove through the crowded streets of Manila was resisted by a security guard. © Greenpeace/ Shailendra Yashwant

20. Jack Weinberg (in the blazer), Von Hernandez, our Filipino campaigner (blue shirt) and Yours Truly (in the sporty orange jumpsuit) waited to be arrested outside the US Embassy in Manila. © Greenpeace/Shailendra Yashwant

21. Since I was the driver of the forklift, I was the first to be arrested. Here I am practicing passive resistance, not struggling in any way but making it as difficult as possible. © Greenpeace/Shailendra Yashwant

22. A shot of the second *Rainbow Warrior* with her banner sails during the tour protesting illegal 'blood lumber' from countries such as Liberia.

23. The note that one of our activists was handed by Liberian stowaways while they were boarding the *Meltemi*. © Ken Lowyck

24. A Guardia Civil (the Spanish military force that performs police duties) jumping into one of our boats attempting to block the *Meltemi's* pilot ladder during our second action against her. © Greenpeace/Daniel Beltra'

25. While the *Meltemi* was able to come into the harbor, we still had activists up in her cranes and rigging to prevent the unloading of the cargo. © Greenpeace/Daniel Beltra'

26. At Vlissingen, Netherlands, to prevent the *Balaban* I unloading illegally logged wood from the Amazon, one of our boats was lifted almost forty feet by a towline being used to manoeuvre the cargo ship. © Greenpeace/ David Sims

27. The *Arctic Sunrise* heading up the Amazon river. © Greenpeace/Rodrigo Bale'ia

28. In many places along the Amazon, people are burning and clear-cutting forest preserves, national parks and privately owned land. © Greenpeace/ Daniel Beltra'

29. Melt pools on the Petermann Glacier, Greenland, reflect the blue of the sky perfectly. © Nick Cobbing/Greenpeace

30. My office has a terrific view. © Nick Cobbing/Greenpeace

31. This polar bear mother might not understand the big picture, but she has a better idea than most of us of the implications if we don't. © Larissa Beumer/Greenpeace

32. This iceberg has a hole through it called a 'moulin', probably a drainage channel for melt water in a glacier, before the iceberg flipped. They often flip suddenly. I see it as a metaphor for climate change. © Nick Cobbing/ Greenpeace

33. Probably taken at the Nioghalvfjerdsbrae, where our observations and findings were indicating an on-going disaster. © Nick Cobbing/Greenpeace
34. The Russian patrol ship/icebreaker *Ladoga*. You can make out the cannon she was firing just above her hull number 058. © Denis Sinyakov/Greenpeace
35. Marco Paolo Weber hanging on the lines the team slingshotted over the rig's heavier mooring lines. © Denis Sinyakov/Greenpeace
36. You can see the machine guns and knives being wielded at us during the muscular response from the *Ladoga*. © Denis Sinyakov/Greenpeace
37. *Arctic Sunrise* being boarded by commandos who were rappelling to the deck from a big black chopper. © Denis Sinyakov/Greenpeace
38. 'Bail denied.' © Dmitri Sharomov/Greenpeace
39. Home sweet home. This cell is very similar to the one I occupied but more "luxurious" because it has a real radiator.
40. A view of the Murmansk prison and the city. And this is before winter really set in. © Greenpeace
41. Maggy in our apartment above my folk's place in Norwalk, CT. This portrait was taken by a local newspaper shortly after we were arrested. © Alex von Kleydorff (TBD)
42. On the day of our arrest, Greenpeace USA staff stood in front of the Russian ambassador's residence in Washington, DC. © Greenpeace/Mitchell Wenkus
43. Support for the 'Arctic 30', comprising the 28 crew, including me and two independent photo/video journalists who were arrested, spread rapidly. Here a group protests outside the Russian embassy in London. © John Cobb/Greenpeace
44. Jude Law, the actor, and Paul Simonon (of the punk band "The Clash" to the right) are protesting in front of the Russian Embassy on October 5th, the Day of Solidarity. © John Cobb/Greenpeace
45. A Day of Solidarity protest in front of the Gwanghwamun gate, the entrance of the Gyeongbokgung Palace in Seoul, South Korea.
46. It's a pretty safe bet that this protest took place at the highest altitude. That's Mount Everest in the background. © Zhou Li/Greenpeace
47. The Kresty prison showing its age. © Igor Podgorny/Greenpeace
48. November 22, 2013. The day of my release. © Dmitri Sharomov/Greenpeace
49. My eldest daughter, Anita, participating in an 'Free the Arctic 30' protest, one of many around the world.
50. My younger daughter, Natasha, pointing to a poster at the protest in Village Creek, where I grew up.
51. Greeting my wife Maggy at the airport in St. Petersburg. © Dmitri Sharomov/Greenpeace

In what we do we have to try to live out what human beings want to be and yearn for, and with every single action, act of confrontation and statement, we have to inspire people's imagination and motivate them to start making their own dreams come true.

–Harald Zindler, *Greenpeace*

What he said.

–Peter Willcox

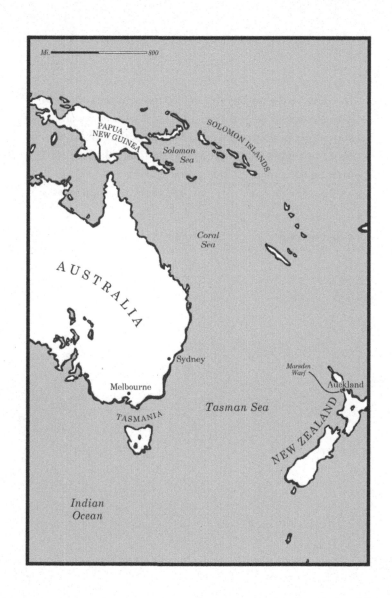

1

"It's Over"

JULY 10, 1985
MARSDEN WHARF
AUCKLAND, NEW ZEALAND
PREPARING FOR AN ANTINUCLEAR ACTION IN FRENCH POLYNESIA

Whump!

A large shiver went through the entire ship and woke me from a dead sleep. I didn't so much hear it as feel it. Disoriented and in the dark, I tried to make sense of what had just happened. As the captain of the *Rainbow Warrior* I knew that whatever that *whump* was, it wasn't good. My sleepy mind slowly began to run through the possibilities. The adrenaline hadn't hit me yet.

Had we collided with another ship? Possibly. *Were we at fault?* I looked out the porthole in my captain's cabin. We were tied up at the dock–Marsden Wharf, in New Zealand–so if there *had* been a collision, at least we weren't responsible. *Well, that's a relief,* I thought, glad to know that whatever had just happened wasn't my fault. Even though I was only partly alert, at least my career survival instinct was intact.

What had caused that sound? It definitely wasn't part of the routine noise of the ship. In fact, *none* of the normal sounds of the ship could be heard. The generator, which supplies electricity to the ship, was strangely silent. The comforting, ever-present hum wasn't there: another sign that something was seriously wrong. The generator is a lot like your pulse or breathing—a ship's basic sign of life. The *Rainbow Warrior*'s heartbeat had stopped. Still, we were at the dock, so how bad could it be?

Strange . . . I reached up in the dark for my glasses, which for the past four years had always been stowed on a small bookshelf just above my pillow. They were gone. *That's really weird.* They'd remained in that exact location through storm-tossed seas and all kinds of actions ("actions" are Greenpeace's term for engagements with the "enemy"), yet they had been dislodged by the *whump.* Another sign of something wrong, but what?

I reached for my clothes, which I had slung over the back of my chair next to my bed, but they weren't there either. I fumbled around in the dark looking for them for a few seconds. I stumbled over the toppled chair. *What the fuck? Earthquake?* Clothes or no clothes, as captain I had to find out what was going on, so I grabbed a towel for modesty and dashed out of my cabin into the hallway.

The emergency lighting was on in the hall in the main companionway—another very bad sign. The five-watt bulbs cast a dull light that was just enough to see by. At the engine room door, a small group of the crew was standing near the doorway and looking down. Davey Edward—our chief engineer—was there. He had rushed to his engine room—right after what seemed to him to be an explosion—worried that something down there had caused it. As I came up to him, he said the last thing I expected–or wanted–to hear. "It's over, she is done with, finished." When your chief engineer says that, you can be pretty sure it's a fact.

Looking down into the engine room, I could see water had almost filled the compartment, and was already rising dangerously close to the main deck where we were standing. It made no sense at all. The ship had a massive steel bulkhead door to prevent flooding between the hold (the wide, open cargo area belowdecks) and the theater. At sea, that door was always closed as a safety precaution. At the dock, however, it was always left open, and something had caused massive flooding in an incredibly short period of time.

Whatever the cause, the effect was clear. Davey and I locked eyes and I knew what had to be done. I said in my command voice: "Let's get everyone off the ship and onto the dock, and then we'll figure it out from there." Even as a relatively young captain, I knew that the safety of the crew was the first priority. Davey and I both realized that if the engine room had flooded, the lower accommodations–which were on the same level–would be underwater too. I hoped like hell that no one was down there, but I had to walk back aft toward the lower accommodations to see for myself.

As I got to the stairs going down, I saw Martini Gotje at the bottom of the steps. He had arrived there first, and had immediately gone to the crew's sleeping quarters in the area that seemed to be in the most danger. Andy Biedermann had gone down right before him, and gotten our temporary cook, Margaret Mills, out of her bunk. I felt, rather than heard, the ship lift under my feet.

Whump!

Another shock wave–less than two minutes after the first.

Was the New Zealand navy firing at us? At the dock? It was the only thing I could think of, and that didn't seem very likely. Whatever was going on, it didn't make sense and it wasn't over. I looked down at Martini and told him to pass on the word to abandon ship. *Abandon ship!? At the dock!?* It seemed like a strange order to both of us, but he did not argue.

I went forward with the thought of trying to go down to the theater. With the water already this high, there was a good chance someone needed help. As I went past Grace O'Sullivan and Nathalie Mestre's cabin and took my first step down, I went up to my shin in water. Not good. Not good at all.

Somewhere along the way, my towel had slipped off. I hadn't noticed, and apparently no one else had. Still, I did not want to hit the dock in my birthday suit. As I got back to my cabin, I felt the boat roll toward the nearby wharf as her bottom slipped down and away from the dock into deeper water. She was definitely sinking, and there was no way of telling how far and how fast she was going down. *Fuck the clothes, I'm out of here*, I thought as the water poured over the doorsill. It was now flooding the *upper* deck. I headed aft to where there were more cabins, shouting "Abandon ship!" as I felt the boat under my feet leaning over even farther. It was just like *The Poseidon Adventure*, but sickeningly real.

We were berthed at the end of a large pier dominated by a sizable warehouse in a remote corner of the harbor. A few small sailboats had been tied up alongside us before the explosions—sailboats that were part of the Pacific Peace fleet that was planning to sail with us to the Moruroa Atoll to protest France's nuclear weapons testing. The *Rainbow Warrior* was going to accompany the fleet as a supply and support vessel. After the explosions, the sailboats had quickly moved a short distance away. There was nothing around us that could conceivably have caused our ship to explode and sink.

The ship had already sunk to the point where I had to climb up off the ship's deck to get onto the dock. As soon as my feet hit the pier, I began counting heads—taking a mental inventory of the crew. Several, I knew, had been onshore, taking some time off before we left for the three-thousand-mile sail to Moruroa. From what I could tell, only Hanne Sorensen and Fernando Pereira were missing. I wasn't worried about Fernando as he was normally a late-night person and loved to go ashore. Hanne was more of a concern.

There is a saying among captains: "In an emergency, no one rises to the occasion. You fall back to the level of your training." I was functioning, but still badly stunned. It all seemed surreal, but it was real all right. I was turning back to look at my ship when Davey grabbed me and told me, "Fernando's down there!"

Fernando was our snapper—the ship's photographer—who had joined the crew in Hawaii four months earlier. I hoped to hell Davey was wrong, and told him that I thought Fernando was still out on the town, but Davey was emphatic. *Shit*, I thought. *If he's down there, he is way down under that mix of diesel fuel and cold, black water.* Davey confirmed that Fernando had gone down with him to the mess (the crew's cafeteria) for a nightcap, and after the whatever-the-hell-it-was happened—like any good photographer in a crisis—Fernando had gone down to his cabin to get his camera gear. Fernando's cabin, starboard and forward, was now deep under the seawater that was quickly filling the ship. Air bubbles were still hissing and boiling as they escaped the hull and emerged through the slowly spreading slick around the boat.

Part of me desperately wanted to find some scuba gear so

I could dive down into the ship to find my shipmate, but it seemed both risky and practically hopeless. (Later, when the police showed up, even their trained divers couldn't make it down through the fuel oil. It took a team of highly trained New Zealand navy divers to retrieve the body, and even they had to wait until the fuel had dissipated. To this day it still haunts me that I didn't make an attempt, but realistically it probably would have meant that the navy divers would have had to bring up my body as well.)

"Peter, I did not know you were so . . . chunky."

I had been so focused on Fernando that it had completely escaped my mind that I was still stark naked. Of course, Margaret—the assistant cook—didn't know that Fernando was most likely dead, and was trying to make light of the situation. I borrowed a sweater from Davey. Both of us were still half-naked (the only clothing I had on was Davey's sweater, and Davey was wearing only pants) but the two of us decided to go back to make sure that Hanne wasn't still on the ship. The *Rainbow Warrior* was continuing to settle and roll over, and water was already pouring into the bridge deck—one of the upper decks. Davey and I clambered up to the top of the stack—one of the highest points of the ship—and removed the aluminum top plate. Normally we should have been able to see almost forty feet straight down into the engine room. Instead, the water was now a mere six feet from the top, covered in a thick layer of oil. Full stop. The diesel fumes, and the reality, hit us full in the face. There was nothing more we could do. It was a terrible feeling.

Still worried about Hanne, Davey and I climbed back down and carefully picked our way over the crazily tilting ship and back to the pier. We still had no idea about what had caused all the damage. No other ship could have collided with us. The fuel oil was diesel, which isn't explosive. The

only explosive materials onboard were the oxygen and acet-
ylene tanks used for welding, but those were stored well forward and far from where the damage had occurred. I was
thoroughly mystified. Davey was too. At first he wondered
if he had screwed something up in the engine room and had
caused the explosion. The second explosion, in a different
location, was a good indication that it was something else
entirely.

"Are there any more bombs aboard?" asked the fire chief
who had just arrived on the scene. *Bombs? Who said anything
about bombs?* Greenpeace was—and is—very much against the
use of any kind of weaponry, violence, or property destruction. There was absolutely no way that we had bombs aboard.
Still, we were all asked to go with the police to the station
right across the road. *Great*, I thought. *My ship has been sunk.
Fernando is probably dead. The police think we did it, and they're
going to interrogate us. And I'm not wearing pants.*

Thankfully, a woman from one of the three small sailboats
that had been tied alongside the *Rainbow Warrior* reported
seeing a very bright flash under the transom of the ship when
the second explosion occurred. (She also brought me a pair of
pants.) To me, that sure sounded like a bomb. Set by whom?
And why?

Certainly, Greenpeace had already made a few enemies
who were against protection of the environment. But New
Zealand was generally in agreement with our principles, and
was definitely supportive of our no-nukes stance, the whole
reason we were there. When we arrived in Auckland three
days earlier it had felt like a homecoming to all of us. New
Zealand was moving toward becoming a nuclear-free zone
(it became official a short time later), and we were greatly en-
couraged by that. We all felt very welcome there.

The police separated the crew around the police station,

and interrogated both Davey and me with some intensity. I wouldn't say that we were being harshly questioned as suspects per se, but when a terrorist act occurs a hundred yards in front of a police station, you can bet your ass the police will be tense and giving you a good grilling.

Each of us was questioned multiple times over the course of an hour. First they asked us to retrace our steps during the sinking of the boat. The more pointed questions were asked later: "Where were you when the explosion occurred?" "Have you seen anyone suspicious near the ship?" "Have you seen anything suspicious onboard?" "Are you carrying any materials that have been used, or could have been used, to make a bomb?"

A short time before dawn, I was brought back to the dock to identify a body. It had taken a team of five navy divers to work their way down into the wrecked ship to retrieve Fernando. He had been in his cabin for about twenty seconds when the second explosion had gone off directly underneath him. The explosion's shock wave had jammed his cabin door closed so that, while he had survived the second explosion, he had drowned shortly after. To make matters even worse, while most of the Greenpeace crew were either single or childless, Fernando would be leaving two young children behind.

My glasses were still in my cabin somewhere under the water, so I had to ask the divers to bring the body closer to the dock and under the lights to identify him. In the faint light of the morning, through the dark oil and shadows under the pier, I had to get practically nose-to-nose with him to be sure. Even then, face-to-face with my dead colleague, what was happening still hadn't completely sunk in. At the moment, however, I had to focus on making sure the rest of the crew was OK, and finding out what the hell was happening and why. The first explosion had occurred under the middle of the ship, and the second had gone off near the rudder and propeller all the way aft. The fact that there were *two* explosions–*just a few minutes apart in two different locations*–indicated this was a deliberate attempt to sink the *Rainbow Warrior.*

At least Hanne was alive, which was a relief. She had gone for a late-night walk and arrived back at the dock after the explosions. She was being kept apart from the rest of the crew. She was distraught, but at least uninjured. I told the police that she was with us, and they let her accompany me to the back room where I solemnly confirmed for everyone that Fernando was dead.

Around four o'clock in the morning the crew was released and everyone went to the homes of various friends around Auckland. The local Greenpeace office also had the presence of mind to take up a collection of clothing for the crew. I was taken to police headquarters downtown.

After police headquarters, I was brought to the harbormaster's office and then escorted back down to what was left of the *Rainbow Warrior.* She was laid over entirely on her side, three-quarters submerged. Davey had been right–twice. My ship was dead and Fernando was dead. Twelve hours earlier something had happened and everything had changed.

At about 10 A.M., I was standing on the dock when the New Zealand navy divers reported that they were able to survey the damage near the bottom of the overturned ship. They could tell from the way the twisted and torn hull was bent inward that the explosion had occurred outside the hull. This, and the fact the explosions had occurred on the side of the ship facing the dock, was confirmation the ship had been bombed by an unknown enemy. The hole from one of the bombs was more than eight feet wide–wide enough to swim through. Hell, it was wide enough to drive a car through. (We found out later that the hull had filled in about twenty-five seconds, at the rate of seven tons of water *per second*.) Whoever had done this was far more sophisticated than a mere vandal or casual vigilante. That meant that Fernando had been murdered. Murdered! Satisfied now that we were victims and not perpetrators, the attitude of the police toward us softened considerably. Little did I know that, right about the same time, the pieces of the puzzle were already beginning to fall into place.

The harbor was normally pretty quiet. Recently, however, a rash of thefts aboard several yachts there caused a few of the owners to set up a nightly crime watch. Late the previous night, just before the explosions, the crime watch had been puzzled to see two scuba divers in a Zodiac inflatable boat approach the beach. As the boat neared the shore, the divers were observed dropping the outboard motor over the side and dragging the boat up the beach where they left it untied. All highly unusual. The divers then climbed into a waiting van and drove off. Amazingly, one of the alert crime watchers had written down the van's license plate number.

The next morning, a Swiss couple stepped into the local airport car rental agency to return the van. The two tourists seemed to be in a hurry, but were insistent on getting back one day's rent on the van. They explained they were flying out a day early because the woman's uncle was sick. Unbeknownst to them, the clerk was staring at a large sign under the desk with an order to call the Auckland police if that particular van turned up. The clerk politely asked the couple to wait while their refund was processed.

The police arrived in short order to bring them in for questioning. The report by the crime watch, including their observation of the divers entering the van and the subsequent explosions, tied the couple to the bombing and Fernando's death. Although they had not confessed, the police knew they were involved in some way. But instead of locking the pair up, the police made a reservation for them in a nice hotel where they could stay before their flight back to Switzerland the next morning. The police were more than gracious, practically apologetic, to the couple. "Please, order room service, use the phone, anything you want. But please do not leave the room, and in the morning we will even drive you to your plane."

Shortly after settling into their room, the couple made a phone call to the Direction Générale de la Sécurité Extérieure, or DGSE. The DGSE is part of the French defense agency in charge of external paramilitary missions and counterintelligence. The couple apologized for missing their flight, and said that they would be on the next one. The police got it all down on tape. They had tapped the line.

The "Swiss couple" were, in reality, French intelligence agents: Captain Dominique Prieur and Major Alain Mafart. The New Zealand police arrested them immediately on passport fraud and immigration charges. Later they were also charged with arson, conspiracy to commit arson, willful damage, and murder. As part of a plea bargain, they pled guilty to manslaughter and were sentenced to ten years in prison (of which they served just over two).

The inquiry also found that a total of at least thirteen French agents had been involved. Operation Satanique (no translation necessary) was a large and complicated mission. The explosives had been smuggled into New Zealand in a moderate-size sailing yacht. Another French agent had infiltrated the Greenpeace office in New Zealand as a volunteer. She had kept the DGSE informed about our timing and plans. She had even used our phones to arrange for the boat and scuba gear used in the attack. Before the actual bombing, the men who had sailed the yacht from New Caledonia to deliver the explosives had sailed back out and rendezvoused with a French nuclear submarine. The submarine had picked up the yacht's crew and then scuttled the yacht. The resulting international scandal led to the resignation of French defense minister Charles Hernu. (The conspiracy went much higher than that. On the twentieth anniversary of the bombing and Fernando's death, a Paris newspaper published a memo by French admiral Pierre Lacoste in which he declared that he had personally double-checked with President François Mitterrand and had gotten the green light for the attack.)

When the news hit that the French government was behind the bombing, the entire country of New Zealand rallied around us. Besides supporting our no-nukes advocacy, they were incensed that the French government had violated their sovereignty with a deadly attack on their soil. The Kiwis brought us clothes, and the car agency that had rented the van to the French agents even granted us use of two of their cars.

A few days later, I was in the courtroom watching the arraignment of the two agents. Unfortunately, I still didn't have my glasses, so all I could see was fuzzy blobs. But I could hear the proceedings clearly, and while I was angry, it still felt surreal. Hell, it *was* surreal.

So what, exactly, had we done to threaten the French government so much? The answer is we were planning to stop a nuclear weapons test in Moruroa, the atoll in French Polynesia where—in the preceding twenty or so years—the French had already exploded dozens of nuclear weapons. As a result of their attack and the death of Fernando, I wasn't about to let the French stop us. Going ahead with our protest was now more important than ever. If the French had attacked us, it was only because they were afraid of the effect we were having. We had seriously pissed them off, but that meant we were making a difference. Rather than scare me off, this strengthened my resolve to fight for our environment.

Within two months, I was heading off to Moruroa, undaunted in carrying out our plan to confront the French and their nuclear testing.

Participation—that's what's gonna save the human race.
—Pete Seeger

2

"Winning the Wrong Lottery"

All we have to decide is what to do with the time that is given us.
—*Gandalf, in* The Fellowship of the Ring, *J. R. R. Tolkien*

So how did I get to the point where my ship and I had become a target for terrorism? Strange as it may seem, it probably goes all the way back to how I was brought up. Not that my parents ever thought, *Gee, we'd like our son to be blown up someday!* But they themselves were committed activists who endured their own challenges and harsh treatment.

* * *

I'm a walking, talking argument for nurture in the nature-versus-nurture debate. I was adopted at the age of three months by a left-wing, antinuclear, antiwar, socially progressive, hardcore-offshore sailing family. Was it preordained that I would become a left-wing, antinuclear, antiwar, socially progressive, hardcore-offshore sailor? While it wasn't really planned that way, I can't argue the point. There were many apparently-by-chance happenings and lucky coincidences with enormous impacts on my life, but here I am—four hundred thousand sailing miles and four decades of environmental activism later—exactly where I want to be, doing exactly what I want to be doing, with exactly the kind of people I want to be doing it with.

My adoptive father, Roger, was a champion sailor with several national championships to his credit. *His* father, Henry Willcox—my middle name was taken from him—was involved in many left-wing/socialist political groups and was one of the biggest builders of public housing in the New York City area. Henry and his wife, Anita, had traveled in 1952 (the year before I was born) to China to attend an international peace conference. When they returned, their passports were confiscated, my *parents'* passports were confiscated, and it was many years before any of us were allowed to travel outside the country again. So what did my grandparents do in response? They organized a speaking tour in the US to talk about the positive things they had seen in China. After that, Henry was an important participant in a class-action suit against the US government, which led to a five-to-four Supreme Court decision on the "right of free movement." It's that kind of perseverance in the face of resistance that runs in my family.

As a result, Senator Joseph McCarthy labeled Henry a traitor, and political pressure was applied against Henry's public housing development company (which was dependent on government contracts). Anita (my eldest daughter is named after her) was an early feminist and an artist who was subsequently blacklisted as a "Red sympathizer." Both she and her husband were forced to testify before the House Un-American Activities Committee (HUAC). Henry had given many of his employees voting shares. After he testified, the employees turned around and voted him out of the company. He was unable to work in the industry again.

My adoptive mother, Elsie, was a union organizer and then a middle school science teacher with a particular interest in environmental science. (She started an outdoor classroom at the school, where a plaque still bears her name.) In 1948, Elsie was a campaign worker for Henry Wallace (FDR's vice president from 1941 to 1945) when Wallace was the Progressive Party candidate in the presidential election against incumbent Harry S. Truman and New York governor Thomas E. Dewey. (My grandfather, Henry Willcox, was the national treasurer for the campaign.) Elsie's position led her to also being called to testify before HUAC in 1957. It was while working for Wallace's campaign that she got to know the American folk singer Pete Seeger. Pete was performing to raise awareness and money for the campaign, and my mother was in charge of coordinating with him and managing his expenses. Pete became a close friend of my parents and would play a very influential role in my life.

Civil rights was a very big deal in my family. As a young child, I was brought by my mother to a civil rights demonstration in Connecticut. I remember picketing at the Woolworth's store in Norwalk. Woolworth's was an American chain of stores that were segregated in the South. In 1960, four African American students sat down at the Woolworth's lunch counter in Greensboro, North Carolina. The four were denied service, which started months of picketing and boycotts. (That section of the counter is now in the Smithsonian Institution, and the store is a civil rights museum.) Henry—Roger's father/my grandfather—had built many housing projects that were racially integrated. He and my father founded the first intentionally integrated community in New England: Village

Creek in Norwalk, Connecticut. Henry and Roger bought
the property and my uncle, who was a lawyer, wrote up the
contracts as the lots were sold. The community, settled mainly
by liberals or socialists, was known as Commie Creek for
years. (Others called it Kremlin Kove.) Real estate agents
often refused to show properties there until at least the late
1960s. Village Creek is now on the National Register of Historic Places. Times sure have changed.

Village Creek is the neighborhood that I grew up in. My father
and stepmother still live there, my sister and her family still live
there, and my younger daughter, Natasha, lives there when she's
not at college. In the sixty-some-odd years since it's been built,
it's become more gentrified. Fewer minorities live there now, but
not because of racism; it's because waterfront property has
gotten so much more expensive. Since fewer minorities can
afford it these days, Village Creek is now mostly upper-middle-
class white families.

In 1965, when I was twelve years old, my father took me
to Montgomery, Alabama, for the culmination of Martin
Luther King Jr.'s civil rights march from Selma. We arrived
the night before the final day, and after a long day of travel
we were quite hungry. We went to a restaurant just outside of Montgomery. I remember seeing a sign on the door
declaring that the restaurant's owners could refuse to serve
anyone they wanted. Having grown up in Connecticut, this
was my first glimpse of the injustice of Southern segregation.

Earlier, on March 7, 1965, on the first attempt to march
from Selma to Montgomery, the protesters had been attacked
and beaten by state and local lawmen at the now famous
Edmund Pettus Bridge. The "Bloody Sunday" images of the
marchers being beaten were seen all over America and the

world. Two weeks later—after a federal judge ruled they had the right to march—they began the march that my father and I joined in Montgomery. Bloody Sunday would later prove to be *the* turning point in the progress of the civil rights movement. The images of the brutality that day moved the mood of the country toward equality. We joined the march as it wended its way through Montgomery. We listened to Pete Seeger sing "We Shall Overcome" at a rally the night before the conclusion of the march, and heard King's speech on the Capitol steps the next morning over the PA system.

I was—even at that young age—struck by the powerful sense of optimism and purpose. We all felt that, somehow, this thing was winnable. Not that it would be easy, or immediate, but that it was *actually going to happen*. The singing, cheering, and the feeling of being part of something right and important is something that I still can recall clearly. No doubt it made a lasting impact on me. In many respects, the march served as a template for Greenpeace's use of civil disobedience and peaceful activism in fighting environmental destruction.

Another parallel between the fight for civil rights and the fight to preserve the environment is that while both efforts have had tremendous impacts and successes, neither effort has culminated in a total victory. Racism is still present (the high rate of incarceration of black males in the US is but one example), just as pollution and carbon emissions are still rampant, but significant battles have been won and progress is still being made on both fronts. We should all hope that further progress continues to be made on both fronts as well.

A couple of years after the march, I was invited to attend a summer camp in the Soviet Union called Camp Artek. The camp was located on the Crimean peninsula—east of Sevastopol—on a mountain near the sea, and operated as an international student center. The leaders of the Soviet Union often sent their children there. (As of this writing in 2015, the camp is in territory that is now controlled by Vladimir Putin.) Being able to share experiences and cultures with kids from all over the world was incredibly stimulating.

One of the most important things I took away from Artek was that the Russian people wanted peace more than anything. This was 1967, during the Cold War, and if you listened to either one of the American or Soviet governments, you thought the two countries hated each other. The Russian people, however, had suffered terribly during World War II. Over twenty million had died from war, starvation, and disease. In the twentieth century alone, tens of millions more had died in the other disasters the Russian people had suffered through. Often, when someone found out I was American, they would say, "Please don't start a war with us. We only want peace." These people had been through decades of hell and wanted nothing more to do with it. Their sincerity came through loud and clear every time they spoke to me: their pleas for peace were genuine and heartfelt. (These people weren't "plants" for the government. That is not to say that there weren't "plants" at the camp; there were. But it was pretty easy to tell who was a government mouthpiece, even for a fourteen-year-old. The "plants" weren't all that subtle about it.) The message of peace was one I was all too happy to take home.

Years later, in a Russian prison, I found that—once again—the people themselves were very sympathetic and likable (even though the judicial system and government they worked for was not).

Activism was deeply ingrained in our family. When I was six years old, the power company announced that they were going to build a coal-fired power plant on the water (in what would now be considered wetlands), right next door to our community. Being sailors and activists, my family and I sailed around the harbor with signs protesting the construction of the plant. It ended up being built, so that was the first–and certainly not the last–of my environmental protests that ended in futility. You win some, you lose some, but that doesn't mean you stop fighting! One of my favorite sayings these days is a quote attributed to Mahatma Gandhi: "First they ignore you, then they laugh at you, then they fight you, then you win."

My father, Roger, tells a story about taking me sailing for the first time. I was about six months old, and I hadn't even stood up on my own yet. Roger was taking the family sailboat to Block Island. While Block Island is not far from the coast of Rhode Island, it is in open ocean, and large swells often sweep in from distant storms in the Atlantic. My father had taken a small crib and lashed it down to the deck behind the cockpit, and that was where I lay until an unusually large wave caught the boat from behind and launched me up in the air. From the way my father tells it, he saw my head come up over the side of the crib and watched me as I caught my first sight of the ocean around us. Wide-eyed with wonderment, I grabbed the side of the crib as I came down and stood there, beaming, holding on to the side of the crib, looking at the waves and feeling the spray coming over the boat. I guess I was a born mariner.

I've raced sailboats for my whole life. And when I'm not racing, I'm generally cruising or sailing as a professional captain. Maybe under different circumstances I would have become a professional racer, or a sailmaker or something like that. Instead, a strange series of coincidences set me on the path that I'm still on today.

As I was graduating high school, the Vietnam War was a

dark cloud hanging over me (as well as the rest of the country). The draft was still in effect: there was a very real chance that I was going to be sent to Vietnam. My family was very much against the war, and had a long history of pacifism as well. Roger had been in the army during World War II, serving most of the war in Hawaii as a supply officer. A few hours after the US dropped the atomic bomb on Hiroshima, Roger was called into his commanding officer's office and shown several glossy aerial surveillance photos of the devastation. The general—the chief intelligence officer for the Army Corps of Engineers—had access to very advanced technology that was an early radio version of the fax. The images had been transmitted from somewhere near Japan and printed out a short time later in Hawaii. The result was that my father was one of the first human beings in the world (outside of Japan) to see the total destruction that atomic weapons could inflict on a city. It affected him deeply, and as a result he went on an anti–nuclear war speaking tour after his discharge from the army. It was at one of these events that he met my mother, Elsie.

The Vietnam War was something I had been against since grade school. At the North Country boarding school for my sixth, seventh, and eighth grades, I used to watch the evening news anchored by Walter Cronkite. I vividly recall Cronkite's report in which he pointed out how much better off Vietnamese villages were under the Vietcong when compared to their lives under South Vietnamese rule. By the time I was a draft-age senior at prep school (the Putney School), Vietnam was a real hot-button issue for the whole country. One day, my history teacher, Sven Huseby, sat down at the lunch table with a *New York Times* under his arm and announced, "If you are a boy born on March 6, 1953, this is your lucky day!" When I asked why, he responded, "Because you're number one in the draft lottery!" "Lucky" was definitely *not* the word I would have used since that was my birthday. It meant I was going to Vietnam.

The professor wasn't being an asshole about the "lucky day"; he didn't even know it was my birthday at the time. Thirty years later I told him the impact his little announcement had made on me. It changed my life. My parents, family, friends, and our surrounding community were all against violence in general, and war specifically, and we all felt that our country had no moral right to fight in Vietnam. Needless to say, I didn't want to "join the army, see the world, meet interesting people, and kill them!" as antiwar T-shirts said at the time.

If I didn't want to go to Vietnam, or jail, I had two choices: flee to Canada, or become a conscientious objector. (College was the third way out, but I was not the best student, nor was I interested in more schooling. I had, in fact, gone to a small, informal college for a semester, but it wasn't my thing.) But, as you can probably guess, I'm not the fleeing type, so I worked toward obtaining CO status. If you were approved as a CO, you could perform noncombatant duty in the military or some other form of approved civil or community service. A good many COs were assigned hospital duties such as emptying bedpans. It wasn't pleasant work, but it sure beat shooting people and getting shot at.

My parents were good friends with Pete and Toshi Seeger. The Seegers had built the *Clearwater*–a ninety-six-foot wooden replica of the historic Hudson River sailing sloops– for the purpose of raising environmental awareness on the Hudson River in New York. The Hudson had been heavily polluted for years, the fish were completely gone in many sections of the river, and the toxins and raw sewage made it too dangerous to even swim in it. *Clearwater* was one of the earliest, and most influential, environmental groups in the world—even earlier than Greenpeace—and I had been sailing on her a few times with Pete and my folks. One of the mates on the *Clearwater* was a young man—about my age—named Bill Siebert. Bill was a draft resister, meaning he was much more active in his antiwar/antidraft stance than I was. As required, I had sent the draft board my application for CO status and explained my point of view, whereas Bill had ignored them completely, burned his draft card, and refused to submit to their authority in any way. The draft board didn't appreciate that, so Bill was arrested right off the *Clearwater.*

My father was actually the one who taught Pete Seeger the basics of sailing. He had taken Pete sailing several times in Norwalk, and Pete had caught the sailing bug. One day, unannounced, Pete drove up to our house in Village Creek pulling a sailboat on a trailer behind him. "Roger!" he shouted. "You've got to take me out and show me how to sail this thing!" So my father and I went out with Pete to teach him how to sail his new boat. Pete, being Pete, brought his guitar along for the sail. That summer, he came over with his boat many times for more lessons. It's fair to say that my father's helping to introduce Pete to sailing contributed greatly to the Seegers' desire to build the *Clearwater.* I guess that—since years later I ended up on the *Clearwater* before becoming a captain for Greenpeace—helping Pete to learn sailing was good karma. One good turn would soon deserve another.

Bill's draft resistance case was being handled by a real hard-ass judge. The judge had given Bill a stark choice: two years of noncombatant service in the army, or five years in jail. Bill wanted nothing to do with the army or the war, so he prepared himself to accept the five-year jail sentence at the next hearing. Then, a remarkable thing happened: on the day of the hearing, the judge suffered a heart attack on his way back from lunch and died on the courtroom steps. Bill's case was transferred to a new judge, one who was far more sympathetic. The new judge sentenced him to only three months in jail, along with two years of public service. Adding to Bill's good fortune (and, eventually, mine!) the judge was a sailor and a member of the Shattemuc Yacht Club on the Hudson River. Shattemuc happened to be a place where the *Clearwater* had spent some time, and the judge was friendly with Pete, so the judge arranged for Bill to do his two years of service on the big sloop. This meant the *Clearwater* was now federally approved for conscientious objector duty. My parents must have told the Seegers about my own plight. The word was passed on to Bill, who then called me to explain I could complete my service requirements by sailing with him on the *Clearwater.* Sailing, drinking wine, and smoking a little pot seemed like a much better alternative to going to war, so I signed up.

As it turned out, just before I was to officially report for duty on the *Clearwater*, Nixon abolished the draft. It was January 27, 1973, and I was in Florida racing on my father's boat in a big regatta when we heard the news on the radio. A large number of draft-age guys were crewing in the fleet and all of us started celebrating and carrying on. Most of the boats carried phosphorus parachute flares (for safety and rescue) so we all started shooting off the flares into the air in an impromptu fireworks display. A very short time later, however, the fun ended when the hot flares began to fall onto the meticulously varnished yachts and their beautiful teak decks. That made for a number of very unhappy yacht owners, but they couldn't really blame us for celebrating.

While I no longer had to join the *Clearwater* to avoid the war, I was still a young man who needed a job, and I loved sailing. Besides, the plans had already been made, and I really liked the Seegers, so off I went. Since I already had quite a bit of sailing experience, they hired me as the second mate. I was twenty years old, being paid to sail, and I could flirt with lots of pretty girls. Life was good.

One of the girls I flirted with was a young crew member named Maggy Aston who came aboard a few years after I became captain of the *Clearwater*. She had signed on as cook, but she also knew how to sail. It was a classic summer romance, so after the end of the sailing season she went her way and I went mine. We stayed in touch off and on over the years. She moved to Maine, got married, and had a son. I got married and had two daughters. In 2011, thirty-six years after being together on the *Clearwater*, I drove to Maine to captain the delivery of an antique gaff-rigged sloop. The yacht had just been restored and needed to be sailed down to Connecticut for her owner. I hadn't seen Maggy in about ten years, so I called her and told her I was going to be in the area. We met for dinner. She was single again, I was single again, and we were both unattached. The old flame was quickly rekindled. We fell in love again, and less than two years later we were married.

The ceremony took place on the island of Islesboro, Maine, in a stone pulpit overlooking Penobscot Bay with her son and my daughters in attendance. It was February and cold and blowing like hell, but for two sailor types like us, the conditions seemed appropriate. Instead of wedding rings, we got tattoos of our entwined hands (from my own design) on our ring fingers.

Within a few months, Bill had burned out, and I was made the first mate of the *Clearwater*. Two years later I made captain. We'd sail up and down the river, taking the public for excursions while teaching them about the environment, or holding fund-raising concerts and the like. Most of the time we were sailing the *Clearwater* up and down the Hudson River, around New York City, or in Long Island Sound, but once in a while we went farther. In 1977 we sailed to Seabrook, New Hampshire, to protest the opening of a nuclear power plant there. The protest included a big concert featuring Jackson Browne, and a large number of environmental organizations were present. (The environmental movement had really taken off by then.) A relatively new group called Greenpeace had sailed a boat up to New Hampshire to join the protest. They seemed like nice people and I enjoyed talking with them, especially the Greenpeace ("Gp" for short) activist Campbell Plowden. Little did Campbell and I know that, within a few short years, we would be working together at Greenpeace. And I certainly could not have imagined that I would be with Gp for over thirty-five years after that.

Sailing on the *Clearwater* during the summers left me lots of time during the winter for other adventures. I continued yacht racing whenever I could, and in 1979 I took some time off from the *Clearwater* to do a stint with Dennis Conner's America's Cup team (the team won the Cup in 1980). After six years on the *Clearwater*, and five years as captain, I felt the need to expand my horizons. I wanted to sail farther, learn new skills, and get experience on a much bigger ship. I had heard about an old square-rigger called the *Regina Maris*.

The ship was operating as a school, paid to take students on voyages to learn marine biology, with an emphasis on whales. While I had been a captain on the smaller sloop, I didn't have the experience yet to be comfortable as the captain of a square-rigger of this size on the open seas, so the *Regina Maris* was a real chance to gain valuable skills and credentials.

It's a small world. (I know that because I've sailed all around it lots of times!) I had been sailing on the *Regina Maris* for a while before I found out that George Nichols—the man who founded the nonprofit that owned her—knew my father. They had sailed together on the Harvard dinghy team. It turned out that my father didn't particularly like him because George had capsized their dinghy while racing in the Charles River. Apparently they were racing even though George had a broken leg in a heavy cast and, understandably, he was having some trouble properly shifting his weight around in the small boat. Roger never really forgave George for losing the race. My father has always been a competitive SOB who, at age ninety-five, still races dinghies solo in the middle of the winter. And wins.

The *Regina Maris* wasn't in the best condition (I used to call her the Rigor Mortis), but I started off as the third mate and was getting good experience. By that fall, I had been promoted to first mate. Earlier that summer, the skipper–Steve Wedlock–taught me the basics of celestial navigation, and then a friend of mine, Andy Chase, taught me many of the finer points. Andy and I attended both the North Country and Putney schools at the same time, and he joined the *Regina Maris* as second mate. A graduate of Maine Maritime Academy, Andy was very well trained in navigation and the handling of large ships. I learned a lot from him, and we are still good buddies today.

Celestial navigation—determining the ship's position using a sextant to measure the angles of the sun, moon, stars, and planets to the horizon—is a technology that really hasn't changed for hundreds of years. Columbus used it, and celestial was still the state-of-the-art for navigating on the high seas as recently as the early 1980s. Now, of course, we have GPS, but I still practice celestial just in case the GPS goes down. In fact, the US Navy still teaches it, and US Merchant Marine deck officers are required to know it as well.

As first mate on the square-rigger, I was getting lots of valuable sea time. (Sea time is the US Coast Guard's measurement of experience on large vessels that allows people to obtain higher levels of certification to captain big ships.) But after nine months on the square-rigger I was unhappy with the organization and its seat-of-the-pants way of planning and dealing with issues. By the following spring, in 1981, it was time to move on.

I happened to see a sailors-wanted advertisement in *National Fisherman* for Greenpeace. Greenpeace had gotten its start in the early seventies when a small group of environmental activists sailed an old fishing vessel from Vancouver toward Amchitka, Alaska. They were going to bear witness to an underground nuclear test being conducted by the United States. This tiny island was home to thousands of endangered sea otters, other wildlife, and the very symbol of the United States—bald eagles. While the activists were intercepted and the bomb detonated, Greenpeace's action had ignited the public's interest. Soon after, nuclear testing was banned on Amchitka, and the island was eventually declared a bird sanctuary. It was the very beginning of Greenpeace's tradition of peaceful protest and bringing the world's attention to important environmental issues. (To this day, Greenpeace abhors violence, property destruction, and aggression of any sort. It is often confused with Sea Shepherd, an antiwhaling organization founded by an ex-Greenpeace captain who was expelled from Greenpeace for not adhering to these principles.)

I had read Bob Hunter's 1979 book about Greenpeace, *Warriors of the Rainbow* (Bob was one of the founders of the organization), and I really liked the idea of direct action and civil disobedience. Having seen the beauty and majesty of whales on the *Regina Maris*, the image of the Greenpeace activists in front of the harpoon gun really got to me. I called the guy who had placed the ad–Steve Sawyer–and after we spoke I sent him my résumé. The *Rainbow Warrior*– Greenpeace's flagship–was in New Bedford, Massachusetts, only a couple of hours' drive from Norwalk, so I went up to meet Steve. He offered me a job as a potential deckhand. As a deckhand, I'd be paid with just beer and cigarettes (and I don't even smoke!). It was a bit of a step down from my previous levels of responsibility, but the crew seemed like a friendly bunch–they were joking around and giving Steve a hard time–and I knew Greenpeace was doing good things. I really believed in what they were trying to accomplish, so I took the lower-level job anyway.

On my first day on the ship, the captain came up to me and said: "Can you paint?" Even though I was twenty-eight years old, had been a professional sailor for about ten years and a captain in my own right, I said: "Yeah, I can paint." (Any real, professional sailor can paint!) The captain led me aft to the transom of the ship where the name "Rainbow Warrior" needed repainting. I was a little apprehensive when I found out I had to paint *lettering*. That was much more complicated than simply painting the hull. But when I saw that the lettering looked like it had been painted by a distracted six-year-old, I figured I could hardly do worse. After rigging up a scaffold and getting a closer look, I realized I was in luck: somebody had already carefully punched the outline of the letters into the steel hull. All I had to do was follow the outlines! The captain was so impressed by my mastery of paint that he made me first mate that same evening. (I found out many years later that another captain—Pete Bouquet—had punched in the outlines.) Who knows how my fate might have been altered if those letters hadn't already been marked out?!

The first action (which is what Greenpeace calls its missions) was to stop offshore oil drilling off of Georges Bank, an area east of Cape Cod, Massachusetts, and southwest of Nova Scotia, Canada, that was, at the time, the world's richest fishing grounds. We sent four inflatables over to the rig with banners, took pictures, and invited some of the local fishing crews to come aboard the *Rainbow Warrior*. We had some TV reporters onboard, and they got footage of us talking with the fishermen and the Coast Guard helicopter that was circling overhead. The action got good coverage and, eventually, drilling near Georges Bank was made illegal. (Put that one in the "win" column, although, decades later, we are still fighting offshore drilling in locations all over the world.) After that, we brought the *Rainbow Warrior* back to the United States, to Stonington, Maine, to have her engines replaced.

When the *Rainbow Warrior* had been built in 1955, she was one of the first trawlers equipped with a diesel-electric (DE) propulsion system. DE systems are essentially a series of diesel generators that produce electricity. The electricity is then supplied to an electric motor that actually turns the propeller. These systems were first developed for World War II submarines, and it was still fairly advanced technology when the R'dub had been built. (R'dub was our nickname for that first *Rainbow Warrior*. Pronounced "ahr-dub," the nickname was derived from the *r* in "rainbow" and "dub" for the *w* in "warrior.") Diesel-electric systems are more efficient if you tend to run the ship at different speeds most of the time, which we do. Traditional diesel-only systems work best when the ship runs at a constant speed for long distances. After over twenty-five years of hard work and countless miles, the original system was on its last legs.

Greenpeace International's headquarters in Europe wanted us to install European-manufactured engines, while we were pushing for General Motors. They gave in when we told them that the engines we preferred were the same type used in the US landing craft at D-Day. That shut them up pretty quick! With the new, far more efficient engines, we were able to double the ship's range to almost ten thousand miles.

We did most of the engine replacement work ourselves. My particular focus was on "scrapping": taking out all of the old bits for recycling. It was ten weeks of hard, tough, dirty work, but my enthusiasm for Greenpeace didn't diminish. (OK, I'll admit it *temporarily* diminished a little bit, but not enough to make me quit!) The skipper at the time, Pete Bouquet, had to return home while we were still in the boatyard. While he stayed with Gp, Bouquet wanted to spend more time with his young family, so he decided not to go on our next extended sail. By the time the R'dub's repower was complete, I was made her captain.

At the time, everyone at Gp was a volunteer. When I was made captain, Gp decided to pay me $300 a month. That made me one of the first paid sailors for Greenpeace. Without any additional living expenses (since I was living and eating on the ship), and no family to care for, the $300 a month was OK by me. While I get paid far more now, believe me, it's nobody's idea of big money. Let's put it this way: the rewards of this job are not financial!

After the Georges Bank action, we brought the R'dub down to New Jersey for an action against National Lead, a company that was dumping millions of gallons of sulfuric acid right off the beautiful beaches enjoyed by hundreds of thousands of people every summer. With the news coverage we stirred up, National Lead stopped the dumping and eventually closed the plant. It was my first action as a captain, and I was off to a good start.

We brought the R'dub back to Boston to await word on what our next campaign would be. We soon learned we would be headed into the sea ice around Newfoundland, Canada, to stop the harvesting of baby fur seals.

When you're on a ship in sea ice, it's nerve-racking; particularly when it's the first time you're doing it. We were going to have to go through more than a hundred miles of heavy ice. As the R'dub had not been built as an icebreaker, there were a number of challenges in making her ice-ready, equipping the ship to safely handle the ice we would almost certainly encounter. One huge issue was that the seawater used to cool the engine could freeze, rendering it inoperable. John Brouwer—our first chief engineer—came up with a brilliant solution. John converted an internal seawater ballast tank into a heat exchanger by running fire hoses between the engine and the tank. The heated water from the engine would keep the seawater from freezing, and the seawater from the tank would cool the engine. It was a closed-loop system; simple, elegant, and foolproof.

Getting into the Gulf of St. Lawrence off of Newfoundland was tough going. Every so often we'd come to a dead
stop and have to wait for the wind or current to shift and
move the ice so we could continue on our way. When we
were stuck, we'd get off the ship and stretch our legs by walking around on the ice. I was walking on the ice when, all of
a sudden, the R'dub's horn sounded an alarm, so I ran back
to the ship to see what it was for. Alarms are usually not
good news, but this one was. There was a big merchant
ship—made for icebreaking—that was moving toward us at
18 knots. (A knot is 1 nautical mile per hour, which is equal
to 1.15 statute/land miles per hour, or—for those metrically
inclined—1.85 kilometers per hour.) The ship had huge, car-
size chunks of ice flying off of its bow. *Boom. Boom. Boom.* As
it passed by, we managed to position the *Rainbow Warrior*
behind the bigger ship into the path it had just cut for us,
hitching a ride behind her. Eventually she outpaced us, but
luckily a smaller icebreaking ship came along and we were
able to follow her the rest of the way to the seal hunting
grounds.

The baby harp seals that are hunted for fur are only a few
weeks old. At that age they are white, with big black eyes and
little black noses. They're very, very cute. During seal hunting season, thousands of baby seals are clubbed to death.
Some are even skinned while they're still alive. The plan for
the action was to get close enough to the baby seals so we
could spray-paint them with green dye. The dye was harm-
less to the seal pups, but it would make their fur unsuitable
for use as a coat. (I am against fur in general, but I especially think that any animal whose parents travel *south to
Newfoundland in the winter to breed* deserves a break!)

There was, however, a law on the books in Canada called
the Seal Protection Act which made it illegal to get close to

a baby seal *unless you were going to kill it.* "Protection Act"? George Orwell would have been proud of that one. The Mounties were waiting for us, so as soon as the team started to paint the seals they were all arrested and charged with violating the Seal Protection Act. We only had time to paint two hundred baby seals, but the action (along with several other actions and lots of lobbying by Greenpeace and other organizations) helped convince the European Parliament to ban the importation of seal pelts. While it wasn't a total victory (seals were still killed for use in other markets), we had struck a heavy blow against those who struck defenseless baby seals. The following year we would stop the killing of much larger, but still defenseless, animals.

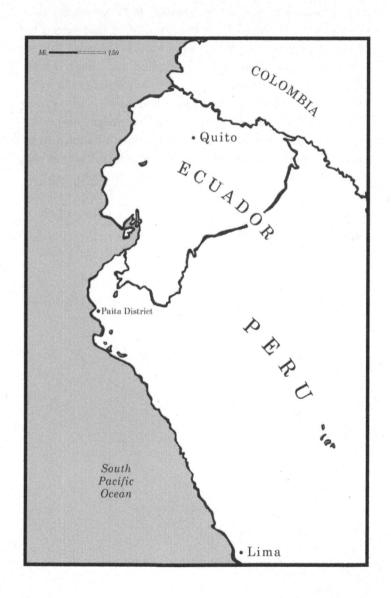

3

Dawn Raid in Peru

DECEMBER 1982

PORT OF PAITA, PERU—NEAR LIMA

ANTIWHALING ACTION

I found myself in Peru, walking around a dead baby whale with a tape measure in my hand. A Japanese-owned whaling ship had caught the undersize southern Bryde's whale illegally and towed it into the harbor at Paita for "processing." A few years before, I had enjoyed an incredible experience on the *Regina Maris* that left a whale-size impression on me: an encounter with humpback whales at the Silver Bank breeding grounds sixty miles north of the Dominican Republic. Three-quarters of the world's humpbacks gather together near Silver Bank to mate. During the season, thousands of them are concentrated in an area of about twenty square miles to breed and calve. Humpbacks are fascinating animals. If you've ever heard recordings of whales singing, it was probably humpbacks. At Silver Bank we could dive off the boat, snorkel around, and actually hear the singing of the humpback whales through the water. We would often drop a hydrophone (an underwater microphone) over the side of the *Regina Maris* and sit around on deck listening to the symphonies that were being performed by the whales every night under the stars. Pure magic.

One day near Silver Bank, a mother whale and her calf–probably a pretty recent newborn–approached the *Regina Maris*, and a few of us jumped in the water to spend some quality time with the pair. It was unusual for humpbacks to come toward a ship: given that whaling fleets were still actively hunting them, their fear was understandable. This mother whale, however, seemed to know that we posed no threat. Maybe she wanted to teach her baby that not all humans are killers.

Floating around within a few yards of these magnificent and graceful giants was a life-altering experience. Ken Balcomb, a cetologist (whale scientist) on the *Regina Maris*, explained to us dumb sailors that whales had originally been land mammals before they returned to the sea. Here, in the water, I was face-to-face with two of my distant cousins. Watching the mother whale teaching her baby how to breach (when whales leap out of the water and slam back with a massive splash), I was touched by this intergenerational moment. At Silver Bank, the very future of the whale on this planet had been right there within reach. Now, in Peru, I was standing on a dead baby whale and fuming at the injustice, cruelty, and stupidity of it.

The International Whaling Commission (IWC) passed a global moratorium on commercial whaling in July 1982. During the preceding decade, Greenpeace and many other organizations had been putting pressure on the IWC to stop the killing. Finally, the ban on commercial whaling was passed (although aboriginal hunting and some "research" hunting was allowed). Japan, Norway, and Russia immediately objected to the ban and continued their hunts. A few months later, in November, Peru—pressured by Japan—announced it was going to allow commercial whaling despite the moratorium. The entire whaling fleet in Peru was owned and commanded by the Japanese (although the crews were Peruvian), and most of the whale meat they caught was being graded and shipped to Japan.

We had been on the *Rainbow Warrior* in the eastern Pacific Ocean looking for tuna seiners (big fishing trawlers) to prove they were killing dolphin. The Pacific is the largest ocean on the planet, and radar and radio waves only travel so far. It was like looking for a needle in a haystack; we were having very limited success in finding the trawlers. It had been a frustrating couple of weeks before we got the radio call from Gp redirecting us to Peru for an antiwhaling action. The whole crew was eager to go.

The best direct actions are inspired by the issue itself. Many of the crew had first heard of Greenpeace during its antiwhaling actions on the West Coast of the US in the 1970s. The famous image of the Gp inflatable in front of the harpoon gun was one of the best Gp actions ever, an action that's hard to top even now. The crew was thrilled by the idea that we would at last be able to drive a boat in front of a harpoon gun. When I had first read Bob Hunter's book *Warriors of the Rainbow*, I was intrigued by Greenpeace's concept of direct action. Doing something real and physical struck a chord deep within me. Most people feel too powerless to have an effect on the world we live in, but direct actions are wonderful educational tools to alert our fellow citizens to a problem, while giving *us* a chance to do something about it. It is a hard combination to beat.

Once, in a misguided effort to get a management job in Greenpeace International's headquarters in Amsterdam, someone
asked me: "How do you motivate your crew to work?" My response was that I had never even tried. If the thought of nuclear
contamination, toxic pollution, or killing the oceans through
overfishing doesn't already motivate someone, what would I ever
be able to say or do to change that? Sure, the hours can be long,
and the pay by commercial standards is pathetic, but it is the
thought of leaving the world in a usable condition for our children
that gets most of us up in the morning and propels us to take
on real risks during these types of actions.

Before entering Paita, we had stopped in Callao, the port
city near Lima, and met with Campbell Plowden, the campaigner. ("Campaigner" is the Greenpeace term for the
person who directs all the activity—actions, lobbying, public
relations, etc.—for a particular issue.) Campbell was the Gp
guy I had first met at the 1977 Seabrook, New Hampshire,
anti–nuclear plant demonstration when I was captain on the
Clearwater. We got along, and worked together, very well.
He is a master planner, and the Peru action would turn out
to be one of the best I've ever been a part of. I was excited to
be working with him.

Campbell had been in Peru earlier in the year, developing relationships with some Peruvian antiwhaling activists.
Despite the Peruvian government's insistence on continuing
commercial whaling operations, the country had a long history of antiwhaling sentiment. One Peruvian activist, Au-
gusto Urrutia Prugue, had been instrumental in bringing the
illegal whaling activity to Gp's attention. Another was Felipe
Benavides, the most notable of the Peruvian antiwhaling activists. Felipe was somewhat famous in antiwhaling circles

for convincing the Peruvian air force to bomb and strafe a Greek-owned whaling fleet in the 1950s. The fleet—owned by Aristotle Onassis—was illegally hunting within Peru's territorial waters. While bombing and strafing whalers is completely and totally against Greenpeace's philosophy, there was no doubting Felipe's commitment, and he was exceptionally knowledgeable and helpful.

Relations between the US and Peru, and England and Peru, were at a low ebb at this time, so we had to be careful. Argentina and England had just ended a nasty little war over the Falkland Islands, and Peru was an ally of Argentina. The *Rainbow Warrior* was registered in the UK, and normally flew the red British ensign (the UK's national maritime flag, also called the red duster), but that would have been like flying a red flag in front of a bull, so we opted for the powder-blue UN flag when we entered Lima. (We kept the red duster rolled up above it, just in case.) To make matters even worse, the US had just enacted substantial tariffs on Peruvian textile imports. Japan, on the other hand, was the biggest foreign aid donor to Peru, with the quid pro quo that the Japanese could continue whaling in Peruvian waters.

To lay the groundwork for our action, Campbell organized a protest in front of Peru's equivalent of the US Senate, and another protest event in Paita on the beach. He also arranged a four-day cruise down the Peruvian coast on the *Rainbow Warrior* with as many journalists and local press as we could cram on board. Campbell was also astute enough to invite some influential members of Peru's opposition party to come along. The idea was to show everyone several alarming examples of environmental destruction that had already occurred in Peruvian waters, and then to make the case that whaling was yet another example of shortsightedness. We also wanted to show them where Peru was doing the *right* things.

The first stop on the tour was a viewing of Peru's anchovy fleet. The seas off the coast of Peru are ideal for anchovies—a family of small, saltwater baitfish that form massive schools. Anchovies are an important part of both the ocean and coastal food chains. Currents bring up huge amounts of the nutrients that the anchovies feed on, and then birds, fish, and other sea life higher on the food chain feed on the anchovies. Twenty years before, Lima had thousands of anchovy trawlers in their fleet. Despite the anchovies' ideal conditions, they had been so overfished that their population crashed badly. (This has happened all over the world for just about every kind of fish that man eats—cod, orange roughy, redfish, etc.) Now almost 90 percent of the anchovy fleet was inactive and rusting away in the harbor. It was a clear and sad example of not only the damage that overfishing did to the fish, but the human and economic consequences as well. (At Gp we have no objection to fishing, just to *over*fishing. We want fishermen to be in business for years to come, but that means it has to be done on a sustainable basis. The results of not doing so were right before our eyes.)

The next stop was the Guano Islands. "Guano," the polite name for bird turds, is an excellent fertilizer. It was once also an important ingredient for making gunpowder, which Peru used in various wars against Chile, Argentina, and Ecuador. They also sold tons of it to the British, French, and Spanish navies. The islands here used to be covered in guano tens of feet thick that had built up over hundreds of years. Since the early 1800s, the guano had been mined and exported all over the world. Guano was an important part of the Peruvian economy for a long time, but the birds that laid the golden poop were entirely dependent on the anchovies. When the fish population crashed, the bird population crashed too. The guano industry had been decimated.

Despite the severe impact on the bird population, there were still millions of birds living there. During the day, the dried guano made the islands appear bright white. But as the sun got low in the sky, the birds came home to roost and the earliest birds landed on the peaks of the mountains—the prime real estate with the best views. Birds that arrived later landed lower down. As the birds settled down for the night, it looked like a giant bucket of black paint had been poured over the tops of the mountains, flowing downward until the entire island was darkened.

For an example of something Peru was doing right for the environment we stopped at the Paracas National Reserve—Peru's first marine preserve. We saw thousands of sea lions and South American fur seals, all flourishing. It was an encouraging sight.

After that we left Lima and headed north for the three-day sail to Paita. This was where the whalers were based, supplying a sizable onshore operation for the butchering and processing of whales. With all of the press attention we had already received, the whalers had to know that we were coming for them. The whaling station, while certainly a big employer in the village, was not a well-loved one. As we had in Lima, Campbell and I and members of the crew got to know some of the locals before the action began. At one point during our reconnaissance, a Peruvian man came up to me and handed me something: two baby sperm whale teeth that he had found on the flense-way (the ramp where the whales' skin is removed and their blubber stripped). I couldn't understand what the man was saying, but the teeth said more than enough to me. Sperm whales were seriously endangered, so hunting them was bad enough. Killing the next generation of them was even stupider.

The new engine on the *Rainbow Warrior* was reliable and

efficient, but it was only capable of moving the ship at about 12 or 13 knots. The whalers we were hunting could go nearly twice as fast, but when they were actually engaged in a hunt their speed would slow down to about 2 to 3 knots in order to keep pace with the slow-swimming whales on the surface. If we were lucky enough to spot a whaler during a hunt, we'd be able to jump into our speedy 25-knot inflatables and re-create Gp's famous harpoon photo. We had no such luck. After several days of fruitless patrolling, we had to switch to plan B: intercepting the whaler in port—which is how I now found myself standing with a tape measure on a dead baby whale.

The whaler had come in towing the whale and we wanted to document the illegality of the hunt. I measured the whale at eight meters (about twenty-five feet), well under the size limit. We also had a one-meter-wide white wooden disk we had fashioned to use as a reference point for photographically documenting the size of the whales being brought in. I've been told that at one point, while I was positioning the disk on the dead whale, I slipped and fell waist-deep into the guts of the whale. (I don't remember this, but I am probably just blocking out what would have been an extremely unpleasant memory.) Strangely, nobody there seemed at all concerned about our presence. It was as if they thought that we weren't going to be able to stop them, no matter what. The fact that the whalers felt they could operate with impunity made us even madder.

A few crew, including Jim Stiles, snuck onto the flensing deck onshore to take pictures. One of the horrifying sights they saw there was a huge whale's heart—about sixty pounds—lying on the floor. Right after that, a beefy whaling station worker brought a big bag over to the *Rainbow Warrior* and dropped it on the deck. We were a little wary since we had no idea what he might be carrying. He kept saying *"barco scientifico"* ("scientific boat" in Spanish), and he handed Jim the bag. When Jim opened it, he saw it contained a baby whale's heart. Among whaling workers the heart is considered a delicacy and it is an honor to be presented with it. The worker had brought the heart to thank us for our work, and he thought we might be able to study it to help the whales as well. We kept the whale's heart in the ship's freezer until many weeks later when we encountered a pod of gray whales off of Mexico. It seemed appropriate to return the heart of the whale to the heart of the sea in the company of his brethren. It was a somber and moving ceremony.

The whaler, the *Victoria 7*, seemed to have a fairly regular schedule, bringing in a catch about every four days. When she left port, we made plans to board her when she returned, to prevent her from unloading her catch. When, however, the *Victoria 7* came back a few days later, she was empty-handed. With no whale to bring in to shore for processing, she anchored in the harbor. Time for plan C: chaining ourselves to the harpoon gun to prevent the whaler from going out for another hunt.

We were fortunate enough to have an experienced harpoon chainer aboard—Patty Hutchison (now Lichen). Two years before, at age twenty-three, Patty had jumped from an inflatable onto an outbound whaler off the coast of Japan. She passed out leaflets to the crew and then chained herself to the harpoon gun. Everyone assumed the whalers would stop and then cut her free, but they just kept going and took Patty out to sea. The Japanese ship steamed toward the whaling grounds for several hours. They told Patty she would be treated nicely if she would just get off their harpoon gun and come inside to get warm. She bravely refused and the Japanese ship had to steam all the way back to port without taking a whale.

Our plan was to have a team of seven activists board the *Victoria 7* amidships (the middle part of the ship), where the sides of the whaler were lower to make it easier to haul in the dead whales. The seven members of the team were Campbell Plowden, Gretchen Hall, Jos van Heumen, Pieter Lagendijk—who would take photos from the harpoon gun—Patty Hutchison, Cindy Stewart, and me. Normally as a skipper I don't get to board other ships. But in this case, with the *Rainbow Warrior* safely at anchor, I was able to get in on the action. Six of us would chain themselves to the harpoon gun and I would climb up to the crow's nest and hang a banner that read *"Salvemos a las Ballenas!"* (Translation: "Let's Save the Whales!") It would be very hard to get me down from there once I reached the top.

Getting everyone to the harpoon gun and then chained on was going to take more time than we were likely to have before meeting resistance from the whaler's crew. What we needed was a diversion, and we came up with the perfect solution. Athel "Ace" von Koettlitz—our English chief engineer—and his very attractive French girlfriend Rafaella DeMandre (I always called her Ralph) would sidle up to the port side of the whaler in one of the Zodiacs and chain themselves onto the whaler. As if that wouldn't be enough of a distraction, we were also betting that Ralph could enchant the whalers enough to cover our actions on the opposite side of the ship.

We boarded the *Victoria 7* early in the morning before they had a chance to leave. Our distraction plan worked without a hitch. Ace and Ralph completely engaged the attentions of the crew; he by explaining the campaign's objectives, and Ralph by translating it—while batting her eyes—for all of the lonely whalers. I clambered up to the crow's nest, got the banner up, and the chain gang got to the harpoon gun with enough time to get locked into position.

The captain, who was Japanese, was incensed. He engaged his engines full ahead, hard astern, and did some doughnuts with the ship, trying to shake us loose or scare us. Athel, realizing that he and the Zodiac were being dragged around dangerously by the whaler, disengaged and went back to the R'dub. Ralph stayed on board the whaler to act as a translator. The Peruvian crew was not about to hassle us and the authorities were nowhere in sight, so the Japanese captain anchored the whaling ship again. We all waited. And waited. And waited.

It was a hot day, and as I sat up in the crow's nest I felt like I was on a spit roaster in the sun. In the afternoon some officials from town came out to pay us a visit. It was pretty low-key. The first thing they said to Campbell was that he did not have permission to be on board the whaler. Campbell knew that they had us there. No doubt about that! Campbell calmly replied that we wanted Peru to honor the whaling moratorium. The officials left. Several hours later the same officials came back to the whaler and told us that they had "checked with the authorities and they are not going to agree to do that." Then they asked us to leave again. And we asked them to stop whaling again. They went away. Stalemate. No big deal, but there was nothing more to do other than wait some more and see what developed.

Night fell. The chain gang each took turns on watch so the rest could get some sleep. We were all getting hungry, thirsty, and a little cold, so some of the crew on the *Rainbow Warrior* came over in a Zodiac with bottles of water, warmer clothing, and food. It was all fairly civil. The whaler's crew even brought the chain gang coffee and a can that they could pee in. They cautioned us that their captain would not approve if he discovered it. (The Peruvian whaling crews were not fond of the Japanese officers at all.) A second Zodiac–with a few other members of the R'dub crew onboard—was chained onto the *Victoria 7*'s anchor chain to prevent her from leaving port.

Someone on the R'dub remembered that it would be Campbell Plowden's birthday at midnight, so they brought over a bottle of rum. After a long hot day in the sun, some rum sounded like a damn good idea. Nothing much was happening, so I climbed down from the crow's nest to share the birthday festivities around the harpoon cannon. I have to admit, I had more than my fair share of rum (after all, I was the only one not wearing handcuffs!). The next thing I knew, I woke up to the sound of Gretchen (at eighteen, our youngest crew member) warning us: "*Something's happening!* Wake up! Wake up!"

The police—blinding us with powerful searchlights—pounced at first light, catching us all off guard. They were boarding the *Rainbow Warrior* and the *Victoria 7* in a coordinated strike. The police were on us in what seemed like seconds. As I was the only one not chained into place on the *Victoria 7*, they immediately arrested me and brought me down to the crew's mess (the dining hall) on the whaler. They left me there, and then tried to figure out how to cut the harpoon gang loose. I'm not sure what they were thinking because they didn't lock me in or handcuff me, so as soon as I could I escaped and climbed back up into my highly defensible position in the crow's nest. That didn't make the police look good at all. Then the army arrived.

The soldiers who came aboard scared the crap out of us. It wasn't their ferocity; it was their inexperience and nervousness that heightened our sense of danger. One young soldier seemed to be shaking uncontrollably, his finger on the trigger of a machine gun. They motioned for the group on the cannon to unlock themselves. Pieter, our snapper, suggested to Patty that she gather all of the keys for the locks. As the soldiers began to get agitated, she calmly threw all the keys overboard.

One of the soldiers or policemen was smart enough to bring bolt cutters, so a short time later we were all officially arrested and taken to the port captain's office. The guards at the port captain's office weren't threatened by us; we had already been around town for a few weeks so they knew we weren't going to be violent in any way. Still, they were annoyed. Campbell suggested that as long as we were being arrested, we should go on a hunger strike. We all readily agreed. The port captain (one of the same men we had talked to on the whaler earlier) seemed to be particularly confused about our hunger strike.

"Please, tell us why you are on a hunger strike," the official said.

"Because you arrested us!" said Campbell.

"But you *wanted* to be arrested!" he said.

"No, no, we just want you to stop whaling!" said Campbell.

The officer went away muttering, probably something about us crazy *yanquis.*

So far, so good. But things were about to take a much more serious turn.

A few hours later, our Peruvian attorney arrived and assessed the situation. First, he was sorry to inform us that under Peruvian law we could be charged with piracy. Peru's definition of piracy at the time was somewhat different from that of most countries and much more broadly defined. The charge came with a *minimum* sentence of three years. Furthermore, there was a three-year-long wait for a trial, and no possibility of bail.

"Will you say you did not board the ship?" our lawyer asked us.

"No!" we said.

"Will you say you did not chain yourselves to the harpoon gun?"

"No!"

"Then you will be found guilty of piracy, and you will be in jail for twenty years. This is not America. This is Peru."

He went on to explain that hunger strikes for political purposes were another serious crime. That was the end of the shortest hunger strike on record. Our lawyer had impeccable timing; it was almost dinnertime anyway. The port captain decided that the *Rainbow Warrior* would be the easiest place to keep us all under guard, so we were escorted back to our ship. It was a very serious little group of environmental activists who went to bed that night. Sleep was difficult, to say the least.

We had a photographer named Duane, from California, aboard the R'dub. He was a skinny character who wore very short cutoffs that often did not cover what they were supposed to cover. The next day, while I was in the middle of giving my formal statement to the magistrate, Duane came flying into the magistrate's office in a severely agitated state. Duane was screaming and shouting unintelligibly, practically foaming at the mouth. From the way he was carrying on, I thought the entire crew had just been killed.

It turned out that during a shift change of our guards, one of the younger soldiers accidentally fired his machine gun as he was stepping aboard our ship. Thankfully nobody was hurt, and the authorities agreed that—from that point forward—the guards would leave the machine guns ashore and only the captain of the guards would be armed with just a pistol. I found the spent shell casing on the deck and stuck it on the light switch in the mess of the *Rainbow Warrior*, where it remained until the boat was blown up in Auckland three years later.

The next day, we were taken to the local magistrate to make statements. It was while we were in the court that we were shown the jail where we'd be held for at least three years if the prosecutor decided to indict us. The primitive three or four rooms had dirt floors sunken down about three feet, with a notable absence of toilets. I'm sure they showed us the prison to intimidate us, and I would be lying if I told you it didn't.

Peruvian jails do not provide prisoners with any food other than bread and water. As a prisoner, you are completely dependent on friends and family to care for you. Six years in a hellhole like this (at least three years waiting for the trial, plus a minimum sentence of another three years) was a very sobering prospect. At the magistrate's office we met some Polish fishermen who were part of a crew that had already been detained for six years. Some of the crew had been jailed, and the remainder of the crew who were free had stayed in Peru to help feed and care for their shipmates in the jail. Many of these Poles had been there so long they had Peruvian wives, and some even had entire Peruvian families! The Poles offered to take care of us if we were thrown in jail, but we really, *really* hoped that wouldn't be necessary.

We also learned that the Peruvian justice system has some additional quirks: you are presumed guilty, and if you're found innocent, the prosecutor can appeal to get a conviction

from a higher court! (At least that was true at the time.) There
was also a sense that the judges were often influenced by
politics and corruption. Sitting on the *Rainbow Warrior* under
armed guard while our future was being decided in such circumstances prompted some very heavy soul-searching. Were
we really prepared to be imprisoned in Peru for six or more
years? Was what we had done worth it? This was my first
time facing serious jail time. I had been captain of the R'dub
for about a year and a half and had gotten very attached to
the ship and my cabin with the (almost) double bunk and the
nice view forward. I was not eager to trade it for a dark, dank
jail cell.

On the plus side, *if we got out*, I knew it'd help me get noticed at Gp's headquarters in Amsterdam. For me, getting noticed wasn't about climbing the corporate ladder so much as it
was about getting the really cool assignments. On the negative
side, if I were sentenced to twenty years, I'd be over fifty years
old by the time I got out. Being convicted would not be a good
career move.

Had we known that simply boarding the whaler could be
considered an act of piracy–with a very lengthy sentence as
the result–we would never have done it. We kept asking ourselves over and over if this was worth it. All of us believed
that killing whales was wrong. But would six years or more
in jail really help them? Couldn't we do more to protect them
if we were free? I suppose we were willing to go to jail for
them, but that certainly didn't mean we were looking forward
to it, or that we wouldn't do everything we could to avoid it!

This stressful state of waiting lasted several weeks. As if
things weren't already bad enough, the whole crew got dys-
entery from eating avocados grown with unsanitary water.
The locals had enough immunity, but all of us *yanquis* got a

serious case of the runs. That experience put me off avocados and guacamole for ten years.

All was not lost, however. We had had some politicians and locals on our side, all because Campbell had done all that relationship-building in advance. The campaign itself—which was getting good press in Peru and internationally—had been effective, and because of that we had gained a lot of additional goodwill in the Peruvian community. *Even some people in the prosecutor's office were on our side:* in the indictment itself they had written "These are well-intentioned but slightly misguided young people who are not out for their own gain." They were basically admitting that we were innocent right in the indictment! You don't see *that* every day.

During the uneventful weeks of detention on the ship, we had an emergency that helped to break up the monotony. Some years before, France had given Peru three nice, new tuna seiners (big trawlers). We heard that, immediately upon their arrival, the trawlers had been stripped of all their good equipment and were now just sitting at anchor and rusting.

The wind would usually build up to a stiff breeze every afternoon, and one day the trawlers broke loose as a group and headed straight for us. It looked to me like the single mooring cable holding them had broken and, driven by the wind, they were moving down on us quickly. We had just enough time to start up our engine, get the anchor up, and move out of their way. This made the port captain exceptionally angry: The *Rainbow Warrior*'s engine was supposed to have been disabled to prevent our escape (although it turned out it was a good thing it hadn't!). The port captain then tried to convince me that it was not the seiners that were moving toward us, but it was the

R'dub that was drifting toward the tuna trawlers. Through a translator, I explained that ships never ever drag *into* a 25-knot wind; they drag *with* the wind. Once the seiners were past us, we re-anchored right away, and he calmed down. I have to wonder if he really thought we would try to escape with three Peruvian guards onboard!

Just before Christmas, the charges were dropped. Much of the credit for our release has to be given to the relationships and politicking that preceded the action. Shortly thereafter, the Japanese-Peruvian whaling industry was shut down and the Peruvian government agreed to withdraw their objections to the IWC ban. There is no doubt in my mind that our action hastened that process and that, as a consequence, we saved the lives of countless whales. It still ranks as one of the best campaigns I've been a part of; thanks in large measure goes to Campbell. While the action had ended well, we had come very close to a disastrous conclusion.

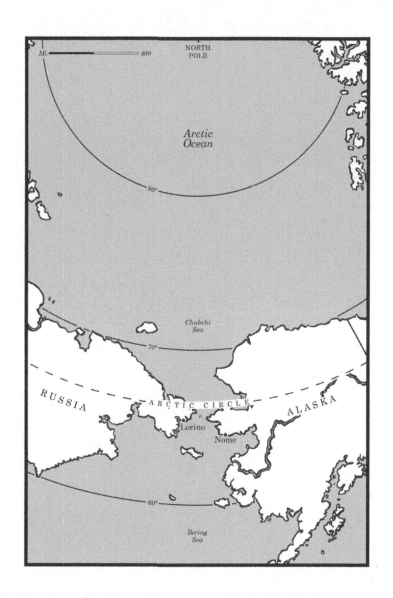

4

The Soviet Whaling "Film Festival"

July 1983

Lorino, Soviet Union—approximately two hundred miles

northwest of Nome, Alaska

Antiwhaling Action

Seven months after the action in Peru, we were embarking on another antiwhaling effort. Our new objective was to document that the Soviets were whaling commercially despite the fact that it had been banned all around the world by the International Whaling Commission the year before. The IWC did allow for indigenous peoples to hunt using traditional methods, and then only for the purpose of sustenance and certain tribal traditions, but the Soviets were using that loophole as a cover for a much larger operation.

A year earlier, Sea Shepherd–the antiwhaling group organized by an ex-Gp'er named Paul Watson–had taken some photographs that proved that the Soviets were whaling on an industrial scale and, worse yet, were feeding the whale meat to foxes, minks, and sables for the fur industry. What a good

idea! Let's turn small intelligent animals into coats by feeding them larger, endangered, and even more intelligent animals. Who thought of *that*!? Apparently, someone in the Soviet
central planning office.

Watson had been thrown out of Greenpeace a few years
before for being too radical and not adhering to Gp's peaceful, no-property-damage approach. While he is extremely
passionate about saving whales, he constantly crossed the
peaceful line as far as Gp was concerned. Sea Shepherd had
taken the photographs at the Lorino whaling base the previous year, but they didn't have a well-developed media arm,
so their action had made barely a ripple. (If a tree falls in the
forest and the media doesn't cover it, did it really fall? In some
ways, Gp could be considered to be a very early social media organization.) Publicity is one of the things that Greenpeace has always been very good at. We were determined to
broadly expose what the Soviets were up to, while saving hundreds of whales in the process.

Our plan was to approach the Soviet Union's international
limit of twelve miles, and when they came out to stop us, we'd
have a showdown with the Soviet navy to capture the world's
attention. This was a very tense time in US and Soviet relations. America had boycotted the 1980 Summer Olympics
over the Soviet occupation of Afghanistan (but had won
the "Miracle on Ice" game against the USSR in the Winter
Olympics). The Soviets would, shortly after this action, shoot
down Korean Air Lines Flight 007, killing 269 innocent passengers. Ronald Reagan's "we begin bombing in five minutes" joke (Reagan hadn't realized that his microphone was
turned on, and the Soviet military went into alert in response),
and the movie *Rocky IV*–both a couple of years later–were
representative of the state of relations between the two super-
powers.

Our arrival in Soviet waters would not be a surprise: we had been cruising up the West Coast of the US holding press conferences and announcing our intentions for a couple of months. Without a doubt, this action was going to be more nerve-racking than any I had been a part of before. The Soviets knew we were coming, so we could expect a welcoming party.

The Bering Sea is a very unforgiving environment at any time of year, but we were lucky that the weather on this 330-nautical-mile passage was a little nicer and warmer than usual. With the warmth, however, came the fog. As we approached the twelve-mile limit off the Soviet coast, we had very poor visibility. Pat Herron—the second mate—woke me when we approached the limit. Eddie Chavies—our campaigner—was called up to the bridge and we both watched the radar intently, expecting that the Soviet navy would enforce their sovereign authority. It seemed they were no-shows. Eddie and I reviewed the situation and we quickly decided to press deeper into Soviet waters.

Eddie and I always worked really well together, and one of the reasons was that we both felt that it was best to have open meetings with the whole crew to involve them in the planning process. The previous night we had called the crew together to discuss what we would do in the off chance that we made it to shore. Someone suggested that we photographically document what was going on at the whaling station and fur farm. Another suggestion was passing out pamphlets about what we were doing and why. It was a typical sort of Gp plan. We asked for volunteers and the usual four or five crazies volunteered despite the fact that we were invading a sovereign nation not known for its tolerance of political protest.

(That whole *Gulag Archipelago* thing could be a real drag. One of our engineers, a woman from Seattle, had decided to remain in the States after reading Solzhenitsyn's book.) We needed a few more volunteers. "Well, some people here do actions, and some don't," I said, throwing the gauntlet down and challenging the crew. Half a dozen more hands shot up.

At 3 A.M. the next morning, we closed on the coast. This far north, at this time of year, the sun never sets, but the fog was still thick and we had visibility of less than a mile. The silvery light in the mist was spooky. Fog always complicates things for sailors, and within swimming distance of a totalitarian nuclear power, it's far more than a nuisance. We inched our way closer to the shoreline of Lorino. We could barely make out the outline of some kind of icebreaking cargo ship anchored closer to the beach. The landing party (Chris Cook, administrative director of GP USA; Barbara Higgins; David Reinhart; Ron Precious, our cameraman; and Nancy Foote) got ready and took one of the inflatables in toward the beach. So far things were going according to plan.

The shore party started taking pictures of the whaling operations and the caged animals, and handed out their pamphlets to the locals and workers there. They weren't being stealthy about it at all. Everyone onshore could see our green ship with "Greenpeace" painted on the side, and they were all probably thinking, *Who are these hippies from Mars and what are they doing here?* They didn't seem to be afraid or angry, but at least one of them decided to call the authorities. Thirty minutes later, soldiers equipped with bayonets showed up and swiftly rounded up the crew.

The onshore crew called on the radio to say that the soldiers had invited them for tea, and that the base commander wanted me to come to shore to "discuss our concerns." All of their film, however, had been confiscated. *Brilliant!* I thought. *We can get photographs of us and the officer talking like diplomats—like adults, not like a bunch of hippies.* The invitation could be an opportunity, or it could be a trap. I wanted to know a little more about what was going on, but that's when their handheld VHF radio batteries died. (Murphy's Law seems to have been inspired by handheld radios, which always seem to die when you need them most.) We needed to get a second VHF radio to the crew onshore, so I asked Pat Herron (the second mate, who was just off the beach in another boat) to bring them his.

Pat was much happier being out of harm's way, sitting in a second inflatable a hundred yards out, but after some "encouraging" language from me he dutifully brought in the radio. As soon as he hit the shore, the soldiers grabbed him, threw his boat into the back of a military truck, and threw him in with the other five captives.

We had two other small outboard boats close by the beach, keeping an eye on the crew who were being taken away. Chris was with a Soviet officer, waving his arms in an exaggerated manner to signal to the two boats to come ashore. The Soviet officer, however, must not have understood any English, because the entire time Chris was motioning for our boats to come in to shore he was shouting, "Get out of here and take the film!"

The crew still had the second handheld and kept me informed as they, and the two boats, were being driven off. That invitation to tea seemed a little less appealing now. I was weighing the option of going ashore when the decision was made for me: a landing craft filled with soldiers heading our way indicated that *we* would be the ones hosting company instead. I could see what looked like bayonets poking up over the sides of their craft.

When our boatswain, Richard Dawson, had heard that all

of the shore party's film had been taken, he had the presence of mind to grab his own still camera, and crewman John Parulis got an extra sixteen-millimeter movie camera to document as much of the action as they could. With a squad of Soviet soldiers approaching the *Rainbow Warrior*, we had to make sure they didn't get their hands on that film. The Soviets had every right to take the ship and all the crew as we had violated their sovereign territory—not just for being inside the twelve-mile limit, but especially for putting people onshore. We could even be considered spies. Not good.

Wolfgang Fischer, a Russian-speaking, German scientist from our Hamburg office, had been assigned to our crew as translator. He was suddenly sweating bullets by the bucketful. I didn't know it at the time, but apparently Fischer had escaped communist East Germany as a young man by going over the wall in Berlin years before. Had he been captured and identified by the Soviets, he would have been thrown in prison for a very long time. If somebody had told me about Wolfgang's situation before the action, I might not have gone into Soviet waters, but as I said, nobody said anything about it until much later. Despite his well-founded fears, he did a fantastic job of translating. I saw Wolfgang at a Greenpeace meeting several years later and he wouldn't even look at me, much less speak to me. I can't really say that I blame him.

"Time to go." With the ship, the remaining crew, and the all-important film at risk of seizure, we had to put the pedal to the metal. Besides, the best way to force the Soviets to release our crew was to expose the illegal whaling and embarrass them in the eyes of the world. "Hard left rudder and full ahead!" The R'dub's new 600-horsepower, 16V92 Detroit Diesel engine was more than up to the task of outrunning the landing craft, so we quickly left them in our wake. But we had no time to celebrate our escape before a military helicopter appeared right over our heads. Green flares—the international signal for "stop, turn, follow me"— arched over the R'dub. We kept going. A voice, in English, came over the radio: "You *must* return. You *must* return." No dice. We kept going. The chopper then swooped in low and dropped something on the deck . . . some kind of a shell. We held our breath waiting for the tear gas, or a flash-bang grenade explosion.

After a few seconds of nothing happening with the shell, someone picked it up and discovered it was a spent flare casing. It had a message inside it. In neatly written, perfectly spelled English, the carefully rolled-up message said "Stop immediately." So what did we do? We kept going.

The Soviets must have been getting frustrated, because after the green flares, the radio announcements, and the written note in the shell casing, we still weren't "getting the message."

A new and ominous contact appeared on our radar: something was approaching fast off our port bow, directly between us and the safety of Alaska. The fog had temporarily lifted to about six miles of visibility, and when I actually eyeballed the ship in the distance I was suddenly struck by the thought that perhaps this had all been a trap, that the Soviets had let us in *specifically to catch us*, to throw us in prison as spies, to take our ship and make examples of us to the rest of the West. Maybe that's why they hadn't met us at the twelve-mile limit. Maybe that was why they let us land on the beach. Whether it was a trap or some kind of oversight, we had to escape, and we had to escape with the film. Not only did our lives depend on it, so did the freedom of our colleagues, as well as the lives of hundreds, if not thousands, of whales.

From the speed of the Soviet ship that was approaching, we knew that we couldn't outrun her, and she was very likely to be a warship. Knowing that we didn't have much time before we were intercepted, we had to have another idea and fast. John Parulis came up with a plan that was pretty "out there," but it was the best idea we had. I looked at First Mate Jim Henry and said as casually as I could in these circumstances, "Hey Jim, you wanna take a boat over to Nome with the film?"

To get to Nome, Jim would have to take an open boat 120 miles across the Bering Strait, which boasts some of the coldest and roughest seas in the world. Depending on where Jim landed on the Alaskan coast, he would then have to hike or jog as far as forty miles—while wearing a survival suit—to get to Nome. It was a slightly crazy plan, but so is killing whales and feeding them to minks. We all felt it was worth the risk, and while it was a long shot, it was the best available option at the time. (Remember this was long before satellite transmission technology. Nowadays, we can beam images all around the world in real time. Amazing stuff.) Once in Nome, Luis Barreto—the assistant campaigner onboard for the action—would take the film down to the lower forty-eight to get it developed and distributed.

To Jim's credit, he agreed to go despite the hazards and the limited chance of success. We swiftly prepared Jim's boat, filling it with spare gas tanks so he would have enough fuel to reach Alaska, and we gave him a compass to find his way east. We also gave him a couple of EPIRB emergency search-and-rescue beacons in case he didn't make it all the way back.

The Soviets saw us launching the boat and had a pretty good idea of what we were going to try to do, so they launched a second, smaller helicopter to follow Jim. Jim had already taken off and disappeared into the fog. With the roar of the outboard and the noise of the helicopter over his head, he couldn't hear us on the radio telling him he was going the wrong way. Instead of Alaska, he was headed for Japan— thousands of miles away in the wrong direction.

With the fog and haze, Jim couldn't use the sun to figure out which direction he was going in, which was exactly why we had given him the compass. Unfortunately, since his boat was filled with steel gas tanks, the compass turned out to be worse than useless. With no way to recall him, we altered course and started chasing Jim and the helicopter that was chasing him. Jim was heading into fogbanks to evade the chopper. We could see the chopper on our radar, but not Jim, and there was no way we could keep up anyway. The chase continued for more than an hour.

Finally we broke through the fogbank just in time to see Jim being hoisted from the water into the chopper full of armed soldiers. What a man's man! When he had seen us coming out of the fogbank, he had thrown himself into the water to distract the chopper while we recovered the film from the boat! At least that's what we thought. It was not, however, quite what had actually happened.

What *had* happened is that the chopper had hovered so low and close to Jim that the rotor wash literally blew the boat out of the water, flipping Jim right out of it. Miraculously, the boat had landed back in the water right-side-up and was still running. That was the good news. The bad news was that the boat was still running, but without anybody at the con- trols it was speeding around in circles. In fact, just after Jim had fallen into the water, he resurfaced just in time to see the boat heading straight for his face. Thanks to either excel- lent reflexes or a strong survival instinct, he had just enough time to push himself off of the bottom of the boat and away from the spinning prop. Unfortunately this caused his survival suit to fill with ice-cold Bering Sea water (is there any other kind?!) and Jim began to get hypothermic. He was probably glad to be picked up by the chopper after that. Once they had Jim inside the cabin, the Soviet helicopter headed back to its mother ship. Jim's part in the action was over.

After freezing his ass off in the survival suit, Jim was OK with being hauled into the Soviet chopper. The suit was so full of water that Jim had to hold on to the hoisting line with all his might so the weight of the water would not pull him back into the ocean. Once he was lifted up and into the helicopter, a soldier immediately stuck a machine gun in his face. Jim just smiled and put up his hands. The soldier smiled back and put down the gun. It was a reaction that would be normal all day. The troops were surprised and wary, but not aggressive.

They took Jim back to the navy ship, but by the time they got him there, hypothermia had made it impossible for him to walk. They carefully carried him out of the chopper and sat him down in a chair. With about twenty people looking on very sternly, the Soviet sailors handed him a big glass of water. So he drank it. Halfway down he felt a terrible burning sensation. It wasn't water at all. It was vodka. (Do not try this at home. Alcohol is *not* the remedy for hypothermia. It can actually make things worse, but in the Soviet Union the solution to everything seemed to be vodka. When in Rome— and when the Romans have big guns—do as they do.) Jim was carried to a cabin, stripped of his survival suit and wet clothes, and then rubbed down with even *more* vodka. Our light-drinking chief mate then slept for the next twenty hours.

As for the rest of the crew being held ashore, they were held in some kind of military barracks. They were not harshly treated, but were being told that they could expect to be there for a very long time.

Since Jim was already in custody inside the chopper, we focused on retrieving the film that was still in the runaway speedboat. It was about this time that someone told me that *all* the film was in the boat. Nobody had thought to keep some on the *Rainbow Warrior* just in case. Things were just moving too fast, including the boat with the film. Somehow we had to stop it, and we had to do it before the Soviets did. The film was not just important for saving the whales; it was vital for securing our friends' release. Bruce Abraham, our third mate who was making his first trip with Greenpeace, came up with an idea.

Bruce had been hired in Seattle just before we left for Alaska. He was a professional seaman with years of experience on research ships. We met one afternoon and after he expressed an interest in joining Gp, I invited him to join us for a short cruise from Lake Union to downtown Seattle. An audition of sorts. As we approached the dock, I could see that a good strong wind was blowing. It was going to keep pushing our ship away from the dock, making it more difficult to get a dock line over the water to one of the rope handlers onshore. The solution was to throw a heaving line—a light line with a heavy weight on one end—with the idea being that we would tie the other end of the light heaving line to the much heavier dock line. Then the dock line handlers could use the lighter heaving line to pull the dock line across the gap between the ship and the pier. With the wind, though, throwing the heaving line would also be tricky. I shouted to Bruce that we didn't have time for a second chance, given the tight quarters we had to work in. It had to be "one and done."

Bruce calmly coiled the heaving line and hefted the weight encased in the rope ball (it's called a monkey's fist) in his hand to better gauge the throw. He made what, at first, looked to be a beautiful throw, but then I saw that the weight was headed for a large plate-glass window and an unsuspecting group of people eating lunch in a restaurant next to the dock. All of us on the bridge sucked in our breaths, anticipating a crash of shattered glass—accompanied by the sound of screaming diners—that would announce Greenpeace's arrival in Seattle. It was all unfolding in what seemed like slow motion. . . .

As the monkey's fist flew over the heads of everyone standing on the dock, Bruce gave a little flick of his wrist, arresting the monkey's fist's dangerous trajectory and causing it to land gently at the feet of the waiting dockworker. It was a masterful demonstration of expertise, and right then and there it instilled in me a great confidence in Bruce. (I would have run up to the bow and hired him on the spot, but my own pride and ego held me back for a full ten minutes.)

Now, with all the precious film in the runaway boat, I was all ears when Bruce suggested a plan.

Bruce recommended that I maneuver the R'dub in front of the speeding boat so that it would hit the *Rainbow Warrior's* side near the stern, which would stop the smaller boat from turning away. Then Bruce would jump from the deck of the *Rainbow Warrior* into the boat about ten feet below. It wasn't a great plan, but it was at least simple and, more important, it was the only one we had. Bruce went up to the bow of the ship and waited until the boat made contact and started to work its way forward. With the same sense of great timing that he had exhibited with the monkey's fist, Bruce leaped over the side and landed squarely in the boat.

Remember all of the steel gas tanks in the boat? Well, Bruce does. He landed right on top of the tanks on his butt. You could instantly see the look of severe pain cross his face, but adrenaline is a wonderful thing: Bruce managed to get the boat under control so we could winch it, Bruce, and the film—the all-important film!—back aboard. Cindy, our cook and medic, determined that he had broken his ankle, and treated it. (The ankle was later found to have been broken in three places. Bruce also ruptured a disk in his back. He would end up enduring a long year of surgery, therapy, and recovery.)

At least now we had the film back, so we set a course toward Alaska. But the Soviets weren't giving up. Soon another ship—the freighter we had seen when we arrived in Lorino—joined in the festivities. It was headed straight for us and it didn't look like it was going to stop. Would the Soviets ram us? We couldn't completely dismiss the possibility. . . .

The freighter crossed our bow with little room to spare in an attempt to head us off. They were calling us on the radio demanding that we stop. (Wolfgang—despite his understandably acute case of nerves—was doing a brilliant job of translating.) The Soviets also hoisted the international code flags to signal "stop." Let's see, we didn't stop when they shot flares from a helicopter, or when they radioed us, or when they dropped a message in a flare shell, or when they had chased us with a landing craft full of soldiers, but they were hoisting flags just in case we didn't already understand that they wanted us to stop. Say what you want about the Soviets, but they can always be counted on to do things by the book. *Our* book said: "Keep on truckin'!"

As the freighter crossed our bow again at close range—less than fifty feet—we turned sharply and cut closely behind its stern. The two ships—the R'dub and Soviet freighter, the *Tanwet*—started weaving back and forth like two skiers slaloming down a hill. The other ship was bigger and faster than the R'dub, but being much longer she was far less maneuverable. It was kind of like a bear trying to catch a rabbit. I could put the engine into neutral, and before the other ship could react, we could easily cut behind the *Tanwet*. But if either one of the ships misjudged just one turn, it would spell disaster for us.

Adding to the pressure was the fact that we were running the ship with our manpower drastically reduced. Our first and second mates, the snapper (still photographer), the shooter (movie-camera operator), and two deckhands were in Soviet custody. The third mate had a broken ankle. Lloyd Anderson—the radioman—and Wolfgang couldn't leave the radio room. Lloyd was working with Wolfgang to communicate with the other ship while simultaneously working the Morse code key to keep Gp informed back in the US. Eddie Chavies—our campaigner—took the wheel so I could run back and forth across the bridge behind him. This made it easier for me to see what the other ship was doing more clearly and to direct Eddie when to turn. It was really freakin' busy up there!

Outwardly, I tried to remain calm. I had read all the Hornblower novels and I try to model my demeanor after his: calmly standing with hands in pockets, hunched over, on deck, deep in thought planning his next move. Always weighing the risks but still being aggressive. Classic Hornblower. It's very likely, however, that Hornblower was *not* the image I was actually projecting at the time, but I'd like to think so.

During the insanity on the bridge, there was a similar level of craziness down in the engine room. The Detroit Diesel was being put through her paces, pushed to the limit. (It's a good thing we had the new engine. The old one would probably have failed, with disastrous consequences for all of us. Especially Wolfgang.) During the height of the action the engine's main cooling line blew out, sending a high, arcing stream of hot water across the engine room. In normal circumstances this would be a fairly easy fix once the engine was shut down. In this instance, of course, stopping the *Rainbow Warrior* was unthinkable. The gang in the engine room figured out a clever way to clamp sheet metal around the cooling line to slow the leak to a manageable level. (They never even told me; they just handled it. I didn't find out about it until very recently.) People *and* machinery were being stressed to the maximum.

During the course of this game of chicken between the two ships, the most remarkable thing occurred: at least twice, we saw gray whales surface directly between the *Rainbow Warrior* and the freighter. It was as if they were returning the favor of our getting between them and the Soviet whalers in years past. At the time I didn't have time to really think about it, but it does seem that the whales understood what we were trying to do and that, in this instance, *we* were the ones being pursued. This was the first time I had seen something like that, but others at Gp have seen this kind of behavior before. And I've seen it several times since in other actions. I truly believe that whales are just as intelligent as we are. You can even make the argument that they're *more* intelligent than humans because they don't fuck up their own environment, *and* they don't kill each other for the right to fuck up their environment even more. So you tell me, which species is smarter?

Several of the R'dub crew stood near the bow to watch the action from the front row. At one point the two ships got so close to each other that the crew all ran aft expecting an imminent collision. Later, I got a lot of pats on the back for the cat-and-mouse game, and I have to admit that as potentially dangerous as it was, it was kind of fun! After about a dozen passes, the Soviet freighter captain realized the futility of his efforts. He called me a nutjob over the radio, and called it quits. We all breathed a sigh of relief. An hour later, we were home free. Then the Soviet destroyer showed up.

By the time the Soviet destroyer arrived on the scene, we were well out of the Soviet Union's twelve-mile territorial limit and into international waters. I asked Wolfgang to call the Soviet destroyer on the radio and ask them if they would confirm that both ships were outside of Soviet territorial waters. They confirmed it. I'm sure that little tactic caught them by surprise, though it certainly didn't stop them.

The destroyer was much faster than we were, and more maneuverable than the freighter we had just been playing with. As they gained on us, it looked to me like they had ropes dangling from some type of outriggers. That signaled their intention to board us on the open seas, like old-fashioned pirates with grappling hooks. I could almost imagine them climbing aboard with knives in their teeth. (In looking at the photos now it seems like the ropes were just normal lines used for launching small boats, but in the heat of the battle I could be excused for fearing the worst!) Lloyd was able to raise the US Coast Guard on the radio—we were now in radio range—and explained our predicament. When they asked us what assistance we required, we replied, "Air support!" They were not amused.

As the steaming Soviet navy ship tried to come alongside the R'dub, we cut sharply in front of them to dissuade them. It was like being in a race where one car is trying to pass another, and the lead car weaves back and forth to prevent the other one from passing. We did this to the Soviet destroyer three times before they too decided to call it quits. On to Nome!

During this whole episode, Lloyd had been sending out updates to Gp in San Francisco through Morse code. We had been unable to establish voice communications through the ham/single-side-band radio, because atmospheric conditions were interfering with that kind of signal. Morse code, for technical reasons, is a much stronger signal, but of course you're only able to communicate in dots and dashes. Lloyd was a very experienced radio operator and had a special Morse code device (a "keyer") which allowed him to "key" messages far faster than a traditional straight key—the familiar telegraph type of device.

In San Francisco, we had another experienced radioman—Richard Dillman—who was equipped with a formidable ham radio rig in his bedroom. Richard would transcribe Lloyd's Morse code back into English before sending the story out on the news wires and networks. Every time Richard sent a message back to Lloyd, the transmitter would draw so much power that the lights in his whole building would flicker and dim. It was like a scene in a B movie.

The action was getting so much media attention that there were TV camera crews in Richard's bedroom getting footage of him transcribing the Morse code messages. Remember, this was long before we had satellite phones or the ability to electronically transmit pictures, but the Morse code messages were very much like modern-day tweets. (I don't tweet, but I do post on Facebook at facebook.com/peter.willcox.7. Check it out.) After we reported we had a Soviet destroyer on our tail, Richard sent us a Morse code message asking "What are your intentions?" Lloyd keyed out our response: "Nome! Unless fired upon!" The media loved it.

When we arrived in Nome our first priority was to get Bruce to a hospital. We anchored in the harbor and got a boat ready to take him in. Naturally, with our outboard mechanic being held in Siberia, none of our four outboards would start. After a half hour of fiddling around, I got one of them going and we brought Bruce in. When we got closer to the docks I could see there was a large and expanding crowd of reporters. That's when I realized just how much coverage our action was getting. Once Bruce was admitted to the hospital, we held a press conference right there that was attended by about thirty international reporters. Pretty heady stuff.

Meanwhile, the Gp office in San Francisco and the media were all clamoring for the film and, of course, we had to get pictures to the IWC conference in England that was still going on for another couple of days. Luis Barreto—as our designated media liaison—had the responsibility of taking the film down to the lower forty-eight. Fortunately, Nome was chock-full of private jets that had been chartered by the media to get up there, so Luis was able to easily get a lift to Anchorage. In Anchorage, Luis was interviewed by Tom Brokaw (via satellite) and from there he was able to board a commercial flight to Seattle.

When they landed in Seattle, the flight attendant came up to him and asked him to come directly up to the front of the plane. *That's more like it!* he thought. They opened the door and at the bottom of the stairs was a man in a suit who walked Luis over to a helicopter—engines idling—that was waiting for him. Cool! By the time he saw a group of Gp campaigners banging on the glass from inside the terminal yelling "No! No! No!", it was too late. He was already in the NBC News chopper and they got the exclusive. (It turned out OK in the end. The chopper brought Luis to the NBC studio in Seattle and he was able to get even more airtime and publicity.) Within forty-eight hours, the IWC conference in Brighton, England, got an eyeful about what the Soviets were doing. And Hans Guyt, John Frizell, and Remi Parmentier—our team of campaigners—made the best use of it. Without our media departments onshore, it never would have been as big a story, and without our lobbyists, there would have been no point to the action at all. It was a group effort, and any one weak link in the chain would have caused it to fail.

Now that "the mink was out of the bag" and the Soviets had been embarrassed all over the world, they were anxious to put the entire incident behind them. But they also didn't want something like this to happen again, so they made a point about how outraged they were with Greenpeace, *and* with the US government for not preventing the incident. When informed that the Soviets were placing blame on the US government, Jon Hinck—Gp's national campaign director in the US—responded to his contact at the State Department: "I trust that you informed them that we are a free society and the citizens of the United States are not under the control of the US government." It was a nice civics lesson, but the Soviets were threatening our people with a lengthy detainment of seven years or more.

At first the Soviets made their own demands, but Jon gambled that as the media pressure built, the Soviets would soften. Eventually, they relented and released what were now being called the Siberia 7. A ship-to-ship handover of the prisoners was arranged, and four days later we cruised out to meet their ship at the international date line. Over seventy journalists, eager to cover the crew's return, joined us on the ship. So many, in fact, that we didn't have room below for all of them to sleep. Bunches of them were sleeping in various places on deck, but they didn't seem to mind that much as they were all swilling vodka and eating smoked salmon along the way.

Telephoto lenses littered the deck like beer bottles at a fraternity party. I'm sure it wasn't hard duty for them.

As for the Siberia 7, the Soviets had treated them fairly well, but there was one strangely ironic aspect to their experience in captivity: they were pretty sure the Soviets had been feeding them whale meat. My guess is that they are the only Greenpeace activists ever to have been fed whale meat (although, to be fair, they didn't realize it until after they had been released).

Chris Cook, one of the Siberia 7 and our US administrative director, headed directly for Gp's US headquarters in Washington, DC. Unbeknownst to him, former secretary of state General Alexander "I'm in Charge" Haig was also on the plane. When Haig stepped off the plane and saw the press waiting there, he naturally assumed it was for him. He straightened his tie and strode over to the podium. He was somewhat taken aback when one of the journalists said wryly, "Not this time, Al. We're here for the Greenpeace guy."

The action itself had ended well. Everyone was safe. Bruce had sustained injuries but they would heal, and the Soviet Union's big lie had been exposed. I have often wondered why Ed and I didn't hesitate when we completely changed the action plan and crossed the territorial seas limit. Any number of things could have happened that would have spelled the end of our Gp careers. Had Jim Henry been lost, or had we not gotten the film out of the inflatable, or had Wolfgang been arrested and detained, I am sure I would have been flown home from Nome, never to sail for Gp again.

We made other mistakes too—like putting all of the film in the inflatable. I had told the crew to "put the film in the boat." It didn't occur to me they would put *all* the film in,

nor did it occur to me to tell them not to. We were just react-
ing in the moment. Still, it was a wildly successful action, and
a great learning experience for me about what being a real
Greenpeace captain was all about. I could hardly wait for the
next adventure.

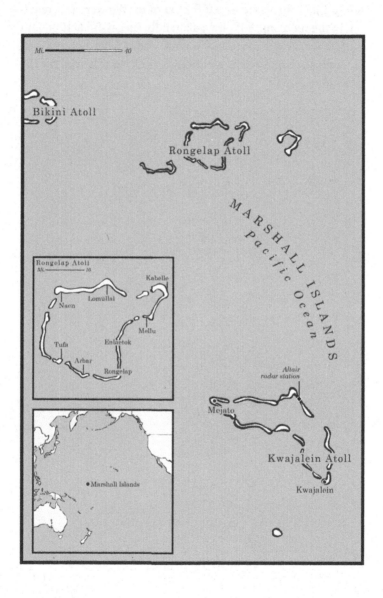

Mi. ⊢━━━━━━⊣ 40

Bikini Atoll

Rongelap Atoll

MARSHALL ISLANDS
Pacific Ocean

Rongelap Atoll
Mi. ⊢━━━━⊣ 16

Naen
Lomullai
Kabelle

Mellu
Enlaetok

Tufa
Arbar
Rongelap

Altair
radar station

Mejato

Kwajalein Atoll

Kwajalein

•Marshall Islands

5

The Evacuation of Rongelap

MAY 1985

RONGELAP ATOLL, THE MARSHALL ISLANDS—IN THE MIDDLE OF THE
PACIFIC OCEAN

HUMANITARIAN MISSION

It was just before dawn on a spring day in 1985, and we were bringing the *Rainbow Warrior* into the Majuro Atoll in the South Pacific; Majuro is the capital of the Marshall Islands. It had been a very long voyage; this was, in fact, the last leg in a series of the longest voyages I had ever been on (let alone captained) so far. I wasn't complaining; the length of the trip suited me just fine. I love the routine of being at sea. Life at sea is far simpler. Being back onshore usually means my life will be ruled by lists. After spending several months in a boatyard in Jacksonville, Florida, I was glad to be on a long ocean passage.

For several years prior to the refit in Jacksonville, I had tried to convince Greenpeace's leadership to equip the R'dub with a sailing rig. Not only would it be the perfect symbol of environmentalism, it would significantly reduce our fuel consumption and costs, *and* substantially increase the ship's operational range. Lloyd Bergeson, a gentleman I met when I had first joined the crew of the R'dub in New Bedford, had retired as one of the top engineers for General Dynamics Electric Boat, a company in Connecticut that builds nuclear submarines. Lloyd was a lifelong sailor, and after he left General Dynamics, he founded Wind Ship Development, designing sails and rigs to help cargo ships cut their fuel costs through wind power. He worked up the design proposal for outfitting the *Rainbow Warrior* with sails, which I took to Greenpeace. It took a long time to get Greenpeace's approval but they finally agreed, and the R'dub had been brought to Jacksonville for the fabrication and installation of her new rigging and sails.

While the R'dub was in the boatyard, we took the opportunity to make other improvements. It turned out to be a very difficult project. Our ship's manager quit right before the work was to begin, and so the entire sail conversion landed in my lap. It was a textbook example of being careful what you wish for, because you just might get it.

Most of the work was performed by the crew, but the welding on the masts, booms, and bowsprit of the rig was done by local companies. Lloyd, our radioman, upgraded the radio room. Bulkheads under the masts were strengthened to support the new loads. Practically the whole ship was repainted, and the engine room was completely cleaned and painted to the point where it was sparkling. To balance the additional weight of the sailing rig and the forces the sails would generate, we had to add twenty tons of concrete ballast in the lowest parts of the ship.

All of this work had to be completed within a very tight deadline. The ship was scheduled to be in New Zealand–

eight thousand miles away—in a few months, and we had a number of stops planned along the way. It took several months of hard, dirty work, but the result of all the effort was an almost completely rebuilt and modernized vessel. Little did we know that, once we got to New Zealand, all of that work would be blown up by the French government.

Note that I didn't say "blown up by the French." I always try to differentiate between the people and their government. I've never blamed "the French" as a country for blowing up the R'dub. No more than I want to be held up for blame for the shameful things the US government has done!

We set sail from Jacksonville, Florida, through the Panama Canal, then on to Hawaii to provision and refuel, continuing on to the Marshall Islands. It was a voyage of almost 11,500 nautical miles, almost halfway around the world, across some of the remotest stretches of ocean on Earth. The weather was mild most of the way and we got a good "downhill sleigh ride" (a yacht-racing phrase meaning sailing downwind at a good speed—the easiest and most enjoyable way to sail). The east-to-west trade winds carried the recently rerigged R'dub thousands of miles without us having to resort to using the engine for propulsion.

The heavenly sail across the Pacific made the work and pressure back in Jacksonville well worthwhile. The burdens and cares of the boatyard blew away in the warm breeze as the new sails and rig brought the Marshall Islands closer and closer. It had been a very enjoyable and successful passage, albeit a very long one, and when we brought the *Rainbow Warrior* into the atoll I was greeted by one of the most beautiful, mysterious, and rare displays provided by nature: the fabled green flash.

The green flash is the stuff of legend for most sailors, and only a very lucky few of us have ever seen one. It occurs when the sun is just below the horizon, in very clear atmospheric conditions and calm seas. The air and the Earth's curvature refract the sun's light and, if its colors are separated under just the right conditions, for the briefest moment, there is a brilliant and pure green flash that disappears in the blink of an eye. It looks like a giant green camera strobe. They're so rare that even after more than forty years at sea, this green flash is *still* the only one I've ever seen.

I'm convinced that many of the people who *think* they've seen one of these rare events have actually just been staring into the setting sun for too long and burned out their retinas. That, or they've been staring at the bottom of a recently emptied rum glass. Generally, green flashes occur only at sunset. This one was even more unusual in that it appeared at sunrise. Sailors consider a green flash to be a good omen and it left me feeling that the task that had brought us to the Marshall Islands was blessed by Nature herself.

Thirty years before our arrival, the Marshall Islanders had seen a different kind of flash on their horizon, a flash that was not a good omen at all. This flash would destroy their lives and culture in just a few days, and they had had no idea what was coming. On March 1, 1954, John Anjain, a local magistrate on Rongelap Atoll, was enjoying his usual morning coffee and looking out over the placid lagoon of the atoll. He later recalled, "In the early morning before sunrise, there was a sunrise in the west. It was a beautiful sunrise, with many red, green and yellow colors. . . . A strong, warm wind like a typhoon swept across Rongelap and filled the entire sky with smoke." The cool morning air suddenly got hot like the noonday sun, and then the entire atoll heard and felt the earthquake-like sound of one of the most massive explosions the world has ever seen.

What Anjain had just witnessed was the detonation of Castle Bravo on Bikini Island–the most powerful thermonuclear weapons test that the United States has ever conducted. (The Soviets–of course–had to one-up the Americans several times later.) The World War II atomic bombs had been measured in kilotons (1 kiloton=1,000 tons of TNT). Castle Bravo was a *thermonuclear hydrogen* bomb, an entirely new type of weapon that produced 15 *megatons* of explosive force–each megaton being equal to one *million* tons of TNT (1,000 kilotons=1 megaton). Imagine *1,000* Hiroshima or Nagasaki bombs detonating 110 miles from your house and you'll have some idea of what the Rongelapese had just witnessed. (Currently, a single US ICBM can contain up to *eight* Castle Bravo–size warheads. And there are hundreds of ICBMs. Not to mention the sizable stockpiles of the other nuclear powers.)

It is estimated that there are almost sixteen thousand nuclear weapons in the world today (according to Hans Kristensen and Robert Norris of the Federation of American Scientists as published in the *Bulletin of the Atomic Scientists*). As of June 2015, the Russians have roughly 7,500; the US, approximately 7,100; France and China, several hundred each; the UK, around 200; Pakistan, India, and Israel, roughly one hundred apiece; and North Korea has a few as well. Experts estimate that there is enough nuclear weaponry to destroy the Earth at least five times. Some even estimate *fifty* times. Destroying the world just one time should be enough, and in my opinion, even *one* nuclear weapon is one too many.

The fireball from the hydrogen bomb reached a diameter of four and a half miles *in less than a second* and was visible over 250 miles away. The mushroom cloud eventually reached a height of twenty-two miles. This new form of weapon turned out to be two or three times as destructive as the physicists had predicted. They were playing with fire, literally, and with a type of fire that even they didn't truly understand.

The afternoon of the explosion, white flakes began to fall on Rongelap, coating the entire atoll and the waters around it with more than an inch of "snow." Children played and swam in it. People drank water from collection cisterns that had flakes of the stuff floating on the surface. Families dusted the flakes off their fruit and ate it. Within hours, the effects of radiation sickness were being felt. It was another three days before the United States would remove the islanders, but they didn't move them to save them; they moved the Rongelapese to *watch them die.*

The United Nations charter requires that the United States, as trustee of the Marshall Islands, "recognize the principle that the interests of the inhabitants . . . are paramount, and accept as a sacred trust the obligation to promote to the utmost . . . the well-being of the inhabitants." Instead, the US used the islands for nuclear weapons tests and to *study the effects of radiation on human populations.* So much for the "obligation to promote . . . the well-being of the inhabitants." These gentle people were being used like they were guinea pigs.

The abuse of these islands began years before that. Bikini Island, captured by the US from Japan in World War II, was considered to be the ideal atomic weapons testing area. It was very remote, sparsely populated, and—probably most important—was far from prying eyes. When the Bikini Islanders were originally approached about using their home as an atomic test range, they were told that they were being asked to leave their ancestral home for *"the good of all mankind and to end all wars."* A supposedly benevolent government telling a people whom it's supposed to protect that they're going to destroy their homes with massive weapons for the sake of world peace is yet another instance of Orwellian audacity. Being a peaceful and easygoing people, the Bikini Islanders agreed to leave. It's doubtful they were told they could never return. In the ensuing twelve years, twenty-three nuclear devices were exploded on, under, over, and around Bikini.

Strangely, the bikini swimsuit was named after the Bikini Atoll nuclear explosions because—in the words of its French designer (Louis Reárd) when he launched it—"Like the bomb, the bikini is small and devastating." I'm not a fashionable guy, but I guess "bikini" sounded better than "Nagasaki suit."

Up until 1954's Castle Bravo test on Bikini, Rongelap had been mostly unaffected by the tests. It had always been one of the most peaceful and utopian places on Earth. The large atoll, almost twenty miles across, provided the ideal fishing grounds: almost perfectly protected by the ring of islands and reefs on the edge, with crystal-clear waters filled with various fish and gentle ripples lapping along beautiful beaches with palm trees full of various fruits and coconuts. Heaven on earth, Rongelap hadn't changed all that much until the "sunrise in the west" that beautiful March morning changed everything.

Right after the test, the Atomic Energy Commission issued a press release claiming that the test was routine and that although some individuals had been unexpectedly exposed to some radioactivity caused by an unpredicted shift in the winds, there were no burns and all were reported well. It is difficult to count the number of lies in this statement.

It's a proven fact (there are many documented reports, investigations, and studies to back this up) that the United States *knew* that Rongelap was going to be in the fallout zone. Gene Curbow–the senior weatherman for the US Air Force on nearby Rongerik–was caught in the fallout himself. Years later, he and several other servicemen who had been stationed there during the test sued the United States after suffering from leukemia, cancer, and other radiation-related illnesses. Their lawsuit stated:

> *The wind had been blowing straight at us for days before the test. It was blowing straight at us during the test and straight at us after it. The wind never shifted. Gene Curbow, senior weather technician on the neighboring atoll of Rongerik, took radio-sound weather measurements up to an altitude of thirty thousand meters before and after Bravo. Curbow and US veterans stationed there have suffered since from a variety of illnesses, including cancer, tumors, heart and thyroid conditions, and urinary and bladder disorders that they say were related to Bravo. Three of them said they had difficulty fathering children or had had sickly offspring.*

Thanks to Curbow, we know that there was no unpredicted wind shift. In a formerly classified document he stated, "These observations were transmitted directly to a command center aboard the USS *Estes*, and the information was made available prior to the decision-making process of to go or not to go." Curbow further testified, "I believe that this action will go down in history as one of the greatest acts of criminal negligence to humanity."

So the military knew the Rongelapese were going to be irradiated. On the day after the blast, Americans wearing protective suits came to the island. They took readings with a Geiger counter from two wells and left after twenty minutes, without saying a word, according to the islanders. The Americans refused to treat them, and there have been admissions and statements that attest to the fact that these poor victims were being used to study the effects of radiation on humans. These studies continued for years, even after the islanders had been returned to their homes on Rongelap. Worse, the government even used the children of the islanders—those who had been born on their temporary island home in the years immediately after the explosion, and who had not been exposed in the initial blast—as a control group to study the continuing effects of the radiation that still lingers on Rongelap years after the Castle Bravo test. These trusting and innocent humans were seen as nothing more than medical test subjects. In my opinion, this is one of the most deplorable episodes in US history, right down there with the Tuskegee syphilis experiments.*

Like their cousins on Bikini, the Rongelapese were a trusting culture and they believed the authorities who told them that everything was safe and that they could return to their island. In 1978, almost twenty-five years later, the US Department of Energy performed an aerial radiation survey of the area. After reviewing the results, the government told the islanders, "Don't eat the fish from the north side of the lagoon, and don't go and pick fruit from that side of the island, either." That's when their trust ran out. Who was going to

---

* The Tuskegee syphilis study was a clinical study conducted by the US Public Health Service from 1932 to 1972 to study the effects of *intentionally untreated syphilis* in African American men in rural Alabama. The subjects of the study were never even told they had the disease; many died, numerous wives were infected, and children were born already suffering from the disease. When the issue was exposed in the early 1970s, it caused a massive scandal.

convince the radioactive fish to stay on the north side of the lagoon? The fish are going to swim wherever they want to. That was a fishy fish tale that no fisherman on Rongelap could believe.

After that, they petitioned the Marshall Islands and the United States governments to evacuate them to a new island home that wasn't contaminated with strontium, cesium, and plutonium. For thirty years they had suffered from high incidences of leukemia, thyroid cancer, birth defects, miscarriages, and even "jellyfish" babies: babies without facial features, with no skeletal structure, and with strangely colored, alien-like forms. Some babies were born alive but died immediately after their umbilical cords were cut. No mother should have to bear that.

Finally, Senator Jeton Anjain of Rongelap–the son of the magistrate who had witnessed the explosion–asked Greenpeace to move his village a hundred miles to the island of Mejato, which–while it did have slightly elevated levels of radiation from the bomb–was a big improvement over Rongelap. Nobody else was going to do it, so we had to. We immediately agreed to transfer their entire population of 350 people, lock, stock, and barrel. Steve Sawyer, our campaign coordinator, dubbed the effort Operation Exodus. It's a heavy responsibility to transplant an entire people and their culture, but we knew it was doable. Any sailor's primary rule at sea is to immediately render all aid to any ship that requires assistance. This island was no different than a sinking ship, only it was the people who were sinking.

Now, after weeks at sea, we were finally entering the port of Majuro, the capital of the Marshall Islands. We were there to pick up officials, journalists, and assorted volunteers to assist with the evacuation and relocation of the village. A welcoming committee composed of people from the local newspaper and other dignitaries greeted us. There were, as expected, no representatives from the US Embassy. They knew we were there and why we were there, and they were not at all happy about the visibility their mistreatment of the islanders was going to get. We provisioned the ship, loaded up additional building supplies, and took aboard a group of local volunteers. The *Rainbow Warrior* was as loaded down as she'd ever been for the three-day sail from Majuro to Rongelap.

Our course from Majuro to Rongelap brought the R'dub close to Kwajalein Atoll, the biggest atoll in the world. The atoll is home to a massive US ICBM missile-tracking base with the ALTAIR radar system—a huge radar dish that's over 150 feet wide. I don't know if it was a coincidence or not, but just as we sailed by the base, the gigantic radar dish rotated around and pointed straight at us. It was like they were telling us, "We have our eye on you. We know what you're doing, and we don't like it." It was not a comforting feeling.

Rongelap has no piers or docks, so we anchored the ship several hundred yards from the beach in the middle of the lagoon where the water was deep enough. Almost immediately a flotilla of small boats came out to greet us. The first boat to reach us was filled with women singing the sweetest-sounding indigenous melodies and holding signs that said "We love the future of our children." That hit me hard, and to this day I often tell people that everything I've done and stood for is for the love and future of *my* children.

Once ashore, Martini Gotje and I started walking around the village in Rongelap getting a feel for the task at hand. My first reaction was, *Oh my God! We've got to move all this stuff!* Literally tons of stuff. The villagers had already started taking things apart but there were dozens of still-standing homes and other structures needing to be moved. There were no cranes on the ship and no forklifts on land: everything would have to be done by hand and by block and tackle. Since we had to traverse over a hundred miles of open ocean between Rongelap and the new island, everything would have to be lashed down carefully so it wouldn't shift or topple over. When we got to the new island of Mejato, we would have to do it all again in reverse. It was going to take several trips back and forth to complete the move.

To make offloading easier, we figured out we could place plywood sheets across the inflatables to increase the surface area, and then pile stuff up as high as we dared. Sometimes the drivers of the boats couldn't actually see over the piles, and others would have to guide them. In some cases the seas were running high enough that when the loaded boats went into a trough between waves, all you could see was the pile of stuff and not the boat underneath.

It took four trips, but we were able to move the entire population from one island to the other in less than two weeks. The only things of value left behind on Rongelap were the livestock (mostly goats) and chickens. The animals were "hot" and the islanders thought it best to start over with nonradioactive animals. It's hard to argue against that.

One afternoon, after several hours of work in the hot sun, I decided to swim back to the *Rainbow Warrior* from the beach at Rongelap. It wasn't far, less than half a mile. One of our inflatables pulled up alongside me just to make sure I didn't become a shark snack. Grace O'Sullivan, one of the R'dub crew, jumped in the water from the inflatable and starting swimming alongside me. Naturally it turned into a race and she beat me back to the ship. Since Grace was a national women's surfing champion and a former lifeguard in Ireland, I didn't feel too badly about it until she climbed up the ladder on the side of the ship and I realized she had beaten me while wearing a full wraparound skirt!

After the last plywood sheet was unloaded, and the final corrugated metal roof was set down on the sand, the grateful Rongelapese held a banquet in our honor. It would be the first official event in Mejato. Every single islander was there, as was the entire crew of the *Rainbow Warrior* and all of the volunteers from Majuro. Everyone was exhausted after two weeks of non-stop work. Brief remarks were made, as were some toasts, but none of us had the energy to either make, or listen to, any long speeches. We didn't need words to share the emotions that were plainly visible on our tired and happy faces. Looking around you could tell that everyone felt that this was a new beginning. I especially remember seeing the many children with severe birth defects, and I hoped that the next generation of Rongelapese would be spared the horrible effects of the radioactive fallout they had been purposely subjected to.

It was, and still is, one of the most profoundly emotional experiences of my life. In many respects, this is why Greenpeace acts to bear witness to these abuses: to shine a light on the terrible things that we do to the Earth and to each other. Sure, Gp cares about whales and polar bears, and coral and seals, but we also care about humankind and our kids, our future grandkids, and so on. Personally, my commitment stems not from my love of the environment alone, but because I want to make sure that future generations have a planet they can actually still live on, a planet that *my children* will live on. The warmth, love, and gratitude that the islanders expressed to us that last night continues to sustain me in my darkest moments.

After that final dinner, we set sail in the direction of New Zealand where we were to join a protest fleet sailing to

Moruroa to stop nuclear testing by the French military–the only country besides the Soviet Union that was still conducting nuclear tests. After seeing the damage and destruction unleashed by the nuclear testing in the Marshall Islands, we were eager to stop it in French Polynesia. But it was on our way there that the *Rainbow Warrior* was to meet her fate in New Zealand at the hands of those same French forces.

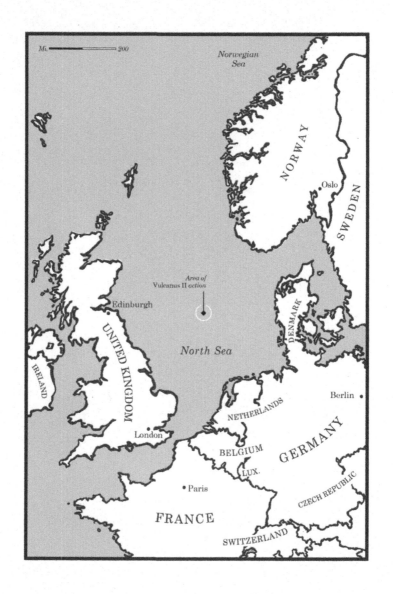

6

Something Is Toxic in Denmark

August–October 1987

Voyage from Auckland, New Zealand, to Moruroa, French Polynesia

Anti-Nuclear Weapons Testing Action

With the *Rainbow Warrior* out of action, I was a captain without a ship. That's like being a fish out of water. Still, after what the French government had done to the ship and Fernando, I was even more committed to carrying out our plan to stop nuclear testing in Moruroa in French Polynesia.

The original plan was that the *Rainbow Warrior* would serve as the mother ship for a group of sailboats that were sailing as the Pacific Peace fleet. The boats would sail into the testing area, putting themselves in harm's way to force the French to stop the test, or at least bring media attention to it. One thing we had learned about the French authorities was that you could count on their overreacting. (Of course, we hadn't counted on them overreacting by bombing our ship in New Zealand before we even *got* to Moruroa!) Now, without the R'dub, the logistics were somewhat more difficult. It would be a 2,571-mile sail—with no stops—and take a month or so to get there. One of the smaller sailboats in the fleet—the thirty-eight-foot *Vega IV*—needed a celestial navigator and radio operator, so I signed on as the mate.

The *Vega IV* was equipped with a new technology called satnav. Satnav was an early version of GPS. It was very accurate (at least for the standards of the day), but it had one big limitation: it could only give you a fix (position report) about once every ninety minutes. Today's GPS technology is even more accurate (sometimes to within centimeters) and it provides continuous fixes. Back in 1985 there were only a few satellites in orbit, so service was limited. As usual with new technology, the hardware could be a bit buggy, so it was important to have a navigator with celestial navigation skills as a backup, skills I had honed over the last several years.

The *Vega IV* was a slow but well-built sailboat. It had been the personal yacht of David McTaggart. In 1972, McTaggart joined Greenpeace and sailed the *Vega IV* (which he temporarily renamed *Greenpeace III*) to French Polynesia to protest atmospheric nuclear testing there. The French authorities eventually lost patience with the delays he was causing and finally rammed his yacht with a navy minesweeper and caused considerable damage. (Remember what I said about counting on the French to overreact?!)

The following year, McTaggart was back and this time the French forces were in no mood to fool around. Within a couple of days of his arrival, a commando team boarded his boat and beat him severely—almost costing him an eye. To cover up the beating, the commandos searched the *Vega* and her crew carefully and confiscated all of the film onboard. They proclaimed that McTaggart had "resisted arrest" and injured himself in a fall. They were, however, completely embarrassed a short time later when pictures of the entire event

were distributed all around the world, disproving their version of the story. Despite the commandos' careful attempt to
eradicate any evidence of their aggression, one of the crew—
Anna Marie Horn—smuggled out some film. The ensuing
firestorm of publicity drove the French to agree to stop atmospheric nuclear testing. It was one of Greenpeace's earliest and biggest successes. Afterward, McTaggart had *Vega IV*
repaired and then donated her to Greenpeace. Now, over a
decade later, we were taking her back to stop the nuclear testing that was still being performed underground.

After the monthlong sail from New Zealand to Moruroa,
we hovered outside the twelve-mile territorial limit. We knew
as soon as we went inside the limit the French military would
legally be able to board and arrest us. Our plan was to wait
until just before they were going to detonate the "shot." The
M/V *Greenpeace* was meeting us there to fill in for the *Rainbow Warrior.* She would act as the mother ship and provide
the communications capability that we needed to get media
coverage for the action.

We had gotten good press when we left New Zealand for
Moruroa, but just sitting around sailing or floating with nothing going on wasn't generating headlines. Knowing the media were going to quickly lose interest, we needed to make
some news. We found some large pieces of driftwood in the
water, lashed them together with empty barrels, and made a
good-size raft. We added a sail and a protest sign. When it
was ready, we made an official announcement over the VHF
radio that we were sending a "secret weapon" inside the territorial limit. A couple of crew sailed the driftwood "weapon" in
the direction of the island. The French navy, probably expecting something like a minisub, got all riled up. With the new
satellite uplink on the *Greenpeace,* we were able to send back
pictures of the "secret weapon" to the media. They loved it.

After the long haul to Moruroa and several weeks of waiting around for the "shot," several of the sailboats that had
made the trip were running low on supplies. To make matters worse, the *Greenpeace* had some generator issues and was
forced to depart for repairs. The French weren't about to allow any of us to provision, so many of the sailboats had to
leave while they had enough food, fuel, and water left to sail
the few thousand miles back home. We stayed on and hoped
that something, anything, would happen soon. Finally, we
heard a radio report on the BBC that an underground detonation of a one-kiloton device had been scheduled. (It is believed to have been a test of a trigger for a hydrogen bomb; it
was the largest test they could perform while we were there.)
It was time to make our move.

We sailed across the twelve-mile limit and got about a half
mile in when we were intercepted, boarded, and arrested.
Chris, *Vega*'s skipper, and I had our hands tie-wrapped, and
then we were all brought to a warship of some kind. Grace—
our Irish surfing champion—and I were in a relationship at the
time, and we were left in a cabin together. We were told we
would be put in separate cabins later that night. Surprisingly,
when the door was locked for the night, they left us together.
It went the same way for five nights. After all the negative
press the French had received after beating McTaggart, and
the international backlash from their bombing of the *Rainbow Warrior*, they were bending over backward to treat us
as politely as they could. We were served nice meals, good
wine, and generally were treated like guests. After a month
and a half of eating canned food in the confines of the *Vega*,
this was practically a vacation.

We had hidden our passports, and that made it difficult
for them to get rid of us. Eventually we were allowed to leave,
but we were banned from French Polynesia for life. (Martini

has been banned for *two* lifetimes, so he's got me beat on that score.) Grace was sent back to Ireland, and I flew to Los Angeles and then on to Ireland to reunite with Grace.

It had been more than six months since I had been in the States. Quite a lot had happened during that time. We had left Jacksonville, Florida, on the *Rainbow Warrior* in March 1985, sailing to Panama and then to Rongelap. From Rongelap we sailed to New Zealand, where the ship was blown up. From there, I sailed to Moruroa on the *Vega*, was arrested, held, and then deported. By the time I got to LA I was a little fried.

I arrived at the LAX airport in a T-shirt and shorts, but as I looked around the terminal I was freaked out by the way people were dressing. I am not a fashion plate by any stretch of the imagination (a clean sweatshirt is dressing up for me), but what people were wearing in LA was truly bizarre. A customs official saw my bewildered look and asked me, "You know it's Halloween, right?" I had completely lost track of what day it was. It was quite a relief to know that aliens hadn't taken over California while I was away.

OCTOBER 1987
MIDDLE OF THE NORTH SEA
ANTI-INCINERATOR SHIP/TOXIC WASTE ACTION

I spent the next eighteen months sailing and working on a forty-eight-foot antique wooden ketch I had been given by my friends Scott and Barbara Herrick. I did some competitive yacht racing with some buddies, and had earned some additional radio and EMT (Emergency Medical Technician)

certifications to widen my skills as a captain. By the summer
of 1987 I was itching to get back into action. Greenpeace
assigned me to the M/V *Sirius*, built in Holland in 1950 as a
pilot vessel. Pilots are specialists who are placed on large
vessels whenever they enter or leave a busy port. The idea is
that pilots are very familiar with the harbor and local traffic
patterns, reducing the dangers of vessels transiting the harbor. (This is mostly true, but I have had some pretty hair-
raising experiences with pilots who've made mistakes.) A pilot
vessel brings the pilot out to the ship when it's coming in,
and takes the pilot off after the ship leaves the harbor area.
The *Sirius* was a rugged, all-weather boat, but in high waves
she'd roll at an alarming rate. There were very few crew members who didn't get seasick on her. I don't ever get seasick,
but on the *Sirius* even I came close a few times. Seasickness
is a very special kind of misery. There's a saying among sailors about seasickness: "At first you're afraid you're going to
die. And then you're afraid you won't."

Another quirk of the *Sirius* is that she was equipped with
an old-fashioned telegraph to the engine room. A ship's telegraph is the pedestal with a dial on it that says "Full Ahead.
Half Ahead. Slow Ahead," etc., and it rings a little bell every
time you move the handle from one speed/direction to the
other. Another telegraph in the engine room repeats what's
being signaled from the bridge. In other words, the captain
is not in direct control of the engines; he's merely communicating orders to the engineers through the telegraph, and
hoping the engineers get the message and respond accord-
ingly.

Shifting from forward to neutral to reverse on the *Sirius*
also required a delay. Different ships have different mecha-
nisms for doing this, but they all take a certain amount of time,
and difficulties can and do occur. This was my first tour on

1. Me steering my family's 36' Alden Coastwise Cruiser *Luau*.
I was probably imitating my paternal grandfather with the pipe.

2. At the helm of the
good ship *Clearwater*,
probably the late 1970's.
Note the eagle's head
carved into the end of the
long wooden tiller.
© MARTY GALLANTER
(CLEARWATER)

3. Maggy Aston (her maiden name. We got married 35 years later.) and me in 1978, my third year as Captain of the *Clearwater*.

4. The Greenpeace version of a 'Seal Team', heading out to spray paint baby seals (to protect them from being hunted for their fur), with the *Rainbow Warrior* in the background surrounded by pack ice.
© GREENPEACE/PIERRE GLEIZES

5. The Soviet warship that chased *Rainbow Warrior* off the shores of Lorino after we engaged with the Soviet freighter *Tanwet*.
© RICK DAWSON

6. Jim Henry in an inflatable on his way to Nome, Alaska, carrying film evidence of the commercial scale whale hunting and mink farms.
© RICK DAWSON

7. *Rainbow Warrior* on her side in Auckland,
New Zealand, after French commandos planted
two bombs on her hull and sunk her,
killing our photographer, Fernando Periera.
© GREENPEACE/JOHN MILLER

8. A New Zealand investigator standing in the hole caused by the
first of the French bombs.
© GIL HANLY

9. Fernando Pereira, probably in the Marshall Islands around the time
of the evacuation of Rongelap.
© GREENPEACE

10. Many children on Rongelap had birth defects. It is impossible to say for sure if radiation caused this particular girl's deformities, but it seems highly likely.
© GREENPEACE/FERNANDO PEREIRA

11. Andy Biederman, our ship's doctor, and a deckhand (centre, wearing shorts) and Davey Edward, our chief engineer (right) assisting one of the Rongelapese.
© GREENPEACE/FERNANDO PEREIRA

12. Rongelapese children on the deck of *Rainbow Warrior*.
© Greenpeace/Fernando Pereira

13. Me at the bow, a knife-edge, of the destroyer after it stopped,
but before the crew aimed their firehoses at me.
© Greenpeace

14. I'm sure the sailors on the bow were enjoying this much more than I was. After a while, someone else took my place and I was brought back to our ship, the *Moby Dick*, to warm up and rest.

© GREENPEACE

15. In October of 1993, we brought *Greenpeace* to the Sea of Japan to prove that the Russians were dumping nuclear waste. Here, Dima Litvinov and I are communicating with a Russian tanker.
© GREENPEACE/HIROTO KIRYU

16. Our activists got close to the radioactive tanker with a Geiger counter, which showed exceedingly high readings.
© GREENPEACE/HIROTO KIRYU

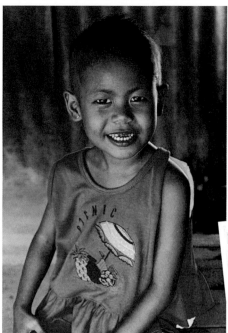

17. Crizel Jane Valencia, a six year old girl, and her family lived in one of the most polluted areas of Clark Air Force Base, Philippines. Crizel was dying from acute myeloid leukemia.
© Jonathan Taylor

18. Although Crizel was terminally ill, this brave and creative little girl made some drawings that we used in our February 2000 toxics tour of Asia.

19. The forklift and container filled with toxic waste that I drove through the crowded streets of Manila was resisted by a security guard.
© Greenpeace/Shailendra Yashwant

20. Jack Weinberg (in the blazer), Von Hernandez, our Filipino campaigner (blue shirt) and Yours Truly (in the sporty orange jumpsuit) waited to be arrested outside the US Embassy in Manila.
© Greenpeace/Shailendra Yashwant

21. Since I was the driver of the forklift, I was the first to be arrested. Here I am practicing passive resistance, not struggling in any way but making it as difficult as possible.
© Greenpeace/Shailendra Yashwant

22. A shot of the second *Rainbow Warrior* with her banner sails during the tour protesting illegal 'blood lumber' from countries such as Liberia.
© Greenpeace/Daniel Beltra

SAVE
THE LAST
ANCIENT
FORESTS
GREENPEACE
SAVE ANCIENT FORESTS!
GREENPEACE

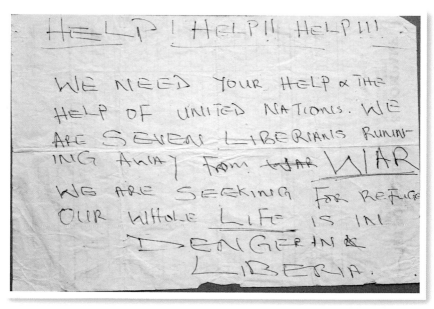

HELP! HELP!! HELP!!!

WE NEED YOUR HELP & THE
HELP OF UNITED NATIONS. WE
ARE SEVEN LIBERIANS RUNN-
ING AWAY FROM ~~WAR~~ WAR
WE ARE SEEKING FOR REFUGE
OUR WHOLE LIFE IS IN
DENGER IN
LIBERIA.

23. The note that one of our activists was handed by Liberian stowaways
while they were boarding the *Meltemi*.
© KEN LOWYCK

24. A Guardia Civil (the Spanish military force that performs police duties)
jumping into one of our boats attempting to block the *Meltemi's* pilot
ladder during our second action against her.
© GREENPEACE/DANIEL BELTRA'

the *Sirius*. I had a problem one of the first times I took her out. We were approaching the dock and I rang for dead slow astern. Nothing happened. There had been a glitch in switching from forward to reverse and the engine crapped out. The engineer had tried to shift it too quickly and jammed some of the gearing. We were in close proximity to a number of ships and other hard, big, and expensive things. Fortunately we were going slowly at the time and I was able to glide into the dock without even scratching the paint. Incidents such as that one did not make me confident in the *Sirius*'s ability to work in tight situations. This concerned me as I awoke the morning before an action in Rotterdam Harbor: I could see that the wind was blowing Force 10 (about 64 miles per hour) on the Beaufort scale.

The Beaufort scale is a way of observing the behavior of waves and other indicators to accurately gauge the speed of the wind. For example, Force 3 is defined as "Windspeed of 7 to 12 miles per hour. Large wavelets. Crests begin to break. Scattered white-caps. Leaves and small twigs constantly moving. Light flags extended."

Force 10 is a very serious tropical storm: "Very high waves with overhanging crests. Large patches of foam from wave crests give the sea a white appearance. Considerable tumbling of waves with heavy impact. Large amounts of airborne spray reduce visibility. Trees are broken off or uprooted, structural damage likely. Wave heights 29 to 41 feet."

Force 11 is close to a Category 1 hurricane. Force 12 is "holy shit" (my term, not the technical term!) with more than forty-six-foot waves.

I've been in one Force 10 or 11 storm: the 1972 Newport Bermuda Race. We were in the tail end of a hurricane with wind speeds of over 70 knots. The boat we were sailing began to fall apart: the deck was peeling off the hull. At one point, the jib began to tear and we had all hands on deck to get it down and get it repaired. I remember thinking to myself, *This is the last time I am ever doing this race!* but I've done it at least a dozen times since then. What can I say? I like a challenge.

The action planned for this morning was to bring the *Sirius* in close to another ship—the *Vulcanus II*—and then board her to prevent her from going out to incinerate a tanker load of toxic waste at sea. When it comes to pollution, most perpetrators use the out-of-sight, out-of-mind strategy: if people don't see it, they won't think about it. The population's ignorance is bliss if you don't care about destruction of the environment. The main objective of Greenpeace is to bring offenses like that into the public eye: "*in* the sight, *in* the mind" is our basic strategy.

A Dutch parliamentary committee was scheduled to visit the *Vulcanus II* for an inspection and we intended to make a scene. In these conditions, however, I was extremely worried about being able to safely handle the *Sirius* in the harbor. One false move could cause us to collide with the *Vulcanus II* and possibly release the cargo of toxic waste directly into the harbor. That would pretty much spell the end of my career, and possibly the end of Greenpeace. For a young captain, that was a lot to contemplate. On the one hand, I didn't want to appear like I was chicken or a neophyte captain unsure of his skills. On the other hand, I didn't want to create an environmental and public relations disaster. Harald Zindler, one of our more experienced campaigners, came up to me and said, "I think it's too windy for the action. Let's take the inflatables." *Thank you, Lord!* I *thought*, but then I *said*: "Only if you really think so . . . that sounds good." Phew. (Nowadays, I have a lot more credibility and experience than I did then. If I feel conditions are too dangerous for something, nobody will give me any grief about it. Back then, however, it was a different story.)

The *Vulcanus II* was boarded by a number of our crew, who were able to delay the ship from being able to take its cargo to sea for incineration. We got some press coverage out of it, but it was a relatively uneventful action up to that point. Our next step was to find her at sea and to photograph her burning the waste while surrounded by a fleet of dozens of Danish fishing boats.

The local fishing fleet was very concerned about the damage that the *Vulcanus II* and other ships like it were doing to the valuable and important fishing grounds in the North Sea. Purpose-built incinerator ships like this one were each burning over a hundred thousand tons of toxic waste a year. The emissions from the ships included dioxin (one of the deadliest substances known), hexachlorobenzene, and octachlorostyrene. Nasty stuff.

Scientists had already proven that these substances were being absorbed into the water and that they eventually made their way to the seabed and into many of the living things down there—including the fish people like to eat. The Danish fishing fleet was outraged that Waste Management (an American firm that owned the *Vulcanus II*) was destroying their livelihood and making a profit from it. While Greenpeace often finds itself at odds with fishermen (Gp has no issues with those who fish sustainably), in this case the Danes were very willing to work with us—and we with them—to stop Waste Management.

The *Vulcanus II* could burn her toxic load in only a small

area in the middle of the North Sea. This area was a "doughnut hole" of international waters outside of the Economic Exclusion zones of the surrounding countries. That meant that no country had the authority to stop the incineration as long as she was in that circle. While that would make it easy for us to find her, stopping her while she was incinerating would be extremely difficult, and potentially dangerous.

We arrived in the circle in the afternoon–before the *Vulcanus II* was scheduled to arrive–and rendezvoused with a fleet of thirty fishing vessels. Most were Danish, but a few had come over from England as well. These boats were generally sixty feet long, designed for two-to-three-man crews and weeklong trips. We called the fleet on the radio and asked the captains of all the fishing boats to meet on the *Sirius* to coordinate our plans.

The *Vulcanus II* was expected to approach the circle from the south at some point during the night. I explained to the other captains that Gp had experience with similar actions, how we planned to get photos and media coverage, and detailed our policies against violence and property destruction. We agreed to have the fishing boats converge around the *Vulcanus II* once we had enough daylight for pictures of the entire fleet engaging in the protest. The fishing captains nodded their heads in agreement. At dusk they returned to their vessels and we settled down for the night to await the arrival of the *Vulcanus II* in the morning. It was a pretty cool sight, drifting in the darkness, surrounded by the lights of the thirty boats that were all going to be part of the action.

Suddenly the fleet's radio blared out, "Hey, the *Vulcanus* is here on the *north* side of the circle and they're starting to burn!" The ship, knowing we were out there waiting for them, had done an end around and come into the designated burning area from the opposite direction. I was on the bridge at the time and I called Andy Booth—the campaigner—up to the bridge so he could be updated. Andy and I agreed we wouldn't approach the *Vulcanus II* until daylight. The Danes, however, had other plans.

I looked out the windows of the bridge a few moments after the radio announcement and saw only the stem lights of the fishing vessels as they headed toward the *Vulcanus* at full speed. "Son of a bitch! They're not waiting for us!" I telegraphed full ahead to the engine room so we could catch up with the fleet before they reached the incinerator ship. The *Sirius* was a little faster than the fleet, but the Danes had a head start. Soon we could see the bright flames leaping from the incinerator stacks and huge columns of toxic smoke billowing into the night sky—lit up by the fires below. We had to be careful not to position ourselves downwind where we would be subjected to the highly poisonous fumes. (During the ensuing action, one Danish boat did get exposed to the smoke, and they suffered serious eye injuries as a result.)

The fishing fleet, as planned, had the *Vulcanus II* surrounded, but it was still far too dark to take any pictures. We could easily see the flames, and the ship itself was lit up with all of her working/deck lights, but what you couldn't see was the Danish fleet showing its support. Someone on the *Sirius* had the idea to set off a parachute flare—a very bright white flare used to illuminate large areas for rescues at sea and other similar situations. (The parachute keeps the flare up in the air for several minutes by slowing its descent.) A crewman went up to the bow to fire off the flare. The next thing I knew the white-hot flare was whistling right toward everyone standing on the bridge deck. We all ducked instinctively. The high winds had caused the flare to take an immediate and hard 90-degree turn into horizontal flight about six feet off the deck. Getting hit in the face with a white-hot flare could easily be fatal. So much for that idea. Getting pictures of the ship would have to wait until daylight. I went to bed. There wasn't much more to be done until then.

A couple of hours later, Willem Groenier, the mate on watch, called me up to the bridge. Something was happening, but he wasn't sure what. Willem reported that, in an instant, the incinerator ship had gone completely dark. No flames. No pillars of smoke. No work lights. All we could see now were two small red lights—one over the other, the international signal for "ship is not under command." That meant the *Vulcanus II* had lost power and could no longer maneuver. What the hell had happened?!

The Danes, apparently, had their own secret plans from the very beginning. The entire time they had been nodding their heads during my briefing, they must have been thinking, *Yeah, right! We're supposed to listen to* you, *hippie-boy?!* They had prepared a long length of hawser (a thick, stiff rope used to dock or tow big ships), by wrapping it with heavy chain. Then they paid out the hawser and chain between two fishing boats so that it was about ten or fifteen feet deep. Instead of waiting for daylight, under the cover of darkness the two boats with the chain approached as close to the stern of the *Vulcanus II* as they could. They positioned the hawser and chain so that the propeller of the *Vulcanus II* caught the rope and chain, wrapping them tightly around the propeller and stopping it completely. For some ships, a stopped prop merely means that the ship can't maneuver or move effectively. For the *Vulcanus II*, it was her Achilles' heel: without the prop shaft being able to turn, *all of her electrical systems went dead*. No lights, no pumps to pump the toxic waste into the incinerators, and no fans to feed the flames, nothing. She was as dead as a doornail. The Danes had it all planned perfectly.

On the *Sirius* we had no idea what had happened, but through the dark we could see some of the *Vulcanus*'s crew on the aft deck trying to pull up the hawser to clear it. They couldn't work it free, so they were forced to call a salvage tug to come out and bring the *Vulcanus II* back to port for repairs. The crew of the incinerator ship got really agitated. They had been told that Gp could cost them their jobs—which was true. I brought the *Sirius* in for a closer look. We got so close that someone on the *Vulcanus II* threw a coffee mug at us and it shattered into a million pieces on the deck of the *Sirius*. In retaliation, I blew our ship's massive horn (pilot ships generally have extraordinarily loud horns to help ships locate them in low-visibility conditions) and I'm sure that we scared some toxic waste out of a few of their crew. By now it was daylight, so we got some good photographs and headed back in when the salvage tug began towing the crippled ship.

There was quite a ruckus onshore when we got there. The action had gotten a lot of media attention, but Gp was having a cow because of the hawser. Gp abhors violence of all sorts, and is strictly against property destruction of any kind. Damaging the propeller was absolutely forbidden. They calmed down after I explained that we had no advance knowledge of the Danes' plan. I had to admit, though, that their plan worked beautifully. The *Vulcanus II* had been stopped cold, and the media jumped all over the story. One researcher found that almost *20 percent of all of the broadcast news in Denmark that day* was devoted to the *Vulcanus II* and the action. This action, along with others by Greenpeace and several other organizations, led to the eventual ban of all ocean incineration of toxic waste in the North Sea.

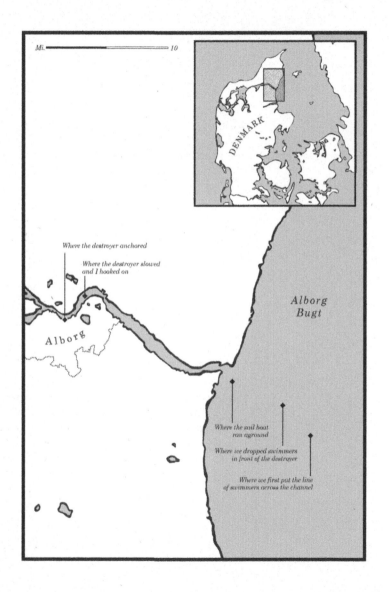

Where the destroyer anchored

Where the destroyer slowed
and I hooked on

Alborg
Bugt

Alborg

Where the sail boat
ran aground

Where we dropped swimmers
in front of the destroyer

Where we first put the line
of swimmers across the channel

Mi. 10

DENMARK

7

"Captain Hook" vs. The Destroyer

Rule number one when jumping in front of a speeding
destroyer: keep all of your body parts on one side of the
bow.

—*Peter Willcox*

JULY 4, 1988

ALBORG, DENMARK—140 MILES NORTHWEST OF COPENHAGEN

NUCLEAR-FREE SEAS ACTION

During the summer of 1988 I was feeling a little shore-bound
after spending a good many months in a shipyard in Hamburg, Germany, helping with the refit and conversion of the
Grampian Fame—a late-1950s North Sea fishing trawler—into
the second *Rainbow Warrior*. The new ship would replace the
one that had been blown up in New Zealand three years earlier. The conversion was taking far longer than had been
originally estimated—eighteen months instead of the predicted six to eight months. The initial schedule had been
overly optimistic to begin with, and then both the rig manufacturer and the piping contractor had gone belly-up in the

middle of the project. The entire ordeal had been very frustrating. My desire to be in action at sea was growing stronger by the day as the project dragged on. Too much time spent in the office is guaranteed to make me an unhappy captain. There was, however, one bright spot in the middle of this dreary period.

Harald Zindler is Greenpeace's mad genius. Some of us call him the Actions Guru because he's the man who has dreamed up the majority of Gp's most famous exploits. He's also an inventor of sorts, creating some of the wildest action innovations we've ever used. For instance, Harald had devised a method of using one 50-horsepower inflatable to lift another 50-horsepower inflatable into the air. We've even used this method to lift pods (portable living quarters for protesters) onto places like offshore oil rigs. He has an entire warehouse filled with a wide variety of equipment and gadgets that I like to call the Hamburg Toy Store. Harald is the Gp equivalent of James Bond's Q, minus the exploding pens. He's also a class-A team motivator.

Harald and I shared a desk in Hamburg and sat right across from each other. I took great pleasure in listening in on many of his conversations, and he taught me a lot about problem solving and thinking things through. One day I heard Harald describing an action he was planning; we were going to try to stop a US nuclear-missile-equipped destroyer from entering nuclear-free Denmark. Two months before, the Danish government had declared the country "nuclear free" and banned nuclear weapons and nuclear-propelled ships from its waters. The US Navy was planning to test that ban with the Adams-class guided missile destroyer USS *Conyngham*. According to *Jane's* (the reference bible for ships and their weaponry), the *Conyngham*'s usual complement of nuclear weapons included one-kiloton ASROC antisubmarine missiles, as well as various other conventional ASROCs and torpedoes.

To save face the Danish government had formally asked the US if the *Conyngham* was going to be carrying nukes during her visit. The US Navy's response was essentially "We can neither confirm nor deny," and the Danish government then decided to assume they would not. Still, everyone was pretty clear on the fact that the ship would be carrying nukes since the navy had gone to great expense to equip the ship to do so. Furthermore, immediately prior to her departure, the destroyer and her entire crew had been put through a comprehensive nuclear weapons certification process. The ship was scheduled, ironically, to arrive on July 4–American Independence Day. After overhearing the plans for the reception that Harald was organizing for the destroyer, I begged him to let me come and join in the fun. I didn't have to beg too long.

One of the additional benefits of participating in this action was that I would get to work with Jon Castle. Jon was one of Greenpeace's most experienced captains, and had a reputation (within Gp, and among numerous police departments around the globe) for being a wizard at cleverly maneuvering large ships in tight quarters during actions. (For this trip, I wasn't going as the captain, but as one of the action team members, instead.) He and I had never really worked together, so I was looking forward to seeing him do his stuff.

Jon was extremely popular with his crews, although he did have a somewhat strained relationship with Gp's administration and management teams because he often—in their opinion—went

rogue. It isn't surprising that this is part of the chemistry and culture of Greenpeace. In many respects, the captains and crews are
paid to break the rules. We're antiauthoritarian by nature, and
administrators and managers are inherently rule *makers*, so it's
understandable when there's a little friction between the two
cultures.

Before any action, we practice with our teams just like any
sports team or military squad would. We replicate the action
as closely as we can, using the exact equipment that we're
going to use, and game-plan the moves that the opposition
might use. We also have the occasional "action camp" in
which we practice various skills, audition new action team
members, and provide an opportunity for various personnel
to get additional action experience in a controlled setting.

To stop the destroyer, we were going to set divers in the
water across the harbor channel that the *Conyngham* was
going to be steaming through. International navigational
rules state that if there is a diver with an international diving
flag in the water, all vessels must stay well away from the area
and slow way down. In theory, that meant that the destroyer
was supposed to stop. As the wise man said, in theory, there
is no difference between theory and practice; but in practice,
there is.

The divers were going to be in the water wearing Gumby
suits, a common nickname for survival suits. These large, un-
gainly neoprene suits are designed to prevent hypothermia
when you're in the water a long time. They look like fluo-
rescent orange versions of the animated character Gumby
from the old American kiddie-cartoon show. While the suits
will keep you alive for a long time in the water, you can't
swim, dive, or generally move around much. You're a sitting
Day-Glo duck. We expected that the destroyer would simply

move through the divers like a skier on a slalom course, but it'd make for some good pictures and possibly slow the ship down enough that we could put plan B into effect. Plan B was me.

As plan B, I would be positioned directly in front of the moving destroyer and attempt to latch on to the bow of the ship. Jan Madsen, the chief engineer on our 110-foot trawler *Moby Dick*, fashioned a piece of hook-shaped rebar with a handle on it that I could use to grab on to the *Conyngham's* bow. (Jan is a prime example of a chief engineer; he can make anything out of anything in a pinch. Sometimes I help him out—but that usually means standing back and cheering him on, or bringing him a beer while I admire his work.)

During our action practice, we tried to work out the best way of positioning me in front of the destroyer's bow, which is not that different from a fly trying to stop an eighteen-wheeler by hovering in front of its windshield. (There's an old joke that goes: What's the last thing that goes through a fly's mind when he hits your windshield? Answer: His asshole. I really hoped that wouldn't apply to me!) The *Conyngham* was over 437 feet long, and 4,500 tons at full load. I weighed a grand total (sopping wet) of about 170 pounds (those were the days!). The other statistic that I was keenly interested in was her top speed: 30 knots.

After experimenting with a few different techniques, I remembered something stupid I used to do as an adolescent kid growing up in Norwalk: I would grab a water-ski towline, lie in the water on my back, and get pulled along—headfirst—by the ski boat, skipping along the surface like a flapping fish getting reeled into a boat. I demonstrated the technique for Harald and he was delighted with it. For added maneuverability, I would wear a scuba suit and swim fins instead of the Gumby getup.

The practice went well. All in all, almost fifty activists were going to be involved. We had six inflatable RHIBs (rigid hull inflatable boats), six divers, support staff, etc., and the *Moby Dick*—which would be the base vessel for the action. We also had another toy—a jet-drive boat we called the Playmobil (named after the kids' toys). Jet boats don't have propellers; their engines shoot jets of water in pretty much the same way that a Jet Ski does, but they're a lot bigger and can carry several crew. They're also exceptionally maneuverable and can be used in very shallow water, which comes in handy in all sorts of ways. The destroyer was expected to arrive at around 5 A.M. We went to bed that night eager for the dawn. At midnight, however, I was suddenly awakened. Jon, the captain of the *Moby Dick*, needed me on the bridge ASAP.

My first thought was that the *Conyngham* was trying to evade us by coming in earlier than expected. It was nothing of the sort. During the night, a thirty-five-foot sailboat and her crew had gone out of the deepwater channel leading into the harbor and had run up hard on the beach. Jon heard their mayday call on the radio and, since we were in a position to be the first to respond, he wanted me to go over to the sailboat and do whatever we could. Glad that Jon had asked me to handle the situation, Jan Madsen and I hopped into the Playmobil and went to investigate.

The unfortunate sailboat was a couple of miles farther out in the harbor. She was caught in breakers that were running three to five feet high, more than enough to be very dangerous to a boat in her situation. They were being mercilessly pounded against the hard sand by the surf, and neither the boat nor the crew would be able to last much longer. We found out later that her engine had failed as she was coming in, and then the wind and waves had driven the boat onto the lee shore. (A lee shore is a shore that is downwind. If you don't have maneuverability, the wind will drive you toward the rocks or shallows and dash you to pieces. It's every sailor's nightmare.)

So it was with some trepidation that Jan and I brought the jet boat toward the beach. Both of us were wearing eyeglasses, and between the dark of the night, and the spray from the wind, waves, rain, and the jet boat, it was damn hard to see. We could easily get caught in the breaking waves and have the jet boat flip over. We rescuers would then become rescuees.

Just where the waves started to break, I turned the Playmobil around and backed her down carefully as close as I dared get to the stricken sailboat. I was amazed at the control I had with the jet drive. The bow rose easily over the waves, and I never felt that positioning the jet boat was a problem. We threw a towline to the yacht and began to pull her off the beach. Every time a wave hit the sailboat, it would lift it up just a little, and we thought we could pull her out, bit by bit, as she was lifted off the sand. I watched the buoys in the channel as reference points, and I swore I was making progress. But an hour later, it was apparent that the sailboat was still hard aground.

Harald showed up in one of the smaller inflatables to see what was going on. He took stock of the situation in about two minutes, told me what I was doing was not working, and asked me if I had any other ideas. My father's way of getting a sailboat off a sandbar was to put a towline on a halyard (one of the ropes from the top of the mast that pulls the sails up) and haul the boat off from its masthead. By pulling on the masthead, the mast is pulled over and down so the keel lifts *up*, and the boat has a much better chance of coming off the bottom. At this point the crew on the sailboat was mostly incapacitated, so Harald got aboard from his RHIB and tied the towline to a halyard. It worked! In five minutes we had the sailboat out in deep water. Then the towline snapped. Shit! The tension on the line whipped it back toward the Playmobil and the line got sucked into the jet drive. Shit! Shit! Shit! We were dead in the water.

If we didn't move fast, the sailboat would quickly end up back on the beach, and so might the Playmobil. Yet another inflatable arrived on the scene, so I jumped into that one to organize another towline to the bow of the sailboat. The other RHIB towed the jet boat back to the ship.

Wolfgang "Womie" Meister, the main manager of the Hamburg Toy Store, was driving the second boat, and I quickly gave him helm orders so I could get the other towline on. We only had a few seconds to get it done, and I guess I was being a little hard on him—shouting orders at the top of my lungs to be heard over the surf. Afterward, while we were towing the sailboat up the channel to safety, he said to me, "Peter, it's very hard to think when you're yelling at me." Since then, I've tried to remember that louder isn't always better.

Finally, the sailboat broke free from the beach and we were able to tow her to safety. Three hours later, around 3 A.M., we got back to the *Moby Dick*. I was tired, all of my adrenaline had been used up, and in two hours I was going to be facing off with a destroyer. Still, I felt pretty good about rescuing the sailboat and her crew. At least that would look good in my obituary if it needed to be written in the next few hours.

"It's a good day to die." That line from the movie *Little Big Man* kept running through my head as I bobbed in the channel waiting for the *Conyngham* to show herself. There were six of us in the water—five Gumbies and me. Each of us had large, orange inflatable fenders with diver flags tied to sticks.

One of the Gumbies was a Swedish gal named Katrin Gunnerson. She had joined Gp about a year before as the radio operator on the *Sirius*. "Sparkies"—an affectionate term for radio operators—are usually grizzled, grumpy, older guys. When I first met Katrin, I took one look at this cute, blond twenty-two-year-old and thought, *How can this sweet young girl really be up to the job?* I was polite, though, and showed her around the ship and introduced her to the crew.

Two hours later I asked her to get me a weather forecast, as we were about to depart on an action. About an hour later she came back, and I expected her to say something like "How do you turn on the radio?" Instead, she said, "Do you mind if I copy down the weather forecast in Morse code? It's easier for me than English." Right then I thought, *Wow! This woman really knows her shit.* She was the real deal. . . .

Before she joined Greenpeace, Katrin had been working on an oil rig with about a hundred men on it. All of them could easily get a satellite phone line from their own rooms, but instead they would all go down to Katrin's radio room and ask her personally to get a line for them. I guess having a continuous line of interested guys outside of your radio room gets a little tiresome after a while, so she joined Gp. Now this brave woman was floating about thirty feet away from me, smiling sweetly, as we waited for the arrival of the destroyer.

The Gp inflatables and support boats had pulled well away from the line of divers. The thinking was that if the destroyer saw boats near us, it might convince them we would be moved out of the way. Without the boats nearby, they would see we were determined to stay in their path. Soon, in the gathering light, we were able to make out the signal masts, antennae, and then the bridge of the *Conyngham* coming up over the horizon. She was quickly getting bigger and bigger. Clearly she had a good head of steam; she was moving fast. Even as she closed on us, we couldn't hear her bow wave or engines at all. It was quiet. Dead quiet. Kind of like the quiet in *Gunfight at the OK Corral* just before the shooting starts. It seemed like the destroyer was on top of us in seconds.

Five blasts of the *Conyngham*'s horn ripped through the morning air, the international signal for "you are in imminent danger, get out of the way." Well, we weren't going anywhere. A few seconds later it looked to me like she was changing course. She was. She blew right through the narrow gap between me and Katrin. As the destroyer passed us I could hear the bow wave, but there was still no sound from her engines or the giant bronze propellers churning just twenty feet below us. The inflatables quickly swooped in, picked us all up, and charged ahead of the *Conyngham* so we could try again. This time, we were going to drop the divers off directly in front of the ship.

Harald positioned the jet boat about a hundred yards in front of the ship and yelled, "Jump!" We were now close enough that I could hear the bow wave. I didn't hesitate, but when I looked up the ship was right there. Rule number one when jumping in front of a speeding destroyer: keep all of your body parts on one side of the bow! This is important. If you get a lower leg—or, worse, a femur—across the bow, you'll be lucky if it's just broken. I didn't have a chance to get the hook on her.

On the next attempt I let the bow come by so close I could touch it. The bow wave slapped me in the head as she went by, my hand dragging along the gray steel hull of the ship.

Once the bow wave passed, it was so quiet that I could hear one of the sailors high above me shout: "Watch out for the propellers!" I tried yelling back "Do you know you're breaking Danish law?" but by then I was already past her stern. Harald came back to pick me up, and that was one of my all-time favorite Greenpeace moments: Harald, looking very concerned, telling me in a stern Germanic voice, "Don't get so close to the bow! You really scared me!"

Harald and I had discussed the potential danger of being sucked under the ship. We both felt that as long as the ship was going in a straight line, the divers and I would be relatively safe if we were able to remain on the surface. The real danger would come if the ship turned; if it side-slipped, we could easily be dragged under the hull and would probably be killed. Harald and I reasoned that the destroyer's captain would not have much room to turn, even if he wanted to, if we confronted the destroyer while it was in the relatively narrow channel. Once the boat was in the harbor she would have more room to maneuver, but by then she wouldn't be traveling nearly as fast. That would further reduce the risk of being dragged under the warship.

We attempted to stop her several more times, jumping off boats in front of the ship and having the destroyer speed past us each time. I felt like a matador trying to stop a charging bull. While we were having zero effect for now, as she got farther into the harbor she was going to have to slow down, and that's when we'd have a real shot at her. The main objective now was to keep her from getting to the dock.

As the *Conyngham* approached the inner harbor, her speed dropped to roughly 6 knots and I was finally able to get my hook on her bow. For my efforts, I received my own modern version of a Nantucket sleigh ride. A Nantucket sleigh ride is an old-time New England whaler's term to describe when they harpooned a whale and the whaleboat—tied to the harpoon by a long length of rope—would be towed by the whale at fearsome speeds as it attempted to escape its pursuers. I had just hooked on to the bow of a 4,500-ton "whale" and was riding along quite happily until all of the destroyer's fire hoses trained on me. Most ships use fire hoses that are pressurized at 100 pounds per square inch. The navy, being the navy, uses 200 psi. That's a *lot* of pressure. The pressure of all those hoses forced me under her bow wave and I somehow got unhooked.

One of the boats quickly picked me up again and brought me back to the bow, where I was able to hook on again. This time, to counteract the force of the fire hoses, I inflated my life vest to keep me above the water so I could hang on. This also reduced the risk of being chummed by the propellers. Finally the *Conyngham* came to a stop, but I didn't know why.

"Come along now, son. You've had your fun. Why don't you swim over and get in our boat before you get hurt?" said a Danish policeman who had just arrived on the scene in a police boat. It certainly sounded tempting, but I could see Womie glaring at me from one of the inflatables as if to say "Don't you dare!", so I stayed where I was.

In the meantime, while we were distracting everyone, Jon had cleverly maneuvered the *Moby Dick* into position where the *Conyngham* was supposed to dock, and anchored there. Jon was so close to the dock that he had to use the engine in short bursts to keep from touching it. In order for the *Conyngham* to get to the dock, she had to be assisted by at least a couple of Danish tugboats, but they were nowhere to be seen. It turned out later that the leader of the local tugboat union had ordered the tugs to stay away from the area as long as we were in the way. (I suspect he was on our side on the nuclear-free issue.) The net effect, however, was that the *Conyngham* was stranded in the middle of the harbor, and she was now going to have to anchor until things sorted themselves out.

The navy sailors were yelling at me to "fuck off" and telling me I was crazy. (I really wasn't in a position to argue.) After a standoff of about thirty minutes, one of the sailors yelled down that they were going to drop one of the giant anchors hanging directly over my head. I calmly asked them which anchor they were planning on using and then worked myself around the bow to the other side. I prayed the guy dropping the anchor knew his port from his starboard. Thankfully, they carefully lowered the anchor chain down link by link (the nautical term is "walking the anchor down" and it's the usual procedure for anchoring, but not always!).

The sailors on the destroyer were now hopping mad. Approaching the harbor, they had all been wearing their dress-blue uniforms in preparation for shore leave. Now, as they were anchoring and fighting us off with the fire hoses, the captain ordered them to change back into their working uniforms. That meant we were seriously cutting into their beer time—and Denmark has some great beers!—so that took all the fun out of it for them. Now they were really pissed.

A few hours later we switched out the swimmers and the boat crews, and I went back to a cabin on the *Moby Dick* to warm up and rest. At 5 P.M., the local police boarded and arrested us. I hid in the aft head and hurriedly put on my wet suit with the intention of jumping off the boat and swimming away, but two of the policemen grabbed and cuffed me just before I made it over the rail. Within minutes we were all rounded up. It had been a great action, but our part was now over.

Our engine room crew had disabled the engine on the *Moby Dick* by hiding a critical part, so there was no way for the officials to easily move her away from the destroyer's berth. Finally, a powerful harbor tug came alongside the *Moby Dick*, tied up to her and then–without even lifting *Moby Dick*'s anchor–dragged her out of the docking area so the *Conyngham* could get in. We were all brought to a local jail and stuffed into a small holding cell. After a couple of hours, we were brought to another facility where we had clean, comfortable bunks and were given a decent meal. I fell asleep as soon as my head hit the pillow.

Meanwhile, the action continued in the harbor. The police had finally cleared the way for the tugs to get to the *Conyngham*, and the tugs started to tow her in the direction of the dock. The commotion and news from the action had attracted a big crowd to the harbor, and many of them agreed with our nuclear-free position. As the *Conyngham* got close to the dock, the locals suddenly began to jump into the water in between her and the dock, preventing her–yet again–from landing. I wish I had been there to see it. Apparently, one silver-haired lady had jumped in wearing her Sunday best and was pictured on the front page of the newspaper the next day.

Eventually, after about eight or nine hours, the *Conyngham* was finally able to dock. But the action got a huge amount of press all over the world.

The destroyer's next port of call was in Cork, Ireland, which was also a nuclear-free port. We had another team of activists waiting there too. I've been told that when the *Conyngham* crew saw them, one of the sailors shouted in a plaintive voice, "Oh come on. Won't you guys just leave us alone?" I guess he was looking forward to a pint of Guinness and a dance with an Irish lass. Funnily enough, a couple of weeks later—and just before the destroyer returned to her home port of Norfolk, Virginia—a sixteen-year-old Irish girl who had been hidden by some sailors was discovered in a compartment above one of the ship's refrigeration units.

One of the best feelings you get in this line of work is seeing other people being inspired into action themselves. We sometimes feel like we are sailing through a sea of human apathy, but when you get a public response like that and see people getting enraged and engaged, it gives you hope that what you're doing isn't as futile as it can sometimes seem. That's what our actions are all about, but only very rarely do we get that kind of instant result. That's one of the reasons that this action is, to this day, one of my all-time favorites.

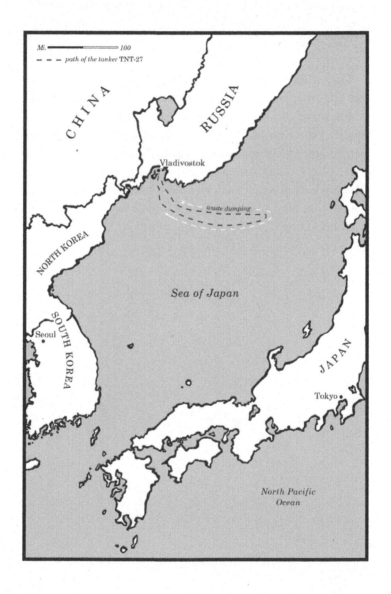

8

Starting a Nuclear Chain Reaction

For over thirty years the Soviet Union had been dumping nuclear waste into the sea, including at least sixteen reactors that had been cut out of decommissioned submarines and other reactor-powered ships, then broken up and thrown overboard. In 1991 Greenpeace attended an international conference in Moscow (along with a large number of other scientists and activist groups) and learned the true extent of the past and current dumping. By the fall of 1992, Greenpeace had executed two actions in the Kara Sea (Arctic, Soviet/Russian waters) that attempted to actually locate the reactors that had been dumped. The Soviet navy had acted quickly and forcefully to keep our activists from locating the reactors, which was proof, in and of itself, that the Soviets were hiding something.

Now that Gp had drawn the world's attention to the issue,

the pressure grew on the Russians to come clean. In the aftermath of the fall of the Soviet Union, the Russian government formed a commission to investigate the issue. The commission was headed by President Boris Yeltsin's environmental advisor, Alexei Yablokov. In March 1993, the commission released a white paper (the Yablokov Report) detailing about forty years of this kind of environmental abuse in the oceans near Korea, Japan, the Kara Sea, and the Pacific near the Kamchatka Peninsula. This activity had even continued for ten years *after* the Soviet Union had signed the London Convention agreement calling for "an immediate halt to all nuclear waste dumping at sea."

While the Yablokov Report detailed exhaustively all of the dumping that had gone on in the past forty years, it also stated that the Russians would need to continue the dumping for at least several more years. Three months later, a Russian admiral admitted that their nuclear waste storage facilities were completely full. We knew this meant that they would have to do some more dumping, and soon.

As the Cold War ended, and many more Soviet-era submarines and ships were decommissioned, the problem was going to get even worse. Besides the reactors and spent fuel rods, thousands of tons of radioactive cooling water were also being dumped—much of it near the prime fishing grounds for the Japanese fleet. The Japanese really love their sushi, and isotopes have a way of ruining it. A new action was designed to prove that the Russians, despite their denials, were still actively dumping nuclear waste at sea.

Relations between Russia and Japan had been belligerent for years. The Russo-Japanese war, from 1904 to 1905, had been a brutal loss for the Russians, and the two sides had tussled over numerous territorial disputes involving the Kuril Islands between Japan and Russia's Kamchatka Peninsula.

(They are still in dispute today.) Because of this long-simmering dispute, the Soviet Union and Japan had never even signed a peace treaty to formally end World War II. Needless to say, the Japanese were no great friends of the Russians. Even so, Boris Yeltsin—the new president of the Russian Federation—was planning a diplomatic visit to Japan in the hope he could convince them to significantly increase the amount of monetary aid for his struggling country. When visiting your neighbor to ask for a cup of sugar (or billions of dollars in aid), it's usually not a good idea to dump radioactive waste in their backyard. But this was exactly what Russia was doing. Not only would we try to catch them in the act, with a little luck, we could prove it while Yeltsin was in Japan.

We knew that the Russian tankers filled with liquid radioactive waste were coming out from Bolshoy Kamen, the nuclear submarine base across the bay from Vladivostok. Vladivostok just happens to be one of the biggest and most heavily protected navy bases in the world. It's the hub of Russia's entire Pacific fleet. The challenge was going to be finding the needle in the haystack: figuring out which of the dozens of ships coming in and out of the port twenty-four hours a day was the ship we were looking for.

Adding to the difficulty was that we had to stay outside of Russia's territorial waters—twelve miles—and that meant that the port was pretty much out of radar range. Unless we were able to pinpoint which ship was the tanker, and had a good idea of when it was leaving the port, there was very little chance of being able to pull off the action. Somehow we had to have an inside man, and some way to discreetly communicate with that person. This required a real cloak-and-dagger approach.

Gp had been cultivating a relationship with a Russian naval officer: Captain First-Rank (similar to the rank of commander)

Grigryan, the chief medical officer for the Russian nuclear navy. The year before, while Grigryan was naked in a sauna at a convention with some Gp members, Grigryan had casually mentioned that the Soviets (at the time, the country was still the USSR) were cutting up and dumping reactors in the Kara Sea. It was the first time that Gp had been made aware of the extent of what was going on there.

A year later, Dima Litvinov—a Russian, and a seasoned Gp campaigner who often does double duty as a translator in actions involving Russia—was sitting in the captain's office and asking him about the next scheduled dumping. Grigryan held up a piece of paper and said, "This has all the information you need." He then made a show of placing the paper in a desk drawer. Grigryan then closed the drawer and announced he had to go to the bathroom. Dima took the hint, opened the drawer, and frantically copied down the information. The document didn't have all the specifics. It was not a detailed schedule, but it did have an approximate date, the name of the ship (*TNT-27*), and a general description of the tanker and the radioactive waste she would be carrying.

It might be surprising to some that a Russian naval officer would share sensitive information like this. Russia was going through a major transformation at this time, and people who had been ordered to do things they didn't agree with felt a little more comfortable about acting ethically. The Soviet/Russian navy had a bad track record of nuclear accidents, and as chief medical officer for the nuclear fleet, Grigryan was in the best position to understand the damage that the radiation was doing to the crews of the ships and the population in general.

Even with the information we had been provided, we needed to know exactly which radar target was the ship carrying the waste, exactly when it was leaving, and where it was going, in order to have any chance of intercepting it while it was dumping. Adding to the complexity of the situation is that Vladivostok has a number of channels that lead in and out of the port. There was no way to monitor every possible exit point. This meant that we had to resort to espionage. We placed a couple of lookouts on a centrally located island to identify the target, and to alert us to the channel it was using to head out to sea. The entire port—the hub of the Russian navy—was a high-security zone, so positioning the lookouts would be tricky enough, but we also needed a way for them to communicate to the rest of us without being located and caught, or having the message intercepted. How could we electronically communicate in secret from inside a high-security Russian navy base?

The answer was an electronic gizmo called an Argos beacon. Argos is a satellite transmission system that had been initially designed to transmit research data (meteorological information, for instance) or location data for migrating wildlife such as moose, bear, or whales. We didn't know what kind of electronic communications interception equipment the Russians might have around their maximum-security navy base, but it was a good bet they weren't going to be listening to whale-watching frequencies. Argos, however, wasn't designed to communicate in full sentences. The team on the ground could only send us brief, coded transmissions. Up to five messages could be preset. The message would then be sent up to a passing satellite, relayed to Gp's offices in Amsterdam, and then relayed back to us on the ship. Hopefully that would be enough to pinpoint when the *TNT-27* was leaving, and which exit from the harbor she was taking. With that "hot" tip, we'd stand a much better chance of catching them "rad-handed."

Radiation was a real concern for all of us. Twilly Cannon, the GP USA actions director, was in charge of radiation safety. Each of us received special training. We were taught how to wear the protective suits and masks, proper use of radiation exposure badges, and how to undress and decontaminate each other. Besides the training, we had a long list of things to be done to our ship, the *Greenpeace*, to minimize the potential of contamination. We sealed her doors with plastic and tape, plugged some scuppers (holes that drain water off the deck) and rerouted others so as not to trap any "hot" water. We cemented the spurling pipes (tubes where the anchor chain goes into the ship). We created a decontamination zone where people who'd be splashed with radioactive water could be hosed down in an area that would be easy to wash down again. It made things very real and got everybody in the right frame of mind. One of the crew members, however, decided she did not want any part of the "hot" side of things. She was probably the only sensible one on board.

Then the waiting began. Day after day, we waited for word about the timing and location of the tanker, but we also knew that there was no guarantee that we'd get any message, or that the tanker would even be identified, and there was no way to communicate with the inside team. John Sprange—the campaigner—and First Mate Pete Sandison and I hovered over the chart tables trying to guess when and where the tanker might appear. A Ouija board might have been in order. We did get suckered once, chasing a ship for about thirty miles up the coast before we realized it was a false alarm, then hightailing it back to our waiting area.

On the *Greenpeace*, Dima and a Russian/Ukrainian volunteer named Nadezhda Mikhaillovna were monitoring dozens of radio frequencies hoping to hear a Russian naval transmission that would tip us off. The two would take turns—three hours on, three hours off—listening intensely and trying to decide if any of the chatter they were hearing was code for information about the tanker. When they heard things like "Mama bear, baby bear is moving now," it was very easy to imagine that they were talking about our target. But after two weeks of highly stressful radio monitoring, when the nuclear waste tanker was ready to leave, her captain simply announced it in plain language on the harbor's main VHF channel as casually as if he was commencing a harbor cruise for tourists.

Finally, we received the report that the tanker *TNT-27* was departing from the nuclear submarine base. She was scheduled to make two dumping runs. The tanker departed during the night, but we were fairly sure we knew which radar blip was hers. When daylight arrived, it was a clear, bright day that made it easy to see the sorry state the tanker was in. Rusting and decrepit, it was obvious that maintaining a ship like that was not high on Russia's list of things to spend money on. She was in such bad shape that she had to be towed out to the dumping area by a tugboat. She was also accompanied by a Russian navy patrol/research ship.

It was almost possible to feel sorry for the Russian navy at this point. Things in that country were really falling apart. Nine months earlier, twenty-five men on one of their outer island posts had died during the winter; their radio had broken and no one remembered that they were on their remote island. Months later, someone remembered to check on them and discovered that all twenty-five had starved to death.

Once the tanker got to the dumping ground, we sent an inflatable over with Twilly, Kiryu Hiroto (our Japanese photographer) and some others—all in hazmat gear—to take some readings with a Geiger counter to confirm the ship was dumping radioactive material. As they got to within thirty feet of the tanker, the Geiger counter gave them some very high readings—7,000 percent above normal background. The team stayed alongside the tanker for about half an hour, photographing the ship and the Geiger counter while recording the radiation levels.

Twilly reported when he got back that he was sure they were dumping, but he couldn't tell how. We guessed that it was via some through-hull fitting under the water. After all, this ship had been designed to carry nuclear waste and dump it at sea. It wasn't until we had a chance to closely examine the photographs that we saw a small fire hose going over the side into the water. The pump was a little gas-powered thing that you might find at any construction site. Apparently, things in Russia were in far worse shape than we thought. Twilly also reported that there were some barrels and boxes on skids—with very visible radiation symbols—that looked like they were poised to be pushed overboard. We followed the ship the rest of the day and through the night. They knew who we were and why we there (the large "Greenpeace" on the side of our ship wasn't exactly subtle), but didn't react in any way.

Still, everything on the Russian ship was radioactive and just being near it was giving us a good-size dose. We were alarmed to see that the crew of the tanker were not wearing radiation protection of any kind. No masks, no gloves, just regular old canvas boiler suits (overalls). It was shocking, and we were truly concerned for them. We were far more protected than they were. Clearly they didn't understand the danger. They were as uncaring about it as if they were pumping out a swimming pool. We were alarmed, however, when the tanker crew turned a fire hose on our crews. We're kind of used to that, but not when the fire hose is shooting radioactive water. Nobody had signed up to get their chromosomes rearranged. In a short time, however, we realized they were just using plain old seawater.

We were getting good footage and high readings, and sent the video and data off using the "Squisher" to our offices in London and Japan for distribution to the press.

The Squisher was a combination video file digitizer and store-and-forward device. It was unlike anything commercially available at the time. Only a very few high-tech military operations had technology with similar capabilities. The Squisher "squished" video using data compression so that the files could be distributed more easily and quickly from the ship. The squished files were sent up to Inmarsat satellites, and then down to Gp's London communications office for distribution to broadcast feeds that reached all over the world. The Squisher didn't always work correctly but, thankfully, it did this time, so video was being sent all over the world in close to real time.

Little did we know how much of a chain reaction we were creating. As the images were broadcast in Japan, the effect was sensational. When the Japanese people learned that the Russians were dumping nuclear waste 150 miles off their coast, and less than 75 miles from their most important fishing fleet, they were as hot as a nuclear reactor in full meltdown. Hiroshima and Nagasaki had never been forgotten and radiation is not something that the Japanese take lightly. All of the major networks were carrying the pictures and the news, and soon there was a squadron of private planes chartered by news crews buzzing in the air over the tanker. At one point our Gp office in Japan had a line of motorcycle messengers outside the door, each of them waiting for the next video to be squished out.

The Russian navy patrol boat that had accompanied the *TNT-27* was flying signal flags. These days, signal flags are not used that much, but they are still good for passing messages when the ships involved do not speak the same language. Each flag corresponds with a number or letter, and different combinations of letters and numbers mean different things. They don't spell out the message letter by letter; a few flags in a particular order have specific meanings. For example "U W 1" means "thank you very much for your cooperation, we wish you a pleasant voyage." (I love hoisting that signal to a navy vessel right after we've done something to piss them off.)

While most of the Russian ship's signals were quite clear, we couldn't find some of their messages in the standard signal book. It was gibberish to us. Several days later we discovered a special section in the back of the International Code of Signals book for "Russian Flags for the Sea around Vladivostok." Everyone else in the world uses the standard system, but they don't in Vladivostok. It didn't matter anyway. We were still going to do what was necessary.

At one point, the Russian frigate signaled "Heave to, and prepare to be boarded for an inspection." I asked Dima to look in the signal flag book and find some kind of response that would confuse and baffle the Russians. Dima selected a message from the medical section of the book: "the patient's penis is swollen and emitting pus."

The dumping story spread all over the world. Crowds protested in front of the Russian Embassy in Tokyo. Russia's ambassador to Tokyo was obliged to visit the Japanese foreign ministry and apologize. And Yeltsin immediately halted all nuclear dumping at sea.

When we sailed back into Tokyo, we got an insanely enthusiastic welcome from the Japanese, complete with helicopters whirling overhead, crowds on the shore, and endless media coverage. Despite Greenpeace's years of actions against Japanese whalers, the whole country was extremely grateful for our defense of their fisheries. The global outrage that followed our action had a widening impact, even after Russia stopped the practice. Within a few months, thirty-seven countries signed the London Convention, permanently banning the dumping of nuclear (and industrial) waste at sea.

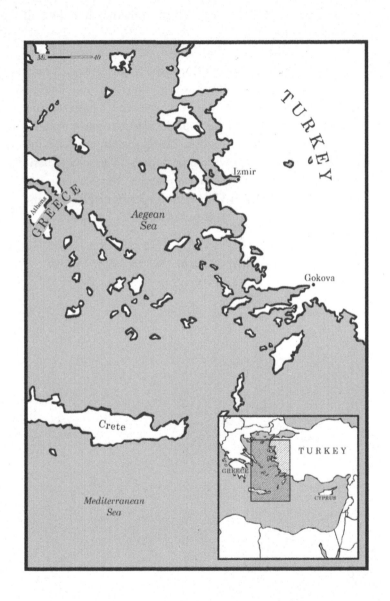

9

"The Caterpillar in the Turkish Coal Chute"

> Actions reinforce the commitment of the activists. This
> should not be underestimated. The chance to go out and
> do something is a terrific energy and morale booster.
>
> *—Me*

August 1995
Izmir, Turkey—205 miles southeast of Istanbul
Anti-Coal Action

Despite our best efforts in planning out our actions, things don't
always go according to plan. You just have to get used to wing-
ing it as the circumstances change. That doesn't mean "don't
plan," but rather "plan on the plan not going according to
plan." Usually, we try to plan any action as far in advance as
possible, but not always. While we often have to make spur-
of-the-moment adaptations as circumstances dictate, at least
we're working off of a pretty solid foundation. This action was
one of those times when our best-laid plans often went awry.

The main reason this action didn't go the way we drew it
up was that we had decided to do it on an impulse. We were

in Izmir, Turkey, doing a series of "open days" (public tours of the ship and related PR activities) when Mario Damato–the director from the Gp Mediterranean office in Malta–decided that we should do a banner action at a big coal-fired power plant in Gökova, Turkey. The plant was approximately a three-hour car ride from Izmir.

The power plant wasn't yet fully operational, but was almost complete. It had been designed and built to burn locally mined coal. All coal has concentrations of heavy metals (cadmium, mercury, etc.) and low levels of naturally occurring radiation. This coal, however, had notably high concentrations of both, but because it didn't have to be transported very far from the mines to the power plant, the coal was very cheap. The plant itself was perched on a hill right over Gökova Bay, a beautiful part of the Mediterranean Sea that would soon be contaminated by the ash and runoff from the power plant.

Our objective was to do a banner action since we felt it would be too difficult to actually disrupt the plant's operation. A banner action is pretty much what it sounds like: we hang a banner in a very visible location and get press coverage. The banner we wanted to hang was going to be monstrously huge–260 feet long and about fifty feet high. Simon Aylof and Mike Fincken–fueled by coffee and cigarettes–led a team of people working around the clock to fabricate and paint it. The ship's fifty-foot-long hold belowdecks wasn't big enough to lay out the whole banner, so they had to sew and paint the banner in sections, letting one section dry and then moving on to the next. (This also kept the banner out of sight of prying eyes.) They added a length of chain along the banner's lower edge to help it hang properly if conditions were windy. The whole thing, despite being made from lightweight nylon sailcloth, weighed over two hundred pounds. Figuring out how we were going to get this unwieldy, rolled-up banner up to the top of the plant, and determining where and how it would get hung from the plant, were critical to the success of the action.

In my view, banner actions are second-class. The best actions are those that don't need a banner at all to explain to the public what the action is all about, the most famous example being the "inflatable boat in front of the harpoon gun" photograph. That action stopped the whalers from taking a clear shot, showed everyone onshore the barbarity of the whaling hunt, and demonstrated the personal commitment of the Greenpeacers who were stopping it. An action like that doesn't need a long caption under the photo to explain what's going on. Another example of a brilliant action was the civil rights demonstrations of African American men and women going to restaurants and demanding service.

Actions also reinforce the commitment of the activists. This should not be underestimated. People get tired of licking stamps and chipping rust. The chance to go out and actually do something is a terrific energy and morale booster.

Clearly we needed to do some serious reconnaissance of the plant in order to plan our approach. That Monday our preliminary scouting team came back to report that the plant had no security, no workers, and only a sixty-foot distance from a low fence to a ladder going up to the top of the main building. It sounded like a walk in the park. It also sounded too good to be true. Apparently, it was. Our *second* reconnaissance of the plant resulted in one person in the hospital missing her spleen, and another with a severely rearranged face.

The second scouting party comprised two Turkish activists—Tolga Temuge and Fulda Balc—who had driven to the

Gökova plant with the intention of pretending that they were engineering students asking for a tour. They never even had a chance. They were firmly rebuffed by the guards at the main gate. On the drive back to our ship, the *Arctic Sunrise*, the two had a major car wreck. Fulda lost her spleen and was stuck in the hospital. Tolga, however, showed up with his nose in an entirely new and surprising location. He insisted that– through his smashed-up mouth and bloody teeth–he was OK and could continue to help with the action. Our ship's medic, Sylvia Huber, put her foot down and sent him to join Fulda at the hospital.

Tolga's report was discouraging. The plant was patrolled by machine-gun-toting guards, surrounded by *two* barbed wire fences with a no-man's-land in between, and then another extensive no-man's-land between the inner fence and the plant. The guards with the machine guns were there to protect the plant from the PKK–a Kurdish rebel group that had clashed with the Turkish authorities many times in the preceding years.

The discrepancies between the "it's a piece of cake" report and the "heavily guarded with machine guns" report were doing nothing to boost our confidence. The group planning the action was showing the strain: one of our more experienced team members, Faik Cimen–an action coordinator from Istanbul–was so upset by the slapdash/ad-hoc planning that he quit the action in disgust. I had never seen that happen before. With the conflicting reports and the clock winding down, Mario asked me to go to the plant to give it a personal look-see. Mario rounded out my team with "Tiger," a local Turkish photographer; and Ziggy, a local volunteer. Tiger didn't speak any English at all, but at least if we got caught he could speak Turkish. Being that I was the only one with a credit card (and it was a personal one!), I rented a car.

Wednesday night, I drove Tiger and Ziggy down to the plant. Ziggy wasn't much of a navigator and we got lost for about two hours. Finally, after I'd been driving for more than six hours, we found the plant. Tiger and I got out of the car near the plant, and I instructed Ziggy to rendezvous with us at 4 A.M. He then took off with the car. Tiger and I started with a look at the western side of plant, which was near a residential area. We tried crawling along on our bellies to avoid being seen, but the neighborhood dogs were doing their job, barking up a storm. Tired of eating dirt to stay out of sight, and not really being able to see much from that side anyway, we decided to check out the east side of the plant, where there was a conveyor belt. The conveyor—designed to carry the coal from the ground up and into the plant—was covered with a roof and walls and went most of the way up the side of the plant. Tiger and I could see there was a walkway alongside the belt for the workmen. If we could get to the conveyor belt unseen, we could go up the tunnel of the conveyor belt without being spotted and then, hopefully, from there we could reach the roof. Getting to the conveyor belt unseen was going to be the hard part. There was a pair of barbed wire fences to get past, not to mention those gun-toting guards on the lookout for terrorists.

In the movies, you always see people snipping barbed wire fences in order to get through. With Greenpeace, however, our mandate is to cause *no damage at all*, and that means cutting through barbed wire isn't allowed. It was either over or under or find a way through without being detected. The fencing around the conveyor belt itself was too hard to scale, and the area was well-lit, but there was a lower section of fence nearby. To get to the lower section we had to crawl through some brush, and then cross a dry creek bed about ten feet deep and thirty feet wide by stepping along the top of a pipe that crossed it. Once across, we found some kind of concrete block or foundation to stand on. With a bit of a boost it was possible to get over the fence without too much difficulty. We got over the first fence, clambered over a small wall in the no-man's-land between the two fences, and then carefully climbed over the second barbed wire fence at the inner bank. We were absolutely amazed that we hadn't been spotted yet, but we still had a way to go.

We tiptoed across 250 feet of grass and roads, and climbed up into the conveyor belt. Its roof and walls would keep us out of sight, so we felt like we had made it past the hardest part (except for the "getting back out" part). From here, it seemed simple enough to make it up to the roof of the ten-story building through the three-hundred-foot length of the conveyor without being seen. Tiger and I were catching our breath when, without warning, bright yellow lights started flashing around us, and a massive mechanical rumble shook the tunnel. The conveyor belt was starting up. Tiger and I almost shit our pants. But nobody had seen us, so we continued up the walkway next to the belt. We found a stairwell at the top that went the rest of the way up onto the roof. It was looking like the plan to hang the banner from the roof could work after all! Once Tiger and I made it onto the roof, however, we found an unexpected and insurmountable problem.

The roof of the plant was made of fairly thin corrugated fiberglass sheets. With the weight of six activists and a two-hundred-pound banner, there was no way the roof could be trusted to hold our collective weight. Having one of us do a swan dive onto the concrete floor fifty feet below us was not going to do the environment any good. We had to find another option. We quietly snuck around the top floor of the plant. It was still night, so there weren't too many people around, but we still had to be very careful. Finally, I saw a potential solution: a series of windows along the top of the plant from which we could hang the banner. With six activists—each working through a window or two—we could get the job done. It would be tricky, but it was our best shot.

Confident that we at least had a workable plan, Tiger and I descended down the conveyor belt, crossed the seventy-five yards of no-man's-land, got over one fence, across the next no-man's-land, then scaled the other fence, tiptoed back along the pipe, and got out undetected. Tiger, who had not said one word the entire night, turned to me on the pipe, smiled, gave me a thumbs-up, and said "*Mission Impossible!*" It *was* kind of like that, but the "should any of your force be caught or killed" bit was the part I was worried about. For tonight, however, the worst was over. All we had to do was find Ziggy and head back to the ship.

Tiger and I walked to the rendezvous point but couldn't find him. We waited awhile, then walked a mile or so down the road hoping we'd spot him. Finally we realized we were walking farther away from the rendezvous location, so we went back. By this time we were tired and cold. We managed to find an empty parking lot that was still warm from the sun, so we laid down to wait. At 7 A.M.—three hours late—Ziggy showed up. I didn't ask him, but I was pretty sure he had fallen asleep. I was pissed, fatigued, and now had to drive at least three hours back to the ship. By the time the three of us got back to the *Arctic Sunrise* it was almost lunchtime. I hadn't slept in over twenty-four hours. I spent the rest of the day sleeping while the banner was being finished. I needed my beauty rest. Tomorrow was the big day.

Once again, being the guy with a credit card, I had to drive one of the cars all the way back to the plant. I drove the car stuffed full of people, and someone else drove the car stuffed with the banner. Even folded as small as we could make it, it barely fit. We started out at 1:30 in the morning. I was having trouble staying focused on the road. At times I thought I was seeing double, and I really didn't feel like joining Fulda and Tolga at the local emergency room.

Four hours later, at 5:30 A.M., we arrived at the plant and stopped the cars near the entry point that Tiger and I had found. It took a few minutes to find it. We all knew that two empty-handed guys making it past all the obstacles without being seen was one thing, but six people carrying a two-hundred-pound, fifty-foot-long rolled-up banner was going to be much harder to overlook. Michael Fincken (second mate, South Africa), Anders Stensson (chief engineer, Sweden), Sylvia Huber (medic, Austria), Gillie "Sprout" Murphy (radio operator, US) and Leonardo Landi (deckhand and cook, Italy) humped the banner and each other over the fences. We then put the banner over our shoulders and started across the pipe.

The gods must have been with us because we all made it to the conveyor belt. We looked up the conveyor belt and it was all clear. We started up, and once again the conveyor did too. Of course, everyone else shit their pants like Tiger and I had the first time. (I guess I should have warned them. Oops!) We kept climbing. A couple of minutes later the belt shut down again. A couple of minutes later it started up again. Was this a sign that someone had seen us? Were they trying to discourage us? Apparently not. Thirty minutes later we reached the top. We were half-expecting a welcoming committee, but none appeared. The action wasn't supposed to start for another few hours, so we had to find a place where we could wait without being discovered.

During our reconnaissance on my first visit to the plant, I had identified a stairwell to the roof as being the safest choice. Unfortunately, there was an open area about a hundred feet wide that we had to cross to get to the stairwell. On our left, about three hundred feet away, was a group of workers doing some kind of lathe work or grinding. Thankfully it was noisy, industrial work that required their concentration, so we were able to sneak behind them unnoticed. Had any one of them simply turned his head, it would have been hard to miss the giant, slinking yellow centipede with twelve legs.

We waited in the stairwell for several hours, praying that none of the workers would need to use these stairs. Some of us dozed off. The rest just chilled. Just before action time, I checked the plant floor and saw that several workers were still there. At noon, as we had hoped, they cleared the floor for lunch and we jumped into action.

To distract the guards outside the plant, we planned to create a diversion at the main gates. With the guards' attention drawn toward the gates, we stood a better chance of making it out of the stairwell, across the shop floor, and to the windows without being stopped. I called the distraction team on the radio and gave them the go sign.

With the plant floor empty, and the guards being kept busy at the front gates, we had no trouble getting to the windows along the top of the plant. These windows opened horizontally from the bottom, but there was a good distance between each window. There was also some kind of structural reinforcement between each set of windows that we had to get the banner around. It was tough going. There were only six of us, and we had to tie the heavy banner onto the rope, pass it out the first window, and then pull it to the second window, and so on. We had no idea how much time we had to do it; we expected to be caught any second. Somehow, with a good deal of exertion, we got the whole banner strung out along the windows. That's when we were spotted. One of the guards on the ground happened to look up. He pointed to us and started shouting *"No!"*, ordering us to stop. (It was amusing to see that because it reminded me of one of my primary rules of being a captain: do not give orders that won't be followed because you will look like a fool when they aren't.) The rest of the workers and guards instantly wheeled around and started running toward the plant. With a rush of anticipation we pulled out the daisy chain of slipknots to unfurl the banner and . . .

There was a snag, in the most literal sense. No matter what we did, we could only get one-half of the banner unfurled. It was supposed to read: "Enough Is Enough!" in Turkish. With the snag, it read: "Enough." Well, "Enough" was going to have to be enough.

This was not the only time we've encountered a banner-unfurling snag. If you do enough of them, sooner or later you're going to have some kind of problem. In the early eighties, there was an action in Seattle at a smelting plant. The campaigner wanted to use a quotation from Chief Seattle. (Others attribute it to the Cree Indians, and still others say it was another tribe. At the very least, it's a Native American saying.) The banner was supposed to hang down from the top of the smelting plant's giant smokestack. The banner said:

Only after the last tree is cut,
Only after the last river is poisoned,
Only after the last fish has been caught,
Only when all the animals have been hunted,
Only then will you discover that money cannot be eaten.

Several intrepid climbers made it to the top of the stack, and the media were all clustered around it when the word came to unfurl the banner. The banner dropped most of the way, but it must have caught on something sharp on the smokestack because the activists couldn't get the last bit of banner to unfurl, so it now read:

Only after the last tree is cut,
Only after the last river is poisoned,
Only after the last fish has been caught,
Only when all the animals have been hunted
Only then will you disco

Shit happens. (Hat tip to Gp'er Jim Puckett, who was there.)

Within minutes we were surrounded by angry workers and a few very tense guards. The workers were probably pissed because we had interrupted their lunch break. The guards were most likely worried that they were going be chewed out or fired for not seeing all of us and the giant banner before we were inside the plant. One very nervous-looking young guard was pointing his rifle at us. His finger was on the trigger and his hands were visibly trembling. Gillie tried to get one last radio message out to let everyone know that the jig was up, but the young Turkish guard with the bayonet charged at Gillie to stop her. Mike stepped in between them with his hands up and stalled the guard just long enough for Gillie to complete her transmission.

While we might not have looked exactly like Kurdish terrorists, we were quite a sight. All of us were wearing white boiler suits and we were covered in coal dust from the conveyor belt. (Boiler suits are denim overalls used for working in the engine room or for other dirty jobs on the ship. They say "Greenpeace" on the back. We usually wear them during actions to identify ourselves as being with Greenpeace. It's considered our action uniform.)

One of the guards was jabbing his bayonet in Anders's direction and shouting "PKK! PKK!" I grabbed Anders, turned him around, pointed to the words stenciled on the back of his boiler suit, and kept repeating softly: "No. Greenpeace." Having the women with us also helped to convince the overly excited guards that we weren't Kurdish guerrillas. Things began to settle down. (This is just one more reason why I like having mixed-gender and mixed-race crews on the ships. Warriors of the Rainbow should be many colors, not just Warriors of the Middle Class White Americans and Europeans.) A short time later we were all gathered, along with the diversion team from the front gate, in an office at the plant, being questioned by the authorities.

Gp trains people that when they give statements to authorities, they should stick to campaign issues and not provide any of the specifics of the action. This keeps them from incriminating themselves without appearing to be uncooperative. After questioning several of us, and getting the same kinds of responses, the police gave up and just took down names and addresses. We had a lawyer standing by, but someone had told him we were already downtown at the police station, so that's where he had gone. If we didn't get in front of the judge by 6 P.M., we were going to have to spend the night in a Turkish jail. (If you've seen the movie *Midnight Express*, you can appreciate our anxiety at the thought.) Thankfully, the lawyer got back to us and, with fifteen minutes to spare, we faced the judge.

The judge was an imposing-looking man with eyebrows meeting in the middle over his nose, and high cheekbones. He would have looked reminiscent of Count Dracula anyway, but—adding to the effect—the judge was also wearing a shiny black cape with a bright red satin lining. In different circumstances I might have said he was good-looking, but he was undeniably fierce-looking. The fact that we had easily and brazenly walked into a high-security facility, *and* were extending the length of his workday with twenty-five arraignments, was fueling his fury. He fumed at our lawyer, Nayon Özkan, who had big beads of sweat popping out on his forehead. I was already getting very nervous, but when the Turkish activists next to me—who could understand every word out of Dracula's mouth—began crying, I began to suspect we were really fucked. Nayon leaned over to me and whispered "Three months." Three months! In a Turkish prison?

Judge Dracula asked us to make statements, and he started with me. I don't remember my exact words (I was, understandably, preoccupied with visions of prison), but I probably said something like: "Very sorry for the disturbance, Your Honor, but the environmental consequences of burning radioactive coal are causing us a great deal of worry. Sir." Mike Fincken, the second mate, was more defiant. Mike stated that he wasn't sorry at all and would do it again without hesitation. I suspect our translator, given the mood of the judge, softened Mike's statement a bit. (I wanted to "soften" Mike as I didn't see much point in further aggravating the situation. "Three months" was still ringing in my ears.)

Eventually the judge let most of us go, except for those of us who had arrived in Izmir in the *Arctic Sunrise.* Upon our arrival in Izmir, we had been given shore passes (kind of like a temporary visa for sailors) that allowed us to visit the town. The passes, however, were only good for Izmir, and we had traveled a long way from there.

While we would be allowed to stay at a hotel that night—a hotel owned by a friend of one of the local Gp personnel—we had to walk two or three miles to get there in our coal-covered boiler suits. I'm sure we looked like a roadside jail gang—and with a less understanding judge, we might very well have been!

After the day's events, punctuated by the long walk to the hotel, everyone looked forward to a good night's sleep before we had to deal with the shore-pass issue the next day. The hotel owner thoughtfully left us a couple of bottles of raki (the Turkish equivalent of sambuca). Anders and I got a room together and had a few pulls of the raki. By the time Anders stepped out of the much-needed shower, he saw me falling onto the bed. He claims I was snoring on the way down.

The following evening, Saturday, at a police station in Izmir, the prosecutor yelled at us for another forty minutes at the top of his lungs because we had ruined his weekend. "Well, we ruined your weekend, but the plant is ruining your environment" is what I should have said, but the reputation of Turkish prisons held me back.

Looking back on it, this action was one of the more exciting ones I've been a part of. While it turned out well (other than the banner snag), I took away some lessons that I still carry today. First, don't do actions involving armed guards, barbed wire, and heavy machinery without a lot of very careful planning and preparation. If I had been sensible, I would have withdrawn from the action like Faik had, especially after the car wreck. Not to mention the point at which I was having trouble seeing clearly while driving to the plant. Then again, nobody's ever accused me of being completely sensible. Second, it pays to really evaluate the site of the action thoroughly before committing to a plan of action. And third, make sure you're not the only one with a credit card.

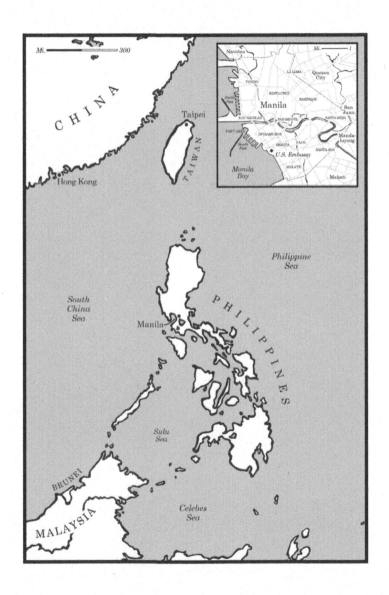

10

Return to Sender

It had been nine years since I had last sailed on the second *Rainbow Warrior*. The ship had a special place in my heart after I spent eighteen months in Hamburg working on her conversion from a North Sea fishing trawler to a Gp vessel. Her three-masted schooner rig (schooners have two or more fore-and-aft-rigged masts, where the rear one is at least as high as the rest) was far more sophisticated than the one we had retrofitted to the original R'dub in 1985.

The new rig had been designed by Peter Schenzle and his team in Hamburg. Schenzle is a leading expert in the use of modest amounts of horsepower in combination with sails on large cargo vessels. I always enjoyed spending time with him, particularly when he talked about using wind tunnels to research traditional square-rigger airflow dynamics.

Schenzle was in charge of an R&D project for a simple and

efficient cargo sailing vessel for coastal and inter-island trade when Greenpeace asked him to design a sailing rig for the new *Rainbow Warrior*. The rig had to be designed so that it could be built, maintained, and efficiently operated in developing countries.

The second *Rainbow Warrior* was more like a sailboat than a motor vessel. There are mariners and there are sailors. Mariners are people who spend time on the sea—whether they're on a motor vessel or sailing vessel. I have served on both, but deep down I'm a sailor. While I'd rather be at sea than on land, I'd *much* rather be sailing than motoring. My favorite sound in the world is hearing an engine stop and then hearing the bow wave burble while under sail. Someone once said that the definition of heaven is taking your favorite moment and being able to live in it forever. I'm not saying there is a heaven, and I'm not saying that if there is a heaven I would even be allowed in, but if there is and if I am, that's the moment I want to be in forever. It's one of the reasons that I had such a fondness for that ship.

Our six-month "Toxic-Free Asia" tour would begin in Malta, and then take us to India, Thailand, the Philippines, Hong Kong, and Japan. I was really looking forward to the trip. One of the perks of my job is being able to sail to all of these wonderful corners of the globe. I had never been to India or the Philippines before, and had not sailed very much in either Hong Kong or Japanese waters. Sometimes you know in advance that certain stints at sea are going to be difficult; cold water, big seas, and hostile governments are good indicators that a trip is likely to be an arduous one. This tour, on the other hand, was shaping up to be a fun and pleasant voyage.

The first stop, in India, was timed to coincide with the fifteenth anniversary of the 1984 disaster at Bhopal that killed thousands of people, and injured half a million more, when a cloud of toxic gas was released from a Union Carbide pesticide plant. It was an entirely preventable accident caused by negligence and lack of maintenance. Fifteen years later, no one had really been punished in any meaningful way, and the disaster area still hadn't been cleaned up.

Next stop was Thailand, where a small fishing village had been fighting off the building of a coal-fired power plant for years. They understood the destruction it would wreak: damage to the coral reefs from the bulk carriers full of coal, air pollution contaminating their food, etc. It was amazing to me that they understood the long-term costs far better than the "more sophisticated and educated" people in Europe and the Americas. The Thais had been demonstrating for a long time, and one of their leading activists had been murdered, but they hadn't backed down. They invited us onshore and we shared a nice lunch together. It was humbling, but heartwarming, to me when they held up banners saying "We trust Greenpeace." Both the Thais and our crew felt good that we were all part of something much bigger than ourselves.

After brief stops in Bangkok and Phuket, Thailand, we set sail for Manila, in the Philippines. This would be the highlight of the tour as far as I was concerned. Banners and ceremonies are nice, and a necessary part of what Greenpeace does, but direct actions are what keep me—and many others in Gp—excited and committed. This next direct action promised to be a doozy: we were going to Manila to bring a little present to the US Embassy there.

The United States had been a presence in the Philippines since the Spanish-American War in 1898. At Manila Bay, when Admiral George Dewey said the now famous words "You may fire when ready, Gridley," he launched the attack that defeated the Spanish Pacific squadron in only seven

hours. In the ensuing ninety years, the US built up a huge
military presence there (with a brief interruption when the
Japanese took over in World War II). Subic Bay, adjacent to
Manila Bay and covering 262 square miles, became one of
the largest US Navy bases in the world. About thirty miles
away—on the other side of Mt. Pinatubo—was Clark Air Base,
which grew to a similar scale and was a critical link in the
supply chain for the Vietnam War. In 1991, however, the Philippine Senate rejected an extension of the agreement allowing the American bases. The following year US forces
withdrew from both bases and turned over the keys to the
Philippine government. As a token of gratitude (my words),
the Americans left behind a toxic booby trap.

Just before the US withdrew from the bases, there had
been a tremendous eruption of Mt. Pinatubo with a mass
ejection on the scale of the famous Krakatoa. There had been
ample warning of the eruption, so the death toll was "only"
nine hundred or so, but thousands of homes had been wiped
out. Most of the population that lived in the area around Pinatubo had been left displaced and homeless. When the US
left, many locals were relocated onto the now empty bases.
Not long afterward, however, reports of significant health
problems began to surface: respiratory ailments and miscarriages, and almost an entire generation of children born inside the base manifested nerve damage, deformities, and
cancers. A local Filipino environmental group, the People's
Task Force for Bases Clean-up, discovered that the US had
left behind a toxic legacy of pesticides, corrosive aviation fuel,
PCBs, asbestos, lead, solvents, waste oil and, to add insult to
injury, UXO—military-speak for unexploded ordnance. In
other words, live bombs.

This wasn't an accident or oversight. The US General Ac-
counting Office had issued a report in early 1992 detailing

the extent of the problem, as well as the expense that would be required to clean it up. Instead, in order to avoid the massive liabilities and cleanup costs from the pollution that the US left behind, it was all swept under the rug. "Swept under the rug" is an all-too-accurate description: much of the toxic material was put into fifty-gallon drums that were placed in shallow trenches and simply covered up with dirt. Out of sight, out of mind. It was only a matter of time before the corrosive fluids and rust ate through the drums and the truth leaked out.

To further the depth of the deception, when the agreement for the transfer of the bases was written, the US included a clause absolving it of any responsibility for the cleanup, all the while assuring the Philippine government that nothing toxic had been left behind. Subsequent studies and evidence clearly showed that the US had left the Filipinos holding the proverbial bag. Greenpeace's action was going to bring that bag back and drop it on the doorstep of the US Embassy in Manila.

Von Hernandez was executive director of our Philippines office. He organized a friendly community-relations event in which he invited about twenty of the suffering children and their families to take a tour of the *Rainbow Warrior* and to enjoy rides around the harbor on one of our fastest outboard boats. One of the children—a six-year-old girl named Crizel— had drawn the poster that we were using to publicize our campaign. Crizel's family had moved into the old motor pool of Clark Air Base after their own home had been destroyed by Mt. Pinatubo. As it turned out, they had moved to a part of the base that was very heavily contaminated. The water the family had been using for bathing and cooking was laden with heavy metals and other poisons. As a result, Crizel had acute myeloid leukemia. Crizel become the poster child for the entire issue. She had already been on local TV, and her drawings had been used by other groups that were involved in the issue.

By the time she arrived at the *Rainbow Warrior*, Crizel was very, very ill. Our ship's nurse–Lawrence "Butch" Turk–thought the girl should be taken directly to the hospital, but her parents knew how important this was for her. They felt that Crizel had been hanging on to life driven by her desire to see the *Rainbow Warrior* and to go for a boat ride. She had been receiving chemotherapy and transfusions every other day, and was so intent on visiting with us that she was willing to skip her treatment that day. Crizel, mustering as much energy as her frail body could, threw a small tantrum to drive home the point. We couldn't refuse her, especially since we were standing near a dockside display of her beautiful artwork.

I took Crizel, her mother, and some other children on one of the inflatables for a harbor tour. Crizel was held the entire time by Lawrence, who kept a close eye on her. Every so often, blood would appear around the edges of her mouth, but it was clear that the ride was a true joy for her. At one point, Crizel was energized enough to take the wheel of the inflatable, and I can still picture the look on her face–the small smile and still-bright eyes–as if it were yesterday.

During the ride, we passed near the USS *Fort McHenry*—an amphibious landing warship. Named after the fort that inspired "The Star-Spangled Banner," the ship had the words from the national anthem—"Home of the Brave"—emblazoned on her transom. Later, when we were back aboard the *Rainbow Warrior*, we were told that the US Navy was threatening to shoot us if we approached the ship again. The supreme irony of the "Home of the Brave" being threatened by a six-year-old girl dying of

leukemia—caused by the US military's own toxic waste!—made
me want to puke.

After the boat ride, Crizel was given a tour of *Rainbow
Warrior*, and then she went to draw pictures with the other
children in the crew's mess (the cafeteria on the ship). Crizel
then went to take a nap in the ship's infirmary while the event
continued at the dock. I went for a short walk to stretch my
legs on land, and when I returned, I passed a mother walking away from the ship carrying a sleeping child. She was
crying. When I got back aboard, the crew rushed over and
told me that Crizel had just died in her sleep on the ship. It
hit me like a ton of bricks. While we felt good about helping
to make her last moments happy ones, I know I was not the
only member of the Gp crew and staff who got fired up about
the upcoming action. Von Hernandez had a great motto in
the Philippines: "Docile people get poisoned. Angry people
get organized." We were angry and organized for sure.

It had been our plan all along to do the action a few days
after the reception for the families. After the senseless death
of this creative, artistic and inspiring little girl, it was good
that we had something to focus our energy on. A few weeks
before, Von had found a PCB-filled transformer in a residential area just outside the grounds of the former Clark Air Base.
It had "Property of the US Government" stenciled on the
sides and a warning sticker that said "Contains PCBs." Perfect. Clearly, since the US had claimed that there was nothing toxic left behind, they must have, obviously, lost track of
it. So we were going to be nice guys and do them the favor
of returning it to the US at its embassy in Manila.

It was easier said than done. First, we were dealing with
toxic waste, so precautions had to be taken; not just for our
protection, but also for the people nearby and in Manila,

since the embassy was downtown. We didn't want to expose
any more Filipinos to the cancer-causing agent inside the
transformer. Rob Taylor, an actions coordinator from New
Zealand, was trained for and very experienced with toxic
waste. He came to the Philippines specifically to supervise
the isolation, containment, and transportation of the toxic
transformer.

Rob had worked out an entire plan. He had shipped in all
the tools and hazmat gear that we were going to need to iso-
late and transport it, and had designed a training program
for all of us to learn how to do it properly. All of that, however, went out the window when he found out—just a few days
before our action was supposed to take place—that the transformer was gone.

With a little investigation, he learned that someone had
taken the transformer to a nearby scrap yard to sell. It had
probably been taken off the base for that reason in the first
place, and it had subsequently been moved and sold. When
Rob arrived at the scrapyard, he found that someone had already started to break it down. There were puddles of PCBs
all around it. PCBs had leaked all along the dirt road from
where it had been transported, and it was a good bet that
whoever had moved the transformer had been bathed in the
powerful carcinogens. It was a real mess. Rob negotiated with
the scrap yard's owner, explained the dangers, and promised
that we'd clean it all up the right way if he let us have the transformer. We not only had to clean up the contaminated areas
in the scrap yard, we also felt duty-bound to clean up the contamination where we had originally found the transformer,
and the contamination along the road where it had been
transported.

All of us who were working around the transformer had
to wear hazmat gear. Here's two things that I've learned about

hazmat gear: 1) It's a great attention-getter. People want to know what's going on and the media show up. 2) It's hot as hell. With the searing tropical sun, each of us could work for only ten minutes or so before having to take the head-gear off and unzip the suit just so we could breathe. It was a massive effort in difficult conditions, and added a full day of work to our schedule. In each location we had to dig up and contain any dirt that had been contaminated by the leaking PCBs. It took several hours to dig up more than three cubic yards of dirt, seal it in fifty-gallon drums, and then put it all in the shipping container with the transformer. We then transferred the container to a flatbed truck and brought it about fifty miles to Manila, close to the embassy. So far, so good.

The night before the action we had a meeting on the ship with the crew and shore-based activists to discuss the over-all plan. I'm a strong believer in going over the plan with all the participants to make sure everyone is on the same page, and besides, you never know who's going to come up with a helpful suggestion or better idea. In my mind this is a criti-cal step in ensuring the success of an action. In this case, we also had a burnt-out action coordinator and we were a little worried about his being up to the task. Action coordinators have to be very detailed and have a thorough understanding of all the parts and pieces that go into an action. They also need to make sure that everyone else knows exactly what they're supposed to be doing and when. Unfortunately, our suspicions about the action coordinator proved correct.

Actions are scripted down to the minute. "Ben," the ac-tion coordinator (I don't want to use the man's real name; he was a good guy who was fried after years of dedication, but on this action he was worse than useless) was supposed to meet us with a van at 9 A.M. to take a team to the container.

Then we'd fasten signs on it that would read "Toxic Waste" and "Property of the US Government" in large letters. We were due to deliver the container to the embassy at 11 A.M.; that's when all of the media would be there. Nine A.M.—no Ben. 9:30 A.M.—no Ben and no word from Ben. Sasha, our engineer, started to get nervous about being able to do what we had to do and still stay on schedule. Without a van, we just started walking toward the staging area. Two miles later the tools were heavier, the signs were heavier, and the van and Ben were nowhere to be seen. It wasn't looking good.

Finally, we were able to use our VHF radio to communicate with the ship (thankfully, Thom Looney—our radio operator, was on watch in the radio room!) to arrange a rendezvous with the truck at 10:30, but we were way behind schedule. Sasha tried to drill some holes into the side of the shipping container to attach the signs, but the battery-powered drill was no match for the hardened steel. The bit was just skidding around and hardly scratched the paint. Time to switch to plan B. (After you do this for a while you become a big believer in always having a plan B. And a plan Z!) We hung the signs up with some galvanized wire. It was now 10:50 and the clock was ticking. We still had to get through three miles of Manila traffic to the staging area, transfer the container to a forklift, and then drive the remaining distance to the embassy.

Months before, when I had first heard about this action, I begged to be the forklift driver. I insisted on it. I had been dreaming about it and thinking about how I was going to do it for weeks. I envisioned taking the container off the flatbed truck, lifting it high in the air so I could see under it, and then zipping down the street, weaving in and out of traffic, skidding around a corner on two wheels right in front of the embassy, screeching to a halt just millimeters from the big iron embassy gates and dropping the container with a loud "clang" and to even louder applause. This was gonna be so *cool*! I couldn't wait.

I had never driven a forklift before, so the forklift rental company's guys gave me a crash course (if you'll pardon the expression). When it came time, I carefully lined up the forks of the forklift with the container—which had been placed at the back end of the flatbed—and slid them under the container. I lifted the container just a bit and backed away from the flatbed, and then elevated the container the rest of the way so I could see underneath. I was just about to start my "run" when I noticed that everyone around me was gesturing emphatically to lower the box. *Maybe they need to adjust the signs*, was my first thought. I hit the lever to lower the container before I remembered how fast heavy loads like this one come down on forklifts. As the blur of the dropping container flashed before my eyes, I remembered to back off the lever just in time to avoid slamming the container on the ground. It stopped just inches from the pavement, but the force of the weight coming down lifted the forklift's back wheels a couple of feet off the ground. The forklift and I just missed toppling over.

Tom Briggs, the ship's boatswain, was shaking his head. Tom had been a medic in Vietnam and had seen more than his fair share of excitement and danger over there. In his laconic Texas drawl he informed me that if I tried to drive with the container up in the air like that I'd "probably tip the whole damn forklift over" when I tried to stop. A little light came on in my head, and I could see the headline in the next day's *Manila Times*: "Stupid Greenpeace Forklift Driver Kills Innocent Family in Bizarre Accident." That wouldn't make Von happy.

Time for that old plan B again, but with the container

down low I couldn't see where I was going. I had to follow Tom's directions as he and another guide walked on either side of me. We must have been quite a sight. All these cars were driving by us, looking at us and thinking, *What the hell are you guys doing?* It wasn't easy to drive the forklift and container on the crowded streets of Manila, but then again nobody wants to cut off a crazy man driving around a shipping container that says "Toxic Waste."

When I got to the driveway of the embassy I could see the press and cameras all over the place. The embassy guards, of course, had no idea what was coming, but they knew something was up. They sure were surprised when I showed up with the forklift and container, so surprised, in fact, that I was allowed to go right up to the gates even though it was a high-security area. I dropped off the package just inches from the gates, backed away carefully, and brought the forklift back to the flatbed truck waiting a couple of blocks away. We told the flatbed drivers to get the hell out of there with the forklift right away. We didn't want to make it easy for anyone else to move the container again anytime soon.

Back at the gates, the crew and local staff were all sitting in front of the container singing songs, including the Philippine national anthem, and holding signs and banners that said "Toxic Legacy," "Return to Sender!", and "Take This Back!" Von and Jack Weinberg were talking to some of the embassy officials and guards inside of the gates, trying to convince them to officially receive the container and the keys to it. Not that we thought they'd actually do it, but it was good footage.

For those who lived though the Sixties, Jack was the guy who first said, "Don't trust anyone over thirty." He was part of the free-speech movement and the first activist arrested in the famous University of California, Berkeley, protests. He has been a committed activist for close to fifty years, and I've always found him inspiring. He's been working on environmental health activism and industrial/chemical pollution issues for the past thirty-five years. He worked with Greenpeace for about ten years during that time. These days he probably says: "Don't trust anyone under seventy-five."

It didn't take long for the bomb squad to show up. And they had the forklift. The idiot flatbed truck drivers were so entertained by the spectacle going on at the embassy that they hadn't left the area as we'd directed. They'd been easily identified and arrested. The police brought the forklift over and tried to convince us to remove the container ourselves, but of course we refused. As intimidating as they looked in their protective gear, we could actually talk to them. Some of them were even a little sympathetic. Just a little. The squad commander asked Von to order the activists—who were blocking the gates to the embassy—to leave. Von, of course, refused and told the commander that the police would have to do it themselves. He also kept reinforcing with the commander that we were nonviolent and would only resist passively.

Eventually they decided to arrest us and clear us out themselves. Since I was the forklift driver they assumed I was the ringleader and should therefore be the first person arrested. I practiced passive resistance and just sat there. Filipinos are generally fairly small people so it took three of them to pick me up, groaning and complaining the whole time. And I was certainly not the biggest and heaviest of our bunch. There were twenty-six of us, many much bigger than me, so the police were going to have a long day.

At the police station, I sat with the local inspector and gave him the whole campaign spiel. When I was done, he said,

"We should be thanking you, not arresting you." Figuring that was my cue to leave, I started to get up but he stopped me. "No, no, Captain. We're not done yet." They had to charge me with something, so they charged me with unlicensed driving of a forklift, driving a forklift on the street, and littering. (Charging *me* with littering was particularly ironic considering all of the garbage that the US left on the bases.) Athena Ronquillo-Ballesteros—one of the local campaigners—told me I was going to be held for questioning, but before I began giving them a statement they suddenly cut me loose and I was free to go. I thought I must have said some magic words. It turns out that I actually had.

At the beginning of the statement the inspector asked if I had a lawyer and I said "Yeah, Ted Te." It turns out Ted Te was the biggest human rights lawyer in all of the Philippines. *Everyone* knew about him. "He's *your* lawyer?!" The cop was so impressed that I had Ted Te representing me on a mere charge of littering that he figured they'd never win the case. (Ted Te is now the spokesperson for the Supreme Court of the Philippines.) "Walk softly and carry a big lawyer" is the lesson I took away from that experience.

The following day, we were splashed across the front pages all over the Philippines and many other countries—including the US—as well. It was a media sensation. Besides the news coverage, there were many editorials written that praised Greenpeace and denounced the US government for refusing to assume the responsibility for the pollution and toxins they had left behind. Days later, the Philippine Senate passed a resolution calling on the Philippine government to push the US to clean things up. Twenty-five years later, the US continues to evade its responsibility.

It was a very long time before I found out what may have happened to the container, the PCB-contaminated dirt, and the transformer. I kept thinking about the ending of *Raiders of the Lost Ark* when they wheel the ark into a giant warehouse full of secret government stuff, never to be seen again: "Our best people are working on it." The truth, however, was that it was probably taken by the Metropolitan Manila Development Authority and kept at a storage facility. They threatened publicly to sue Greenpeace over the container, but never did, as they were secretly sympathetic to our campaign. Eventually, with the help of the UN, the Philippine government instituted a PCB destruction program (one that did not use incineration) and it is believed that is how the container and transformer were finally disposed of.

11

When Push Comes to Shove

Many countries feel that burning toxic waste is a good idea: out of sight, out of mind. Instead of a large, highly visible pile of waste, or leaking barrels of corrosive goo, the waste is burned and released into the air where it "disappears." Voila! Problem solved, right? Except it doesn't really disappear, it just becomes invisible. Releasing the gases into the air just spreads the problem around so everyone can suffer the effects. And you still have the hazardous ash to dispose of in some way. The solution to pollution is *not* dilution; it's stopping the pollution in the first place. In the case of this kind of mixed waste, the right way to handle it is to reduce it, reuse it, or recycle it as much as possible.

Worse yet, incomplete burning of the waste creates dioxin, one of the most lethal poisons in the world. Releasing dioxins in the middle of the North Sea (like the *Vulcanus II* did) indirectly harmed the human population who were eating the polluted fish. In Sweden, the giant incinerators were *on land right near where people live!* The people had no idea of the dangers that were lurking in their air.

Our objective was to stop a delivery of 3,700 tons of mixed waste from Holland that was going to be burned in the Igelstaverket power plant in Södertälje, Sweden. 3,700 tons was just a small part of the over 110,000 tons that had been burned the year before, and Sweden had just applied for a permit to burn *three times that amount.* Greenpeace's position was that burning this waste was inefficient and dangerous, so to bring attention to it, we were prepared to stop the ship from delivering its cargo to the plant.

Södertälje is a suburb about twenty-five miles outside of Stockholm. To get there, the *Greenpeace* had to transit a very narrow, thirty-five-mile-long channel. It's the most direct way in, but it's a very tricky route with twists and turns and very little margin for error. Like most large ports, this one required that a pilot come aboard all vessels coming in or going out. The pilot is the local guide who's familiar with the waters; they pilot the same route day in and day out. Sometimes I feel that they're not necessary, and sometimes they're necessary but a pain in the ass, but in a channel as tricky as that one, it was a very nice feeling to know that a local expert would be watching over my shoulder.

About an hour before we were scheduled to meet the pilot, we radioed ahead to confirm. The dispatcher told us that despite our previously arranged–and confirmed–reservation, "no pilot is available." Since we had followed the proper protocols for arranging one, the dispatcher had no objection to our proceeding without one. *Gulp!* I knew we could do it, but it would be a little stressful since I had never come up this way before, and it was nighttime. As a comparison, it's like when you're driving on the highway in the pouring rain at night; you do it all the time, but you'd rather be driving in better conditions and it makes you tense up a bit.

Days later, after the action was over, we learned from the harbor police that the dispatcher had taken it upon himself to decide that we "did not deserve a pilot" even though we had reserved one. The harbor police were very upset with the dispatcher, and his lie almost cost him his job. Apparently he wasn't too happy with the fact that we were going to protest one of his paying customers. That's understandable, to a degree, but he is not supposed to editorialize. His job is to supply pilots to everyone to reduce the danger to shipping, the harbor, and the environment. Period. Deciding not to provide a pilot was like an air traffic controller deciding not to assign a runway to an inbound plane simply because it's from a country with politics he disagrees with. You just can't do that.

Navigational aids are different all over the world. The shapes, markings, or colors of the buoys can be different. Each lighthouse or lighted buoy has light-signature-distinctive colors, flash intervals, etc., so that you can't mistake one navigational aid for another and run aground. In some parts of the world, the colors of the buoys are even reversed. Imagine driving in a country where red means go and green means stop! In Europe, Africa, and Asia, *green* buoys are used on the right-hand side of channels on the way into harbors, and in North and South America, the right-hand buoys on the way into harbors are *red*. You really need to know the exact system that the particular country uses.

In the channel we were in, Sweden uses something fairly unusual called sectored lights. These are lights on towers that are divided into red, green, and white sectors. The idea is that as you steam up a channel, if the light stays white (or red or green, depending on which part of the channel you're in), then you are in the middle of the channel. As you approach the light you are aiming for, you begin to look for the next light. When the next light changes to the correct color, you turn toward that one.

The radar was almost useless. There were so many small islands all around us that it was impossible to tell which was which on the radar display. Helen Perivier, the chief mate, was doing the navigating in the chart room off the bridge while I was on the helm. She would call the course out, the timing to the next turn, etc., and also direct me when to use the searchlight to find unlit nav aids. (If you remember the scene from *The Hunt for Red October* where Sean Connery is leading the Russian submarine through "Red Route One," you'll have a good idea of what things were like on the *Greenpeace*: "Ten seconds to turn. Five seconds to turn. Turn, 10 degrees left to course 340. . . .")

At times the islands were so close to the ship that the starboard running light (running lights are at the bow of almost every kind of boat, with red on the port side, and green on the starboard) was reflecting on the nearby leaves of the trees. It was a little hairy and took a lot of hard concentration. About halfway up the channel, Marco the cook called up to the bridge to tell us he had just baked some fresh rye bread. I thanked him but told him, "We're a little busy at the moment." I looked up and realized that I had just overshot a turn and had to put the wheel hard over to get back into the channel. Phew. You can't be distracted *at all* in these circumstances. After a long, tense passage up the channel, we dropped anchor at 3:30 A.M., Monday morning. We were exhausted.

Pelle Petterson, our action coordinator, had conceived a highly coordinated attack. It was like the Greenpeace version of D-Day. To paraphrase Winston Churchill, "We would fight them in the air. We would fight them on the seas. We would fight them on the beaches. . . ." Over eighty Gp activists from all over Europe were converging on Södertälje to stop the ship full of waste—the *Aries*. We were going to have swimmers in a line *across* the channel, climbers suspended in the air below a 131-foot-high railroad bridge *above* the channel, inflatables and RHIBs all around the target ship *in* the channel, and the *Greenpeace* blocking the channel as well.

Since we didn't know when the *Aries* was going to be coming in, we had to be prepared for her arrival by day or night. Eight climbers rappelled down to a height of about fifty or sixty feet off the water and set up suspended shelters (like the ones used for super-high mountain climbing) that they could sleep in. They also hung a huge protest banner under the bridge. The swimmers were all going to be holding on to a rope that crossed the entire width of the channel, and the *Greenpeace* would be behind them physically blocking the channel as well. At 9 A.M., everyone was in position and ready.

Lo and behold, the *Aries* came into the channel during the day. They didn't seem to be expecting us. We radioed to them when they were about four miles out and informed them we were going to block the channel with everything we had. She kept coming, but not all that fast. We suddenly realized, however, that while we were blocking the *Aries* from coming into her berth, she was turning toward a different pier not too far away, one that was outside of our blockade. That was *her* plan B. Since we didn't want her in Sweden at any dock at all, I had a brainstorm to prevent her from reaching her fallback pier nearby.

The *Greenpeace* does not have a bow thruster—a sideways propeller in the bow that helps to turn ships more quickly and more precisely. In the past, we had used inflatables and

jet boats as makeshift bow thrusters by having them push on
the bow of the *Greenpeace* in the right direction. I told some of
the crew I wanted them to do the same thing to the *Aries* to
push her away from the other dock. They got right on it, and
it worked like a charm. With three 50-horsepower outboards
pushing on his bow, the captain of the *Aries* couldn't steer the
ship and he backed down. Defeated, he said he was going to
go anchor outside our blockade. Round one to the good guys.

After things cooled down, we sent a team over to the
Aries to chain themselves to the anchor chain. This would
prevent the *Aries* from sneaking into the harbor without us
knowing, and the anchor team could warn the rest of the activists that the *Aries* was moving again. It would also mean
the ship would need to call the police to remove the activists
from the anchor chain, and that would buy us even more
time. As a result, all of us (with the possible exception of the
team suspended from the bridge!) got a good night's sleep.

The police had assured the *Aries* that they would be able
to "clear the way" the next morning, on Tuesday. There was
no way that any of the local cops or harbor police were going
to rappel down to the climbers and arrest them, so in the
morning a SWAT team was brought in from Stockholm to
clear the climbers from the bridge. By noon, however, the
police had arrested Dieter Ertwiens (the ship's electrician)
and our ship's surgeon, who were both on anchor-chain duty,
and the cops had taken the inflatable off the *Aries*'s chain as
well. In the not-so-smart-department, however, we had left
the rope we were going to string across the channel in the
inflatable that had just disappeared with the police. Duh.

The ship's surgeon was brand-new to Gp. The week before, he
had set some kind of record for the shortest time between becoming a Gp crew member and being arrested. He had come

on board, enjoyed a bowl of soup, joined in the action, and was
arrested—all in fifteen minutes flat. Impressive! Now, a week later,
he'd been arrested again. The guy was on a roll!

As the *Aries* was getting ready to get under way, a good-
size police boat came alongside the *Greenpeace* and informed
us that we were expected to stay out of the way. Fat chance. I
told him we couldn't promise that, and he just smiled. He
had something up his sleeve. When the *Aries* began to move
down the channel, we moved into a blocking position, but
then a Coast Guard cutter jammed itself against the stern of
our ship and began pushing on us just like we had pushed
on the *Aries* the day before. The big difference in this case was
that we had 3,000 horsepower at our disposal, much more
than he had.

When the *Greenpeace* had been built in 1959, she was the
world's largest and most powerful salvage tug. Her engines
are big enough to tow or push a ship many times her size.
The big diesels are an older, exposed-rocker-arm type like
the ones you might see in World War II–era U-boat movies
(*Das Boot* comes to mind). The engineer has to keep oiling
all these little oil cups on the engine, and when the engines
are running hard–and they were running very hard now–
there is a fine mist of oil that ends up covering everything in
the engine room.

The *Greenpeace* is not a very maneuverable ship. She takes a very
long time to turn. To many of us, she is known as the Black Pig.
One time, in Rotterdam, we had a pilot come aboard who
thought very highly of himself. We had to leave the dock and
turn around 180 degrees in the narrow channel to head out to
sea. I told the pilot about how I thought we should do it, but he
disagreed and told me he was going to show me "how it was

done." We did it his way and almost got into serious trouble when we couldn't complete the turn within the width of the channel. When he realized we were heading straight toward the opposite bank of the canal at a pretty good speed, his voice got *reeeeeally* high and tight. I had to bail his ass out of trouble, and that was the last word I heard from him all day. Remember what I said about some pilots being a pain in the ass. . . .

The Pig is called the Pig for a reason. Not only does she have a very wide turning radius, it takes about thirty seconds to shift from forward to reverse. To change direction with direct-drive diesels like these, you have to *stop the engine*, reverse the cams, and then *restart* the engine. If you're in a hurry and do it before the cams are ready, you can jam it up, and it takes quite a while to clear the problem. Because the Pig had two engines, we could usually save a few seconds by leaving one engine set for forward, and the other astern, but with only one engine engaged at a time. It's complicated and tricky, but you do get used to it. That doesn't mean I like it, though. With the Coast Guard cutter playing with us, we were using both engines in forward and reverse.

You could tell that the captain of the Coast Guard cutter had never run a tugboat. No matter which way he pushed on us, we were either going into the channel in forward, or into it in reverse. When he turned our stern into the channel, we just backed up in front of the cargo ship, and vice versa. At one point I had the engines in full reverse—something I had never done before. I've always babied these old engines, but we needed all the power we could get. At one point I was able to push the Coast Guard ship into the channel so that *they* were blocking the *Aries*. That was pretty cool, if I must say so myself. After playing War of Tugs/Tug of War for a while, they realized that trying to push us out of the way was hopeless. Still, the *Aries* was approaching and when it got close I was afraid that either the Coast Guard cutter or our ship could hit the *Aries*, so it was time to back off. We never want to cause damage. We retreated to a neutral corner to watch how events would play out. Within minutes we were boarded by the SWAT team.

I said earlier that I admire Jon Castle for the way he handles boats, and this tug of war was right out of Castle's playbook. He had successfully employed that little trick several times before. Many athletes these days are wearing wristbands that read "WWJD," meaning "What Would Jesus Do?" I have an imaginary one that says "WWJD—What Would Jon Do?"

When we're being boarded we generally lock all the doors to keep the other guys out, especially the doors on the bridge. We don't want to make things easy for them, but we don't want them damaging the ship or risking injury to either the crew or themselves. When it appeared they were going to smash a window to get in, I just smiled, opened the door politely, and offered them some coffee. They immediately relaxed and we all enjoyed salmon chowder together while we watched the rest of the show.

It still took another two and a half hours for the *Aries* to make it to her destination. Helen, Erkut Ertürk, and a Dutch woman were still in the water trying to stop the ship. The police were trying to pull them out with boathooks (long poles with hooks on the end). While the police couldn't pull them out of the water, they *were* poking holes in the activists' survival suits. After the swimmers began to get hypothermic from the torment of the frigid water, they finally agreed to get into the police boats.

Erkut Ertürk was our Turkish outboard mechanic and a super guy
to have on board, as outboards are the lifeblood of Greenpeace
actions. Erkut, however, was given the nickname of Jet Lemon.
He got this name when we were talking about girls one night
and teasing Ertuk about a date he'd just gone on. Of course we
wanted to know if he "got any," and he replied in his accented
English that he wouldn't tell us because "I am a gentleman." With
his accent, however, it came out like "I am a Jet Lemon." The
name stuck. Besides, "Jet Lemon" is much easier to say than "Erkut Ertürk."

The *Aries* had been able to get past the next line of defense
(the swimmers), but we weren't done yet. As she came close
to the dock, we had three waves of activists ready to board
her from a flotilla of inflatables. They were quickly arrested
by the police, who were streaming in through the main gates
of the wharf area, some of them accompanied by dogs. Activists would be arrested, released, and then show up an hour
later and board the ship again. The cops were beginning to
lose it, and got rough with some of the activists. Eventually,
someone on our side called off the action because things were
really beginning to spin out of control. Some of the more experienced members of the team said it had been the roughest
action they'd ever been a part of.

Besides being one of the roughest, largest, and most
complex actions I've ever been in, it was also one of the most
successful. By nightfall, we heard on the news that the Swedish Environmental Protection Agency had "confirmed" that
the incineration plant did not have a permit to burn the type
of waste that the *Aries* carried. The *Aries* was sent back to
Holland. Knockout in the third round!

12

Al-Qaeda, Guns, and Diamonds

February–May 2002

Sète, France; Salerno, Italy; Vlissingen, Netherlands

"Save Our Ancient Forests" Anti-Conflict Timber Actions

I was in Majorca on September 11, 2001, when my ten-year-old daughter Anita told me that a plane had just flown into the World Trade Center. My sister Bani's husband and her father-in-law were at work right across the street. I was already concerned about them when the second plane hit and the whole world instantly realized it was no accident. (I found out later that the father-and-son pair started running uptown just as the second tower collapsed. They were badly shaken up, but unharmed.) While al-Qaeda had been heard from before—from the 1993 attack of the World Trade Center, the attack on the USS *Cole,* and other incidents—it was 9/11 that made it a household word. You wouldn't think that a committed-to-nonviolence organization like Greenpeace would cross paths with al-Qaeda, but on this campaign we would— at least indirectly.

In 1991, Charles Taylor—the "president" (read: dictator) of Liberia—promoted a civil war in neighboring Sierra Leone by supporting a rebel militia called the Revolutionary United Front. Taylor's purpose for the war was to gain control of Sierra Leone's diamond mines. The money from the diamonds was being used to support the illegal arms trade that extended to the Taliban, al-Qaeda, Viktor Bout (the world's biggest arms trafficker), Libya, and many other terrorist organizations and regimes. The long civil war—marked by atrocities such as mass rape, slave labor, amputations, and executions—sparked international outrage and eventually a UN ban on "conflict diamonds" or "blood diamonds." While it didn't stop the trade completely, the ban on conflict diamonds had an unintended side effect: a tremendous surge in illegal logging in Liberia's old-growth jungle, and the clear-cutting of stands of endangered and rare trees. Liberia had turned from "blood diamonds" to "blood lumber" to raise cash, some of which went into Taylor's pockets, and some of which was used for weapons deals or to support rebel efforts in other countries. In the four years between 1997 and 2001, illegal timber exports had increased thirteenfold! Greenpeace had already decided to focus on the illegal African timber issue during the end of 2001 and for 2002, but the tragedy of 9/11 added to the timeliness and urgency of the campaign.

Taylor had even provided exclusive logging licenses to companies controlled by a Dutchman named Guus Kouwenhoven—an alleged former drug smuggler, arms dealer, and general all-around asshole. The first company was called Oriental Timber Company, and the second was named, ironically, Evergreen Trading. Taylor had even granted Kouwenhoven permission to log government land that had previously been set aside as a national land and wildlife preserve. It was a nest of vipers that was enabling environmental destruction and human rights abuses on a massive scale.

Most of the illegal timber was being brought into France and China, where once manufactured into finished products, there is no way to trace the wood's origin or to determine its legality. Greenpeace's objective was to stop the ships from unloading their "blood lumber" and to raise the public's awareness that the picnic tables and other consumer products they were buying were supporting torture, rape, death squads, and deforestation. (Greenpeace has no objection to logging if it's done in a sustainable and environmentally sensitive way. Liberia, however, was one of the worst offenders in the world.)

The first of a planned series of actions was to take place at the port of Sète, in France. It would be a few days before the ship we were targeting—the *Agia Irene*—was scheduled to arrive, so we used that time to practice for the action. One of the critical components of many successful Gp actions is the ability to rapidly deploy our RHIBs, and to be able to rapidly retrieve them as well. We've often been able to get a good jump on our targets and/or the authorities by being far faster at these skills.

Since we planned on boarding the ship carrying the timber, we practiced various boarding techniques, as well. In many respects, boarding techniques haven't changed all that much from the days of pirates and square-riggers, but we've managed a few refinements. We have twenty-foot-long poles with big hooks on the end. Attached to the hooks are rope ladders. When boarding a ship from an RHIB (which is much lower in the water than the ship), we use each pole to reach up and place its hook over a railing or some other part of the ship's hull. Then we pull the pole out from the hook, leaving the hook with the ladder dangling down from it to our RHIB. It's a fairly simple but highly effective gizmo. If the other ship's crew is really determined and aggressive, boarding can be a very tough thing to accomplish, but most of the time the crews don't want to tangle with anyone: they'd rather let the authorities handle us (which is OK with us!).

Sometimes when a ship is waiting for a pilot to come aboard, it will have a pilot ladder hanging over the side and we can scramble up that way. Other times we occupy the pilot ladder to prevent the pilot from coming onboard to bring the ship in. It all depends on the weather, the timing, the type of ship, etc., and we often have to make split-second decisions as events unfold. This was one of those times.

The *Agia Irene* arrived a couple of nights after the *Rainbow Warrior* did. Most of the large ports in the world work close to twenty-four hours a day. A ship standing still is a ship losing money, so ports will generally start unloading or loading a ship as soon as it arrives. In Sète, however, the longshoremen refused to work at night, so that meant that the *Agia Irene* had to anchor out in the harbor until the next morning instead of heading straight in to the dock. This made her a relatively easy target for our boarding action.

When a ship is anchored, there is usually at least one person on duty to keep an eye on things. It's called being on anchor watch. The person on anchor watch generally monitors the radar and the GPS to make sure the ship's anchor isn't dragging or that another ship isn't dragging down on you. Generally it's pretty boring duty; they're not on high alert looking out for a group of environmental activists attempting to storm aboard. But you never know. We were anchored fairly close to them, certainly close enough for them to identify who we were, so we had to expect we wouldn't be entirely unexpected.

At 4 A.M., we quietly launched the inflatables. Doing this in the dark makes things a little trickier, but that's why we had practiced so hard beforehand. Once all five boats were launched, they started moving as a group toward the cargo ship. When they got about halfway there, the radio crackled to life; the *Agia Irene* was reporting there would be a delay in being ready to take on the pilot. *Uh oh! They were on to us!* I was about to recall our squadron when the voice on the radio went on to say that they were having trouble starting their engine. That was a real stroke of luck for us. Whether they were distracted by the engine problems, or whether they were just generally clueless about how Greenpeace operates, we were able to take the ship by surprise.

Two activists climbed the *Agia Irene*'s mast and derricks and tied up a huge banner that said "Save the Ancient Rain Forests." Another team stuck a large iron bar through the anchor chain. In truth, the thickness of the iron bar would probably not have stopped them from raising the anchor—the winches they use are much too powerful—but it did send a signal that we didn't want them raising the anchor. The iron bar could also be removed quickly and easily in case the *Agia Irene* did need to move for safety reasons: if there was a fire onboard, for instance, or a storm. Yet another team occupied the pilot's ladder. The *Agia Irene*'s crew seemed pretty calm about the whole thing, and the boarding action had gone smoothly and according to plan. With everyone in place, we knew that the ship would have to wait for the police to clear all of us off before they could move.

We raised the anchor of the *Rainbow Warrior* and began to circle the other ship, taking pictures of the action teams with the banner and the tons of illegally cut logs sitting on her deck. The activists had poured red paint on the logs to indicate the wood was "blood lumber." The images were then digitized and sent to our PR people. The adrenaline rush of the boarding had worn off and we were now in the sitting-in phase, which always feels like it's a bit of a letdown. It was February, it was wet and it was cold, and the activists on the ship were miserable. We shuttled boats between the *Rainbow Warrior* and the cargo ship, resupplying the activists with water and food, occasionally rotating activists on or off the cargo ship, and bringing dry clothing. Every so often a police boat would come our way and we'd all jump into action mode: the activists on the cargo ship would scramble around and get themselves ready, we'd launch our inflatables, and then nothing would happen. This kept up for two days.

Phil Dunn's job on the *Rainbow Warrior* was outboard mechanic, but he has a wide range of skills: welder, engineer, and artist (he hand-painted many of our banners). He's also good with the industrial sewing machine we use to fix sails and make banners. He was a great resource to have onboard. Phil wasn't satisfied with the arrangement we had on the *Agia Irene*'s anchor chain, so he put the downtime we had to good use and designed and built a platform that could be fixed to the chain. The platform was about the size of a bed, and it would be 1) much more comfortable for the activists to stay on, and 2) be that much harder to remove. The biggest challenge in designing the platform was that the anchor chain itself is flexible; it moves as the wind and current affect the ship. Sometimes the chain is slack and hangs straight down, sometimes it's taut and at an angle to the ship, and sometimes it's even pressed against the side of the ship if the wind and current change or are opposed to each other. It would not be a good thing to have one of our crew get juiced between the chain and the hull of the ship. By the afternoon of the second day, Phil had designed the platform, built it, and installed it on the *Agia Irene*'s chain about six feet up in the air. It was practically a patio! The police still hadn't shown up. We knew they would eventually; they always do. It was a matter of when, not if. Maybe they were waiting for a special squad or something. . . . Late that afternoon, however, the police arrived in force.

The "French Fleet" was led by a large harbor tugboat painted navy/battleship gray, a large pilot ship, and an assortment—a half dozen or so—of smaller vessels. As I've mentioned before, whenever we're dealing with the French authorities we know we can expect an overreaction. Once again we were right. We responded by launching our RHIBs and readied a new wrinkle that we felt would throw the French police for a loop: inflatable canoes.

There was a race between the police flotilla and our flotilla to get to the pilot ladder first. If we got there first, we would be in a better position to prevent the pilot from getting aboard, and to prevent the police from clearing our crew from the anchor chain and the ship's rigging. As the two fleets converged, the French began pumping tear-gas grenades into our boats. Tear gas is exceptionally unpleasant stuff, but it's not generally dangerous. But when you start lobbing the shells into boats with exposed plastic tanks full of gasoline, it's a different story. Our teams in the boats were throwing the hot shells out as fast as they could, but I remember that after the action we found that one boat had at least five shells still in it when we pulled it from the water. Any one of them could have caused a catastrophic explosion.

The enemy had clearly planned their response thoroughly. Phil had been in an inflatable just under the platform when the police arrested him and cut his fuel lines. After the police had apprehended him, they simply let the boat drift away. Dmitri Sharomov, our Russian second mate, dove into the icy waters and swam over to the RHIB to retrieve it. A French police boat tried to stop Dmitri, who had not realized that the fuel line had been cut. Dmitri cranked up the engine and made his getaway, but then the gasoline that was still left in the engine ran out. Thankfully, given the spilled gasoline that was sloshing around Dmitri's boat, the French didn't lob any more tear-gas shells at him since he was now away from the action and dead in the water. Within a few minutes, however, Dmitri had somehow repaired the fuel line and he went right back in the fray. Now that's dedication!

On the *Rainbow Warrior*, I had a major adversary on my hands: the French tugboat had squared off with us a short distance away, staying between the *Agia Irene* and us. The big gray tug was probably packing more than 4,000 horsepower—way more than the 1,200 horsepower the *Rainbow Warrior* had—and they had a very efficient propeller design that was far more responsive and maneuverable than our setup. It wouldn't even be a contest. There was nothing I could do except watch. The crew on the tug just smiled smugly and kept us out of the way.

Within about thirty minutes of the police fleet's arrival, the *Agia Irene* had been completely cleared. She raised her anchor and began moving toward the dock. It was time for us to mount our next line of defense: a line (the nautical term for a rope) that would be strung across the channel with a number of activists in the inflatable canoes and RHIBs holding on to the line. As the *Agia Irene* and her convoy rounded the harbor entrance and saw the mayhem we had in store for them, the radios started squawking in loud, rapid French. The cargo ship came to a stop and even more loud, rapid French came from the radio. (I don't speak French, but I'd guess that most of their words wouldn't be printable in a family newspaper.) We knew that this action wouldn't stop the unloading for long, but every delay makes a point and gets us more media coverage. The French police were, once again, ordered to "round up the usual suspects." A half hour later, the channel was cleared of boats, activists, and the rope, and the *Agia Irene* was able to proceed toward the dock. But we had another little surprise waiting.

A number of our inflatable canoes had been repositioned from the outer harbor to the area directly in front of the dock. This would make it very difficult for the *Agia Irene* to tie up. What made the canoes particularly effective in a situation such as this one is that they are very slow. With the outboard-powered RHIBs, a ship can assume that the RHIBs have the power and speed to get out of the way of the bigger vessel in a hurry. With the canoes, however, the cargo ship's captain had to be much more careful. To make it even harder for the police to round them up, the activists flipped the canoes over and hid under them. When the police tried to pull the canoes out of the water, the activists hung on to the upside-down seats to make it harder to lift both the activists and the canoes out.

One burly policeman in a wet suit jumped into the water and tried to get Beatte—our second engineer—out from under her canoe. He didn't reckon with her fortitude and determination, and after a serious struggle he weakly made it back to the police boat looking a lot less cool and tough than he had before. I found out later that, during the struggle, Beatte had accidentally kicked him in the testicles. I'm sure it was an accident, since Gp is against violence of any kind, but I have to say I actually felt sorry for the guy.

Adding to all of the chaos and spectacle (which is exactly what we wanted), the police were still lobbing tear-gas canisters and flash-bang grenades. A couple of them landed in one of our RHIBs right between two plastic gas tanks. The driver of the boat, Bernard McCloud, grasped the two canisters and threw them overboard before they blew up his boat. In the process, however, he got distracted (understandably so!) and his boat collided with the big navy tug. The collision resulted in a seriously gashed elbow for one of his crew. Eventually, however, the water between the ship and the pier was cleared, and the *Agia Irene* was finally able to dock.

After the three actions and several hours of fun, only two boats and a handful of activists made it back to the *Rainbow Warrior*. One of the two was, thankfully, our press boat. They had been close to the action the whole time, but they had been careful to avoid getting caught up in it themselves. They came back with great shots and footage of all the activity. We brought the two boats back aboard the *Rainbow Warrior*, and began checking the equipment, cleaning up, etc. I figured we'd pick up all of the arrested crew in the morning. Then the phone rang. It was the police, asking for me. "Captain, if you would come in and make a statement, we can release your crew back to you tonight."

"No." I said, "That's OK. You can keep them tonight, and I'll pick them up in the morning."

Silence.

"Ahhh, Captain, this is a joke, right?"

"Yes, OK, I will be right in," I said.

I took an inflatable in to the police station. I wasn't expecting to find the crew behind bars (the "cop shop" was far too small to incarcerate the number of people that had been apprehended), but I figured they'd all be giving statements, getting fingerprinted, arraigned, processed, that sort of thing. I've been in many police stations in many different parts of the world, but when I stepped into the police station at Sète, I was completely unprepared for what I saw.

There was shouting. Squealing. Stacks of pizza boxes.

Wine bottles everywhere. Cops and activists taking pictures with each another. In short, I stepped into one hell of a party! No wonder they had been insistent on my coming in; I hate to miss a good party. Pascal Simon, the local police chief, introduced himself and handed me a glass of wine. "Captain, welcome. This is not our best wine, but it is quite good, and I hope you will enjoy it." I was still trying to jack my jaw up off the floor.

After a couple glasses of wine and pleasant chitchat, Pascal asked me to make an official statement. I was happy to. It always amazes me when police really listen to campaign rhetoric, but being able to talk about campaign issues is why I study all the background material before beginning a campaign. I launched into the story about Charles Taylor, Guus Kouwenhoven, the disappearing ecosystem, and how it was hurting the Liberian people. I went through it slowly so that it could be translated for the person taking down the statement. When I finished, Simon looked up at me and said, "I did not know Greenpeace cared about people. I thought it cared only about animals." I was very happy to set the record straight about that. I explained that "Greenpeace does care about animals, and trees, because we believe a healthy environment is necessary for people to live well. But the people of Liberia were the reason for today's action. Citizens of Europe must understand the effects of buying this tropical hardwood." A few minutes later we were all released, and headed back to the *Warrior*.

The next day, tired from the actions and the after-party, we brought the *Rainbow Warrior* into Sète to provision and do a public "open day" on the ship. While we were at the dock, we learned that *another* cargo ship with illegal lumber—the *Meltemi*—was heading into port. We quickly got back into action mode and cruised outside the harbor to meet the

second ship. She was much bigger and faster than the first
one, and the seas were too rough for a boarding action to be
conducted safely. The ship's captain knew she'd be vulnerable
if she anchored, so he took her straight into the harbor at
full speed, and didn't slow down until just before she arrived
at the dock. We never had a chance.

It was while we were watching them unload the next day
that the first of the stowaways were discovered. There were
a total of seven, all half-starved, tired-looking men who had
tried to escape Liberia on the *Meltemi*. A few had been found
during the passage from Liberia, but a least a couple of them
had managed to stay hidden under the logs during the three-
week voyage from Liberia. Our activists had discovered them.
The Liberian men were emaciated and in terrible condition.
The activists gave the men some soup and water, and then
helped the crew of the *Meltemi* take the refugees down to a
cabin with the stowaways who had been discovered earlier.
Ken Lowyck saw an arm sticking out of a porthole, waving a
note. It was one of the previously discovered stowaways asking for help. The Greek captain of the *Meltemi* was at least
somewhat sympathetic and had treated them kindly and fed
them well. He told us that most fishing and cargo vessels
simply throw stowaways overboard while they're still at sea.
There's less explaining to do and no paperwork to be filled
out if there are no stowaways when you get to port.

The captain also told us of an incident on an earlier trip
when his crew found three Liberian stowaways before the
ship had even left the port of Buchanan in Liberia. He called
the local authorities, which in Buchanan are militias that are
controlled by the logging industry. Militiamen tied the hands
of the first two men behind their backs and, as they were sub-
duing the third, the first two—with their hands still bound—

threw themselves into the water and drowned. Suicide was a fate better than being taken prisoner for these men. It was a perfect example of the human impact that we were bringing to light in this campaign.

In Sète, however, the stowaways were in a different situation. The politics and law of refugees is not an area that Greenpeace has expertise in. We knew enough to realize that if we made a big issue out of the stowaways, it would actually be harder for them to find sanctuary in Europe. We alerted Amnesty International to the stowaways' plight—this is exactly what the organization focuses on. They worked behind the scenes but were not able to help the men at all. The would-be refugees were returned to Liberia. I doubt that they lived for very long once they were brought back.

The *Meltemi* was going to be leaving the following day for its next stop at Sagunto, Spain. She was faster than the *Rainbow Warrior*, and we calculated that we needed at least a twelve-hour head start to beat them to the next port. Looking at the charts of Sagunto (which is on the southeast side of Spain on the Mediterranean Sea) and the weather forecast, it appeared that the conditions would be too rough for a boarding action in open water. We would need to commence the action close to the port. Sagunto is a busy port, which made planning even more difficult. There is quite a bit of coastal shipping traffic in and out of the port. Sagunto lies along the route between Barcelona and Valencia, and it's also fairly close to Gibraltar. Every ship entering or leaving the Mediterranean has to pass through the straits there, and many pass close to Sagunto. Trying to pick out the *Meltemi* on radar was going to be damn hard to do. On the plus side, it would be hard for them to pick us out too.

Our colleagues in France informed us when the *Meltemi*

had left, so we had a rough idea of when to expect the ship's arrival. To camouflage ourselves, we rearranged the navigational lights on our masts so that at night we'd look more like a fishing vessel. Normally, our masthead light is about seventy feet in the air; since fishing boats have lights that are not even twenty feet off the deck, lights fifty feet higher than that would make us stick out like sore thumbs. Maintaining the element of surprise would give us the best shot of preventing the pilot from boarding the *Meltemi* and bringing her in.

We identified the *Meltemi* eight miles out and scrambled to get all of our inflatables in the water. The cargo ship wasn't ready for us at all. We were able to get three climbers up into her rigging and blocked the pilot from coming aboard without too much effort.

In response, the captain of the *Meltemi* retreated a few miles out to sea and anchored. We had, once again, successfully achieved a delay in the unloading. The Spanish paramilitary police (Guardia Civil) came out to have a chat. This was Saturday night, and they wanted to have Sunday off, so they said they'd come back on Monday. That was cool with us.

Sunday was a picture-perfect day, so we put up the banner sails. Banner sails are lightweight pieces of cloth that are painted with giant murals of a healthy forest and a dead one. We use them when we do port visits and as a way of "dressing ship" (nautical terminology for decorating a ship with flags and such). In this case, we were going to sail around the *Meltemi* and get some good pictures of the banner sails—which had a "Save the Ancient Forests" message—in front of the cargo ship. It was shaping up to be a pretty relaxed day, until we received a report that a whole pack of police boats was headed our way. Our shore team, which was not expecting any action after the police had said they were taking the day off, was out to lunch. Literally. We were lucky that one of our boats, which had gone in to pick up photographic supplies, was in the right place at the right time to see the entire "Spanish Armada" headed our way. We had swallowed the "we don't want to work Sunday" bait—hook, line, and sinker. Caught flatfooted, I made yet another dumb mistake.

Our pilot-blocking actions had been on a hot streak lately, so we swung into action and sent teams over to the *Meltemi*. Not the smartest move. With eight or ten police boats on the scene, we were significantly outnumbered. In less than thirty minutes the pilot ladder was cleared and the pilot on board. Our climbers, however, were still in the rigging. By Sunday afternoon, the *Meltemi* was at the dock, but she still couldn't unload the blood lumber with the climbers in her rigging.

The climbers were in positions that made it incredibly difficult for the police to extract them, particularly if the ship was anchored or under way. At the pier, however, the authorities had a few more options. Twelve police vans showed up Monday morning. They also brought along a fire truck with a hydraulic arm and bucket. Between the fire truck and the cranes on the pier the police were able to bring our climbers down, but not without some difficulty. One of the funniest sights I've ever seen is a policeman in the bucket attempting to catch one of our activists as he was scrambling around the cargo ship's rigging. It was like trying to catch a greased pig. Eventually, however, the *Meltemi*'s rigging was cleared and she could unload. Still, the score up to this point was that we had stopped two ships from unloading for a total of three days, with lots of good press coverage in two countries. Not bad at all, but we weren't done yet. We were off to Salerno, Italy, to stop another shipment on a vessel far faster and larger than either of the first two.

We stopped in Genova, Italy, to provision and then continued to Salerno.

The next target was the *Sassandra,* which was a RORO. RORO is short for a roll-on, roll-off ship. They're generally used for transporting cars. ROROs are much, much bigger ships, with very high sides, and they travel at twice the speed of the *Rainbow Warrior.* Boarding the *Sassandra* while she was in motion would be almost impossible. We needed an entirely different approach. A RORO's Achilles' heel is that, in order to unload, a ramp in the transom (the broad, flat rear end of the ship) has to open up. The ramp hinges at the bottom and drops down so it can then be used to roll on or roll off the cargo (hence the term "roll-on, roll-off"). If we could stop the ramp from deploying, we could halt the cargo. The best opportunity for that would be when the *Sassandra* slowed to take aboard the pilot.

Using our grappling hook/pole contraptions, we were able to get a few climbers up on the ship's transom. Personally, I was getting a little more aggressive with each action. I had made a weak attempt at blocking the channel with the *Rainbow Warrior,* but then I followed the ship, the inflatables, and the police boats into the harbor. Going into a harbor normally requires a pilot and going in without one can get you into big trouble, but nobody seemed to notice.

There were police helicopters buzzing low overhead, and police boats were trying to lasso our outboards to stop us. There was one point, when all the small boats were flying around and the *Sassandra* was almost at the dock, that I thought about rushing in with the *Rainbow Warrior* and stealing their parking space like a Friday afternoon at the supermarket! But with a very strong wind blowing onto the dock, I did not think the *Rainbow Warrior* would make a good fender. One of the inflatables, crewed by some activists who had joined us from Germany, rushed between the *Sassandra* and the dock, but their boat was crushed between the enormous ship and the dock. Fortunately the activists were unhurt. The rest of us all slowly pulled back and left the action to the climbers.

While we hadn't prevented the *Sassandra* from getting to the dock, they still couldn't unload with our activists on their transom. That evening the police arrived, assessed the situation, and decided they needed to call Rome to request a specially trained squad to deal with the climbers. That was an automatic twelve-hour win for us. For the climbers, however, it was another twelve hours of freezing hell and snow. The cold, and the exertion, meant that our climbing team was running on metabolic fumes. We had to get them something to eat or they'd face serious consequences. Frank—our action coordinator—had a great idea. He found a big, bulky jacket and taped about a hundred chocolate bars to the inside of it. He also stuffed a bunch of nuts and water bottles in the pockets. He looked remarkably like a suicide bomber.

Frank went over to the *Sassandra* and told the guards there that the BBC wanted to interview one of the climbers, and that he had brought a phone with him for the interview. The guards let Frank onboard, and did so without even searching him. Honestly, I can't believe that they couldn't tell he was hiding so much stuff, so there is a least a pretty good chance that they knew what Frank was doing. Maybe they were sympathetic. Maybe they were lazy, or maybe just clueless, but they didn't stop him. One of the climbers—our ship's doctor, Janine Bonnet—actually suffered some frostbite in her toes, which tells you just how harsh the conditions were.

The next day we were served with an injunction, so it was time to go. Once again, we had added to our tally with another couple of days of delays. Our total so far was nine "ship days." Next stop was Scheveningen, Holland, a two-week passage, where we would meet up with the newest addition to the Greenpeace fleet—the M/V *Esperanza*—a converted icebreaker.

From there the two ships would sail to Vlissingen, Netherlands, for another action, this time against a ship carrying
ancient rain-forest lumber from the Amazon.

We met the *Esperanza* in Scheveningen, the seaport of The
Hague, Holland. Scheveningen is impossible for foreigners to
pronounce, and very difficult even for a native. The story is that
pronouncing it was used as a test during World War II to determine who was a Dutchman and who was a German spy. Supposedly there were many Dutchmen who lost their lives because
they didn't say it right.

When we got to Vlissingen, the plan was for the *Esperanza*
(being the faster of the two Gp ships) to intercept the cargo
ship—the *Balaban I*—at the pilot's boarding area, and we would
head for the channel to prepare to block the ship if it got that
far. Thirty minutes after arriving on station in the channel
we saw the *Balaban I* steaming in our direction, with the *Esperanza* behind it.

I maneuvered the *Rainbow Warrior* in the channel to block
the ship, but things immediately started to get dicey. Different ships have different types of steering systems, and the
type on the *Rainbow Warrior* was one of the more complicated
styles. We were in close quarters, and with most of the available crew out on the inflatables, I was trying to steer the ship
while keeping an eye on the *Balaban I* at the same time. Well,
a couple of times I forgot about the quirks of the *Rainbow
Warrior*'s steering and got way too close to the bigger ship. It
was far more dramatic than I had intended. All they could
see were the masts of our ship disappearing beneath their
bow, and they must have thought I was completely crazy. My
head was about to explode, but then I caught my breath.

We slowed down. I figured we could get into his dock before he did and we could stop him there. We beat him in, and took up our position between the *Balaban I* and the dock. Besides the *Rainbow Warrior*, we had inflatables with us, and there were activists in the water as well. But the *Balaban I*– with a tugboat and a towline on his bow, and another tug and towline on his stern–kept coming. I yelled to the cook to put out the fenders (big rubber bumpers) to protect the ships, but he freaked and hid in the galley. (Some cooks enjoy being in actions, some don't.) Megan Houlihan, our Web designer from Vermont, dropped her cameras and rushed forward to put the fenders in place.

Meanwhile, one of our inflatables had run over the forward tugboat's hawser while the rope was slack and under the water. Just as the inflatable had gone over it, the line– pulled by the several-thousand-horsepower engines of the tugboat–had been drawn taut, and now the inflatable was thirty or forty feet up in the air, having caught the towline on the shaft of the outboard engine. Dima Sharomov fell out of the boat and into the water. Miraculously, when the inflatable came down, it was upright and still running, so the recently ejected Dima climbed right back in and rejoined the action.

As this was going on, the *Balaban I* and the *Rainbow Warrior* made contact. It felt like the fenders were in place, but I wasn't sure. I hoped there hadn't been any damage, but there was no time to check. I looked up to see the bow of another ship, one that was already docked, directly in front of where we were heading. It was gonna be close. The line handlers on the dock were watching wide-eyed, but I'm sure my eyes were even wider.

I wasn't the only captain who felt things were getting too close for comfort. The captain of the *Balaban I* ordered the tugs to pull him back out into the channel, and to turn him around. Wanting to stay between him and his berth, I called for one of the inflatables to push on our bow to help us do a U-turn. The *Balaban*'s pilot, however, called us on the radio to tell us they were calling it a day and were heading back to the anchorage. I was damn glad to hear it. My knees weren't shaking but just about everything else was. We motored out to the anchorage, and moored in front of the *Balaban I* just in case.

On the way out we were boarded by the harbor police. They were very calm and congratulated us on a good action. While we were going through the paperwork, Cees, our young Dutch radio operator, came up to the bridge with some sort of problem. "That's it!" I said. "I have had it!" I turned to one of the cops and said in a joking way, "You have a gun. Would you shoot this guy for me?" The cop looked at us very seriously and said, "No, I cannot do that. But here, you are welcome to use it." Cees went running back down the stairs. That was a good laugh after an intense day.

The next day, we were handed an injunction and the *Balaban I* was able to get in and unload her cargo, but we had accomplished our immediate goal: we had delayed the ship from unloading. The crew had performed brilliantly, and I had pushed the envelope harder than I ever could have imagined just six weeks before. The performance was a direct result of the three good actions down in the Mediterranean and a kickass campaigner—Tim Birch—who never stopped pushing us to do more.

If you get the impression that the tour was a complete success, however, you would be only partly right. The entire tour was aimed at affecting a UN conference in The Hague the following week. But despite our good actions and tremendous publicity, the issue got nowhere at the conference.

A couple of years after this, and several other similar actions—along with the efforts of numerous governments and other organizations—a United Nations Security Council ban on the illegal-trees-for-arms trade was finally pushed through. But the larger problem of illegal logging and the clear-cutting of endangered, old-growth forests continues in many locations around the world. Seven years later, I went to see another example of this kind of logging at one of its biggest sources—the Amazon rainforest.

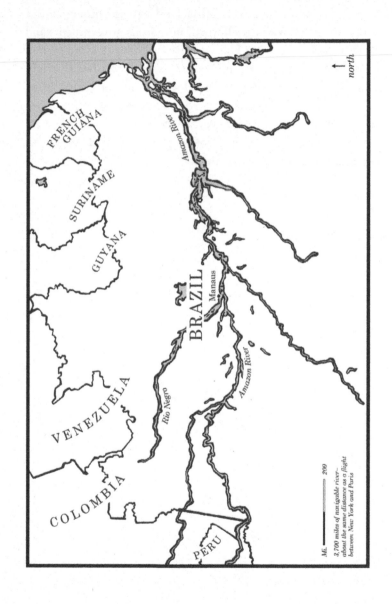

north

FRENCH
GUIANA

SURINAME

GUYANA

Amazon River

BRAZIL

Manaus

VENEZUELA

Rio Negro

Amazon River

COLOMBIA

PERU

Mi. 200

3,700 miles of navigable river—
about the same distance as a flight
between New York and Paris

13

Icebreaking Up the Amazon

Spring 2009

Amazon River, Manaus, Brazil

"Save the Rainforest"/Antislavery Expedition

If you do an Internet search for the "world's longest river," half of the results will say it's the Amazon, and the other half will say it's the Nile. I'm staying out of it, but regardless, the size of the Amazon is hard to comprehend. 3,700 miles of it are navigable, about the same distance as a flight between New York and Paris. At the mouth of the river, it's roughly two hundred miles wide—as wide as the Thames River in England is long. (Farther upriver the Amazon narrows to about two or three miles wide.) During the rainy season the river empties at a rate of three hundred thousand tons—the equivalent of a supertanker full of water—*per second*. Whether it's the longest river or not, it's unquestionably the largest and most powerful. It's also the most important in many ways—over one-third of all known species in the world reside in the Amazon biome.

As we approached the mouth of the Amazon, all of those facts paled in comparison to this one: *more than 1,500 environmentalists have been murdered in the Amazon.* Landowners (often government officials) sanction the clear-cutting or slash-and-burning of the Amazon forest for profit, and to protect their profits they resort to violence.

"Landowners" is really the wrong word. "Land grabbers" is more like it. They will destroy other people's private land, government land, forest preserves, parks, and any other place where they won't get caught or where they can avoid punishment. Most of the Amazon is so remote it is virtually impossible to maintain the rule of law. One of Gp's primary strategies for protecting the rainforest is to help the actual landowners map out their lands using GPS, and to document the illegal taking of their land, forest preserve, etc. Two years before, one of our Gp ships was stormed by a mob that had been riled up by the land grabbers. The ship had been heavily damaged.

The environment itself also offers a number of dangers: dengue fever, malaria, and yellow fever are just a few of the things there that can kill you in unpleasant ways. (In fact, our chief engineer, Dave McEvitt, got "the denguey" a few days into the trip and had to be replaced.) The river itself considerably magnifies the risks. When you're on a ship in the river, if you get in trouble, there is nowhere to go except up the river or down it. As a consequence you can easily be trapped or ambushed, and if the ship is captured nothing but jungle justice can be expected. Where there is the rule of law there's some predictability and, therefore, a way to evaluate the risks. The deep Amazon rainforest is as lawless as anyplace on Earth. If you get stuck on a mudbank (and navigational charts are almost useless upriver because of the shifting sediments and other obstructions), or suffer a breakdown, things can go bad in a hurry.

I'm often asked if Greenpeace ships carry any arms or defensive weapons. We do not—with one exception. When dealing with organized authorities, such as the police or a navy, the lack of weapons onboard makes us safer. Our philosophy is that if the authorities believe you have weapons onboard, they will be more likely to act aggressively and use weapons themselves. In the Amazon, however, when you're far more likely to be facing an angry mob of vigilantes, being unarmed makes you very vulnerable. We were unarmed.

The *only* time Greenpeace ships carry weapons is when we are in Arctic polar bear territory, and then only because *we are required to by law*. By making it mandatory that all ships and helicopters carry a defense against polar bear attacks, it is hoped that the number of air rescues and icebreaker rescues (both of which are very difficult, dangerous, and expensive) will be greatly reduced. It makes sense, but I'm always nervous about having a rifle onboard. When we do, we keep it locked up at all times. I think I have only taken it out once, as a precaution, and I would only use it if a crew person were in imminent danger of being eaten by a polar bear. Even then I might wait until someone's been gnawed on a bit. . . .

We were taking the *Arctic Sunrise*—an icebreaker—up the Amazon. Was I expecting an iceberg in the heart of a tropical rainforest? Of course not, but waterlogged tree stumps have been known to punch through the bottoms of ships, killing the crew. This happens when the ship rides up over the top of a half-sunken tree trunk. The lower end of the trunk gets stuck into the riverbed, and the upper end impales the bottom of the ship. As the weight and momentum of the ship carries it forward, the tree trunk is driven up through the hull like a torpedo. With an icebreaker, there's at least an armored hull between your ass and the tree.

Needless to say, we all had a lot on our minds as we approached the mouth of the Amazon. Eighty miles out from the mouth of the river, the ocean begins to turn brown from the sediment pouring out of the river (roughly thirteen billion tons per year). Thirty miles closer and it was like sailing in mud. It reminded me of a quote about the Mississippi River that is often attributed to Mark Twain: "Too thin to plow, too thick to drink."

The *Arctic Sunrise* has two charting systems. The first is our tried-and-true British Admiralty paper charts. The second system is a state-of-the-art electronic GPS/chart system with two linked flat-screen displays. Both the paper and digital charts have warnings all over them that the Amazon has constantly shifting hazards and that the channel buoys may be missing or moved. Lovely. (It turned out that the old-fashioned Admiralty charts were far more accurate. The digital charts seemed to show us sailing through grasslands many more times!)

Most ports and waterways have pilot pickup points before the entrance to the harbor. In this case, the pilots were to be picked up 175 miles up the river, and there were plenty of hazards to avoid before we got there. There was one narrow and twisting section of the river we were particularly concerned with, and as we were approaching that section we anxiously noted that there were a number of missing or misplaced buoys, and—as it was nighttime—we could tell that many of them were missing their lights. This was getting interesting.

The decision to make the approach at night was not looking too smart. Lighted buoys greatly simplify navigation at night, but we apparently couldn't rely on that. The tide cycle had been the determining factor to go at night. The incoming tide pushes against the outward flow of the Amazon, making progress against the river's current that much faster. Thankfully, as we got closer to the narrow, shifting part at around 10:30 P.M., we noticed the green buoys were all showing their lights, and the red ones seemed to be in the positions the Admiralty charts had indicated. (Score—the old-fashioned paper charts: 1; newfangled digital charts: 0.) After the narrow section of the river, navigation became a little easier. With the strong flood tide of over 2 knots overcoming the river current against us, we were ahead of schedule and decided a good rest was in order. We had to wait until morning, anyway, for a Brazilian navy inspection of the *Arctic Sunrise* before proceeding farther up the river.

The inspection the next morning went smoothly, and we then backtracked seven miles to the general anchorage to pick up two pilots the next morning. (Due to the three-day length of the cruise, we needed two so they could stand watches.) We found a pleasant spot with a nice breeze to keep the bugs away and, being that it was Christmas Eve, we decided to have a barbecue on deck. When it comes to barbecues it's hard to beat an Argentinian, and we had several on the crew. Barbecues are also great morale boosters and team-bonding occasions. This was the perfect time and setting to relax before the rigors that lay ahead. The mood was pretty relaxed and everyone was looking forward to the next few days. Most of us had never been to the Amazon before.

In good weather we have barbecues once or twice a month. Beer and wine can be purchased. It is a standing order that supporters' money does not get used to buy alcoholic drinks, or even soda, for that matter. Obviously, "supporters' money" means

"Greenpeace money," but calling it "supporters' money" helps everyone remember where it came from and how it should be used. Instead, the crews run their own bar. If you want a beer after work, you can grab one out of the refrigerator in the lounge and make a check mark by your name. The bar is always run by the boatswain, and it can be a big job. I think the bar was stiffed only twice by crew members who left the ship without paying. I won't name them, but I know (and they know) who they are! I'm sure that both had simply forgotten to cover their tabs, but I never let either one of them forget it!

After a short delay in getting the pilots aboard (and neither was happy about having to work Christmas Day), we started upriver. It was incredibly beautiful, not at all like I had imagined it. I had expected it would be dark and closed in (maybe I was thinking of the jungle river in *Apocalypse Now*), but it's a very wide river, miles across in places, and it has the open feeling of the ocean. The current, however, forces you into close proximity to the banks on the *insides* of the turns because that's where there is far less current against you. The *outside* of the river bends is where the current runs strongest. With 3 knots of current "on the nose" (against you), it makes a big difference when your best speed is 10 knots. Sometimes we were only a boat length away from the bank. (A boat length, in this case, is 162 feet—the length of the *Arctic Sunrise*. Reading "162 feet" on a page sounds like plenty of distance, but let me tell you that in the real world—especially *that* part of the real world—162 feet is perilously close.) There's little room for error. Here's an example of what I mean: the *Arctic Sunrise* has an alternate steering mechanism close to the glass at the forward edge of the bridge that is used to guide the ship through the ice. It's a small box with a four-inch tiller arm that you steer with. One day on the river, a photographer accidentally leaned on the tiller arm and the ship turned and immediately ran into the riverbank. Fortunately it was soft mud, and after all of the tree branches were cleared out from the open windows of the ship, the *Sunrise* was able to back off the bank unharmed. The tiller arm was dismounted after that!

The Gp office in Brazil is in Manaus, and it took us five days to get there. We tied up to the dock that is used by all of the riverboats. There are no roads in the Amazon, so pretty much everything, and everyone, gets moved by boat. During the day the river is very busy with traffic. At night it slows down, but the dock is in continuous use twenty-four hours a day. Since the seasonal tides in the Amazon can be as high as forty feet, the docks need to be floating docks (as opposed to a fixed dock that remains at one height). The floating dock we were on is by far the biggest I've ever seen; it has a capacity of over fifty trucks with room to spare. Even large cruise ships can tie up on it.

The campaign team at the office briefed us on what was going on in the Amazon, and some of the dangers we might expect. Just getting to the office made a major impact on us. The word "security" is used a lot around here. Gp campaigners have frequently received death threats (remember that about 1,500 environmentalists have been killed in the Amazon jungle). There is a guarded entrance with heavy gates. It was a hot day, and when we got into one of the campaigners' cars I instinctively rolled down the window to let some heat out before the air-conditioning kicked in. "Peter, roll up the window. Roll up the window *now*!" As I rolled it up, I could see that the thick, tinted window was bulletproof glass. All of the Gp vehicles there are fully armored, and have features like bulletproof Kevlar battery boxes. For good reason.

I remember when Paulo Adario and Anne Dingwall went to set up the Manaus office. Anne is Gp's international chief of security. When you think "chief of security," I'm sure that Anne is not the kind of person you're likely to picture. She's an elegant, white-haired lady whom a Spanish newspaper once described as having "the body of an aging fashion model." She's well trained, very experienced, and has taken security/evasive driving courses and other security training. She was in charge of designing the office and all of the walls, gates, security systems, etc. Anne is not to be underestimated.

The campaigners told us that 17 percent of the Brazilian Amazon has been cut down—roughly an area the size of Texas or France. Twenty percent of all the world's oxygen comes from the Amazon biome. Clearing the rainforest for cattle grazing creates a long list of different types of environmental damage. Burning the forest makes Brazil one of the top greenhouse gas emitters in the world. Seventy-five percent of Brazil's total greenhouse gases comes from burning the Amazon forests. Burning the forests of Brazil, Indonesia, and the Congo produces one-fifth of all the greenhouse gas in the world. I remember being at anchor in the Strait of Singapore fifteen years ago. The burning forests in Indonesia cut the visibility down to three or four miles. It looked like fog but smelled like wood smoke, and the smoke covered an unimaginably wide area.

Once the forests are burned, they are opened up for cattle grazing, but because the nutrients have been burned with the trees, cattle grazing is only good for about two years. Then the land is turned over to soy farmers. But the land is too poor to produce crops, so chemical fertilizers and toxic pesticides are added in great quantities. The fertilizers and pes-

25. While the *Meltemi* was able to come into the harbor, we still had activists up in her cranes and rigging to prevent the unloading of the cargo.
© GREENPEACE/DANIEL BELTRA

26. At Vlissingen, Netherlands, to prevent the *Balaban I* unloading illegally logged wood from the Amazon, one of our boats was lifted almost forty feet by a towline being used to manoeuvre the cargo ship.
© GREENPEACE/DAVID SIMS

27. The *Arctic Sunrise* heading up the Amazon river.
© Greenpeace/Rodrigo Bale'ia

28. In many places along the Amazon, people are burning and clear-cutting forest preserves, national parks and privately owned land.
© Greenpeace/Daniel Beltrá

29. Melt pools on the Petermann Glacier, Greenland, reflect the blue of the sky perfectly.
© Nick Cobbing/Greenpeace

30. My office has a terrific view.
© Nick Cobbing/Greenpeace

31. This polar bear mother might not understand the big picture, but she has a better idea than most of us of the implications if we don't.
© Larissa Beumer/Greenpeace

32. This iceberg has a hole through it called a 'moulin', probably a drainage channel for melt water in a glacier, before the iceberg flipped. They often flip suddenly. I see it as a metaphor for climate change.

© Nick Cobbing/Greenpeace

33. Probably taken at the Nioghalvfjerdsbrae, where our observations and findings were indicating an on-going disaster.
© Nick Cobbing/Greenpeace

34. The Russian patrol ship/icebreaker *Ladoga*. You can make out the cannon she was firing just above her hull number 058.
© Denis Sinyakov/Greenpeace

35. Marco Paolo Weber hanging on the lines the team slingshotted
over the rig's heavier mooring lines.
© DENIS SINYAKOV/GREENPEACE

36. You can see the machine guns and knives being wielded at us during
the muscular response from the *Ladoga*.
© DENIS SINYAKOV/GREENPEACE

37. *Arctic Sunrise* being boarded by commandos who were rappelling
to the deck from a big black chopper.
© Denis Sinyakov/Greenpeace

38. 'Bail denied.'
© Dmitri Sharomov/Greenpeace

39. Home sweet home. This cell is very similar to the one I occupied but more "luxurious" because it has a real radiator.

40. A view of the Murmansk prison and the city. And this is before winter really set in.
© Greenpeace

41. Maggy in our apartment above my folk's place in Norwalk, CT.
This portrait was taken by a local newspaper shortly after we were arrested.
© Alex von Kleydorff

42. On the day of our arrest, Greenpeace USA staff stood in front of the
Russian ambassador's residence in Washington, DC.
© Greenpeace/Mitchell Wenkus

43. Support for the 'Arctic 30', comprising the 28 crew, including me and two independent photo/video journalists who were arrested, spread rapidly. Here a group protests outside the Russian embassy in London.
© John Cobb/Greenpeace

44. Jude Law, the actor, and Paul Simonon (of the punk band "The Clash" to the right) are protesting in front of the Russian Embassy on October 5th, the Day of Solidarity.
© John Cobb/Greenpeace

45. A Day of Solidarity protest in front of the Gwanghwamun gate, the entrance of the Gyeongbokgung Palace in Seoul, South Korea.

46. It's a pretty safe bet that this protest took place at the highest altitude. That's Mount Everest in the background.

© ZHOU LI/GREENPEACE

47. The Kresty prison showing its age.
© Igor Podgorny/ Greenpeace

48. November 22, 2013. The day of my release.
© Dmitri Sharomov/ Greenpeace

49. My eldest daughter, Anita, participating in a 'Free the Arctic 30' protest, one of many around the world.

50. My younger daughter Natasha, pointing to a poster at the protest in Village Creek, where I grew up.

51. Greeting my wife Maggy at the airport in St. Petersburg.
© Dmitri Sharomov/Greenpeace

ticides get washed down the streams and rivers. The fertilizers upset the balance of nutrients in the water, and the pesticides are very persistent too. All these chemicals seriously affect the communities of indigenous people because their water and food are being poisoned by the cattle and soy farms upstream. The damage adds up: the Earth's capacity to absorb carbon dioxide has been reduced, its ability to generate oxygen has been reduced, the burning itself adds huge amounts of CO_2 to the atmosphere, and the people who live there are being poisoned. The devil must have really scratched his head for a while to come up with that one!

Another very surprising fact I learned is that the Amazon is not as fertile as you might think. All of the rainforests' nutrients are in the roots of the trees and the vegetation itself, not in the soil. It's a perfect system of natural recycling until you disturb it. When you burn or clear-cut the rainforest, you completely remove the nutrients, and it takes a *very* long time for it to recover. Some experts believe it can take longer than a thousand years! Most of the nutrients in the Amazon don't even originate there; they come from the Sahara in giant dust storms that cross the Atlantic. Even more amazingly, almost 90 percent of the nutrients in the Amazon come from one small part of the Sahara—the Bodélé Depression in Chad. One of these storms passed over us one time when I was on a sailboat in the British Virgin Islands in the Caribbean. The dust reduced the visibility to two or three miles, and this was after the storm had already crossed thousands of miles of the Atlantic!

Besides the environmental damage, there is a direct human cost as well. According to a number of NGOs (nongovernmental organizations, of which Greenpeace is just one), there are upward of a quarter-million slaves being forced to burn the rainforests and work the industrial-scale, *corporate* farms.

These are people who were promised good-paying jobs if they left their families and homes. Once they arrive, there is no way to get back. The slaves are made to work for food and live in pitiful conditions. Brazil, of course, has very tough laws regarding slaves: if a company (I cannot call them "farmers"; it is too much an insult to real farmers) is found with slaves, they must pay the slaves the wages they're owed within two years. Nothing else. With that kind of law, why would anyone pay the slaves?

GP Brazil uses a plane for aerial surveying and surveillance as part of a GPS mapping project. It's a ten-passenger Cessna turboprop Skymaster. A few of us from the *Arctic Sunrise* were taken along on one of the flights. As the captain of the ship, I was given the copilot seat. (Being captain does have certain privileges.) I have a glider pilot's license (although it's not current) and I have some experience with flying, so the pilot—Fernando Bezerra—let me fly the plane for a while (under close supervision, of course). He was careful to warn me about not flying into the hundreds of vultures that live along the shoreline of the river. If a vulture comes through the cockpit window, it's gonna hurt both you and the bird.

The Amazon can be one of the most beautiful places on Earth, and that makes it even more painful when you see huge swaths of the rainforest being permanently destroyed for the sake of a few seasons' worth of crops. The runoff, erosion, smoke, loss of habitat, and real old-fashioned slavery are heartbreaking. These lands will never be the same, and we're losing two hundred thousand acres of land every day– 150 acres lost every minute of every day. Seventy-five million acres a year. At that rate, at least 80 percent of tropical rainforest ecosystems will be destroyed by the year 2020.

Worse, the amount of carbon that will be released is more than all the CO_2 from all the planes, trains, trucks, and automobiles in the world.

We've made some progress in Brazil, and in several other regions of the world, but the fact remains that this is still an ongoing scourge. São Paolo is the biggest city in Brazil, with a population of twelve million. It's the twelfth biggest city in the world. And—at the time I am writing this—it is just a few months away from running out of water *completely*. One of the main contributing factors is that the destruction of the rainforest has completely altered the local climate patterns. Now there is far less rain, and when it *does* rain the water runs off the bare land instead of being held in the rainforest. This is not a disaster waiting to happen; it is a disaster *that is happening already*! The impact is being felt all around the world, not just in South America. A few months later, I would see undeniable evidence of how the effects of environmental impacts spread around the planet, all the way to the glaciers of Greenland, far above the Arctic Circle.

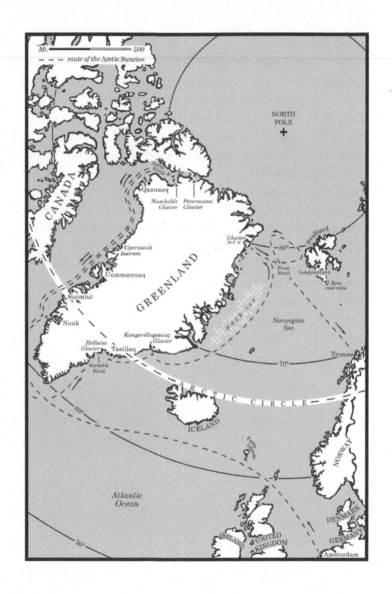

14

Glacially Fast Climate Change

JULY-OCTOBER 2009
GREENLAND—445 MILES FROM THE NORTH POLE
CLIMATE CHANGE RESEARCH EXPEDITION

I had mixed feelings about our upcoming research expedition to Greenland. On the positive side, we were going to document climate change—an issue near and dear to my heart. The United Nations Climate Change Conference (commonly referred to as the Copenhagen summit) would be discussing future climate change initiatives. The *Arctic Sunrise* would be hosting a team of noted climatologists, glaciologists, oceanographers, and other scientists who would be measuring the rate of glacier movements and melting, as well as the effects of warmer Atlantic currents coming into contact with the floating parts of the ice sheets.

The data they collected would provide hard evidence to the conference of the most dramatic impacts of global warming. While Greenpeace would be providing the ship, crew, and support, the scientists would be performing their work with complete independence. They had designed and planned the research, and would be recording, reporting, and interpreting the results without any input from Gp.

I always enjoy the educational components of trips like this one, and I had a chance to learn from the best. This expedition could turn out to be the most important of my career. Another plus was that I had never been to Greenland before, so I was really looking forward to the experience. Those were the positives.

The expedition's *challenges* were colossally big. Literally. Let's start with the fact that we were headed into the birthplace of most of the Atlantic's icebergs. Heard of the *Titanic*? We would also be sailing in some of the most remote waters in the world. If we ran into trouble, we couldn't expect much help in a hurry. This part of the world is one-mistake territory. You're only going to get one chance to make a mistake before the ship is in mortal peril.

Safety experts investigating maritime disasters generally analyze error-chain recognition, tracing backward from the big, culminating disaster through a series of smaller problems and decisions that snowballed into a major mess. When the *Titanic* sank, it was caused by a long error chain, a series of unfortunate decision making, some as early as her design when it was still on the drawing boards. Others were made in the shipyard when she was built, all the way through the decisions that were made about the *Titanic*'s course and speed just moments before she struck the iceberg. The error chain for that disaster stretches for years. Even *after* the collision, decisions were made that caused the death toll to rise considerably.

In one-mistake territory, preparation becomes exponentially more important. Missing one spare part for a critical system on the ship could sink your expedition in the truest sense of the word ("for want of a nail . . ."). You have to be ready to break the error chain either by preventing the problems in the first place, or by keeping the problems from snowballing. As captain, that's an additional worry on your mind. Besides all of the redundant spare parts and safety gear, we also needed to pack a far larger load of provisions than normal, just in case we got stuck in the ice. We weren't worried so much about being stuck in the ice all winter (although that has happened to many Arctic/Antarctic expeditions throughout history) because the *Arctic Sunrise* is a powerfully built icebreaker. But we could easily imagine getting stuck for several weeks. Suresh Babu Bhaskaran Pillai, our Indian cook, had to commandeer the ship's sauna to store the extra food.

We left Amsterdam and sailed through the Pentland Firth between the Shetland Islands and the northern end of Scotland. The Firth is well known for having some of the fastest currents in the world and, mostly by luck, we happened to time the tide correctly and were making over 16 knots with the kick from the current. After exiting the Firth, we had a five-and-a-half-day run to Greenland. It's a funny thing to consider, but technically we were crossing the Atlantic in less than six days, three or four times faster than a Southampton-to-New York transatlantic run.

There are some other navigational oddities this far north. For one thing, the North Magnetic Pole would be relatively close, which causes problems. Magnetic compasses don't point "true north," i.e., toward the North Pole on a map; they point to the North *Magnetic* Pole. The North Magnetic Pole moves around (a few miles northwest a year), and depending where you are on the Earth, the difference between the direction to the true North Pole and the North Magnetic Pole is different. This is called magnetic variation. The closer you get to the North Magnetic Pole, the more useless a traditional compass becomes. And we'd be very, very close to it. For instance, if you're north of the North Magnetic Pole, your compass will point south! Thankfully, most modern ships have gyrocompasses that are unaffected by magnetism or nearby metal objects. They have been known, however, to lose their accuracy from time to time, so you're supposed to check them against a magnetic compass. If you can't rely on the magnetic compass, you might have a gyrocompass error and not know it. And if the ship loses power, you might lose the gyrocompass completely, and then you'd have to rely on the old magnetic compass. It's fairly unusual for a ship to lose power completely, but guess what? We had some fuel pump issues with one of the ship's generators on the way to Greenland. It had gone down for several brief periods before we even got there (which is why we have two generators). The blackouts didn't affect the gyrocompass, but it was a stark reminder of that whole error chain/one mistake thing.

Communications technologies at these latitudes are also problematic. Satellite phones and uplinks/downlinks generally work on one of two technology platforms. Inmarsat phones have better bandwidth and can be used in most places in the world that are between the Arctic and Antarctic Circles, but their satellites don't cover the polar areas. The other system, Iridium, covers those parts of the world, but its bandwidth is far more limited. You can make a phone call easily enough, but sending data or pictures with the Iridium system is like trying to send a jigsaw puzzle through a small pipe. To get the bandwidth we'd need, we had to use a system with eight separate Iridium phones wired together in parallel. Staying with the jigsaw puzzle/pipe analogy, it would be like taking all the pieces of the puzzle, sending each piece through one of eight separate pipes, and then instantly reconstructing the jigsaw puzzle at the other end. Pretty slick. I had never seen anything like it.

I was very fortunate to have Arne Sorenson aboard as our ice pilot. Arne has done something like twenty expeditions in the Arctic and a slightly larger number than that in the Antarctic. He's lived in Greenland, and had been a captain with Greenpeace for almost twenty years. After retiring as a captain, he became an ice pilot. He is probably one of the most experienced ice pilots in the world, and ice is where experience really means something. There are many different kinds of ice, and they move and behave in different ways. An ice pilot needs to "read" the ice and have the big picture in mind in order to keep the ship out of trouble. Should we go up this "lead" (an area of open water in the ice), or will we get cut off and trapped? Is this ice going to get too thick for us to ice-break our way through?

Ice pilots are also able to recognize the many different kinds of ice. "Grease ice" is new ice in a very thin layer, easily breakable. As it gets thicker it becomes "sea ice," which is breakable by a ship the size of the *Arctic Sunrise* up to a thickness of about five or six feet. "Multiyear" ice is much harder and tougher to break, so even if it's not that much thicker than the first-year sea ice, we might not be able to break through it. Multiyear ice loses its salt as it ages (go ask a scientist why; I can't explain it) and that's what makes it so much denser and stronger. Telling the difference between first-year ice and multiyear ice can be a matter of life and death. I was confident that Arne would keep us out of that kind of trouble. This was only my third trip into the ice, and I was looking forward to learning more about it from one of the best.

❧

We saw our first ice as we approached Cape Farewell near the bottom of Greenland. It was "old" Arctic ice pushed down against the land by the ocean current. Arne directed us around it; we'd have plenty of ice breaking ahead of us. (Arne's first rule of ice breaking is "if you can go around it, do so.") We arrived in Greenland just a couple of weeks after the summer solstice, so we had daylight twenty-four hours a day. Luckily, none of us ever got tired of the view. Greenland's coastline is amazingly dramatic. Mountains rise up straight out of the sea. Glaciers come down to the water. Breathtaking.

Nuuk, the capital of Greenland, was our first port, and we came in right on schedule. The police seemed unusually nervous, even putting up a fence to prevent us from getting off the boat or letting the public get on without going through a checkpoint. We've done anti-coal and anti–offshore drilling actions in Greenland before, but never had any serious run-ins with the Greenland police, so it seemed strange. The extra precautions were explained when we were told that the Danish royal family was on a Danish naval vessel tied up around 160 feet away. (Greenland is a territory of Denmark's, but over the last few years Denmark has been allowing them more autonomy.)

Our first objective was the Petermann Glacier. Petermann is at 81 degrees north, on the northwest corner of Greenland. It's about forty-three miles long and more than nine miles wide. Jason Box, a glaciologist then from Ohio State University, was expecting a giant piece of the glacier to break off at any moment. Predictions were that the chunk breaking off could be twice as big as Manhattan. To get there, we'd have to cruise 1,300 nautical miles up the west coast of Greenland, with a good chance of some serious ice breaking to get there. When we were planning the expedition, Jason told us that there was a fifty-fifty chance of being able to get through the ice in July. As we made our way north, we encountered a good-news-is-really-bad-news scenario: There was no ice. None. We didn't encounter *any* ice until we got to the main body of the glacier itself. This was the first of many bad signs—if you're concerned about climate change—we were to see in the coming weeks.

There was another ice issue that we needed to keep an eye on. At the northern end of the Nares Strait there is an ice bridge, the edge of the tough multiyear polar cap ice, the really hard stuff. As the summer progresses, this ice bridge breaks up and huge slabs of sea ice weighing countless tons march south through the strait. Nothing can stand in the way. We'd keep an eye on that with satellite imagery, but given that we had already seen clear evidence of the water being warmer than expected, there was a good chance that the bridge would let go sooner rather than later. When it did, we'd have to get the hell out of there and fast. Just in case, Arne selected a couple of hidey holes in case we got caught with our pants down.

We made good time up the west coast of Greenland, averaging about 11.5 knots. Of course, when you're unimpeded by ice it's easy, much easier than it really should be. The scenery of the coastline was spectacular but bleak. There wasn't one tree, village, or anything to break up the monotony, but it was beautiful nonetheless.

Jason wanted to set up some remote cameras and GPS sensors on the Petermann Glacier to record the big chunk breaking off, but we had to make sure we got out of there before the ice bridge broke up too. On the way there, Jason gave us all a Glaciers 101 course. He showed us some of the camera footage he had taken of Antarctic glaciers and explained that glaciers are slow-moving rivers of ice. He also explained a peculiarity of Greenland's geography and geology: because of the tremendous weight of the ice and snow on the island, 80 percent of the interior land has actually been pressed down below sea level. He described the glaciers as being like champagne corks: if the front edges of the glaciers melt, the seawater would actually flow back into the interior "bowl" of Greenland. Then all of the interior ice would melt and Greenland would look like a giant atoll, an inland sea surrounded by a ring of land. (Millions of years later, freed from the weight of the ice, the land would slowly rise again.) When you realize that most of the interior ice sheet is more than six thousand feet thick, you can begin to appreciate the resulting rise in global sea levels. Greenland has 11 percent of the ice surface of the Earth, containing almost three million *gigatons* (that's three million billion tons!) of ice. If it all melted, scientists have calculated that the global sea level would rise over twenty feet!

Warming sea temperatures accelerate the melting of marine-terminating glaciers (meaning glaciers with ends that float on the surface of the ocean) since water conducts heat over twenty times more efficiently than air. (This is why humans become hypothermic in 70-degree water in as little as two hours, but an air temperature of 70 degrees is considered to be a perfectly comfortable room temperature.) As the seas get just the tiniest bit warmer, they melt the undersides of the ends of these glaciers even more rapidly, and the sea rises. Compounding this rise is the fact that water expands as it gets warmer, and that makes the sea level rise too. Compounding *that*, as we lose sea ice, more of the sun's energy is absorbed by the darker water instead of being reflected back out into space by the white ice. (The measurement of this reflectivity is called the albedo.) Adding to that, as the permafrost (land that's been frozen for thousands of years) thaws, the vegetation trapped in the frozen soil begins to rot, *releasing more carbon dioxide and methane into the air and accelerating the global warming process even further.* Each part of that process reinforces the other, and it is gathering momentum in a vicious cycle. The evidence was all around us.

We got to Petermann without incident and set up cameras and GPS sensors using the *Sunrise's* chopper. Since we hadn't had to do any ice breaking, we decided we would continue up the Nares Strait to 1) get a look at the conditions at the ice bridge, and 2) see if we could make a complete transit of the strait. To our knowledge, no surface vessel had ever managed to accomplish that in June. (Later in the summer, it generally becomes passable.) Unfortunately, or fortunately–depending on your point of view–we were unimpeded by ice and made it all the way through, setting the world record for the earliest passage of the strait. (I wish I could say I am proud of that record, but I am actually dismayed by it.) At the northern end of the strait, we were only 445 miles from the North Pole.

Many people have asked me why we just didn't go to the North Pole, since we were so close. The *Arctic Sunrise*, as good an ice-breaker as it is, is not nearly strong or powerful enough to make it anywhere close. The multiyear sea ice that was stopping us was already twenty feet thick. Even with the helicopter loaded up with extra fuel, it would still be a one-way trip. And that would make for a long, cold walk back.

Before I left on this trip, a friend of mine gave me the book *The Arctic Grail: The Quest for the Northwest Passage and the North Pole*, which details the many people who have died in those quests. I highly recommend it. The British made a number of fatal attempts to find the Northwest Passage. During one of our shore excursions we stumbled upon a small group of unmarked graves. The graves were probably not expired Northwest Passage explorers, or the rescuers who died trying to find them. More likely they were whalers' graves. Nobody knows for sure, but

the graves certainly illustrated the potential lethality of our sur-
roundings.

A few days later, after completing our expedition to the
ice bridge and back, we returned to Petermann and were able
to tie up to the actual face of the glacier.

The edge of the glacier was about twelve to fifteen feet
high above the water. The surface had rounded humps that
reminded me of sand dunes. Since the wind forms the surface of the glacier, I guess you could call them ice dunes. Scattered among the ice dunes were pools that looked like liquid
turquoise. These were small freshwater lakes of melted glacier that captured the light from the blue sky above and reflected it back. In some of these pools, the salt water had
intruded, and the water took on a greenish tint from the phy-
toplankton that flourished there.

Many of the pools had a fine black powder on the bottom.
It's called cryoconite. It's a combination of carbon and soot
from dust storms, wildfires, and man-made pollution and
bacteria. (Some of the scientists told me some of it was cosmic
dust, but they might have been teasing me.) The stuff feels
like sand, but it is completely black. It heats up and melts farther down into the glacier, frequently in perfectly round circles. Scientific measurements demonstrate that cryoconite is
becoming more plentiful, and because it's black and ab-
sorbs heat, it's yet another contributing factor in the accel-
eration of glacial melting.

Flanking the giant glacier were sheer cliffs more than three
thousand feet high. The glacier, when it was far thicker than
it was now, had carved them to a smooth polish. The cliffs
stretched back toward the beginning of the glacier as far as
the eye could see, more than fifty miles. Numerous waterfalls cascaded thousands of feet from the tops of the cliffs–

down past the walls of stratified limestone in various colors and shades—and dashed themselves on the glacier below. At midnight this far north, the sun happened to be in line with the cliff walls, and it cast long shadows along the faces of rock connected by the undulating white glacier below them. There are no words that can describe it. You'll have to look at the pictures, but even then the photos (as good as they are) pale in comparison to the reality.

Alun Hubbard—a Ph.D. at Aberystwyth University in Wales and secretary of the British branch of the International Glaciological Society—was one of the scientists aboard. Alun had devised a method of towing radar arrays from kayaks to measure the thickness of the glacier. There was a river of meltwater flowing down the glacier, so the kayaks were brought upcurrent with the helicopter and then paddled 10 miles back. The radar measured that the glacier was over six hundred feet thick at that point. Two years later Alun was going to return and take new measurements to determine the exact rate at which the glacier's thickness was being lost.

The helicopter was flying all the time, shuttling the scientists and their instruments around to various parts of the glaciers. One afternoon Jason came up to the bridge to show us pictures of a pod of narwhals that they flew over on the way back to the ship. Narwhals are the small whales with the giant, spiral "tusks" that come out of their forehead. In ancient days, narwhal tusks were passed as "unicorn horns" and sold for big money. When Jason told us that narwhals were only a few miles away, the crew was pissed off that nobody had thought to call us on the radio so we could go over and see them. None of us had ever seen one before.

This faux pas was inexcusable, but not quite as bad as letting a shipmate sleep through the meteorological phenomenon of

Saint Elmo's fire. Saint Elmo's fire can be formed in humid conditions when static electricity is collected by a ship's rigging. The
static gets discharged as a glowing blue ball of light that dances
around the rigging. Many sailors regard it as an ill omen since it
usually coincides with thunder and lightning storms, but if
someone doesn't wake you up to see it, killing them would almost be justifiable homicide. Similarly, not being able to see the
narwhals was a severe test of my belief in nonviolence.

After Petermann, we moved to the Kane Basin to study
the Humboldt Glacier. The Humboldt was creating some impressive icebergs. You've heard the expression "the tip of the
iceberg" and it's a very accurate description; only 10 percent
of a floating iceberg's mass sits above the surface. The seawater, however, melts the iceberg under the surface faster
than it melts in the air, so eventually the iceberg's shape
changes enough so that it becomes unbalanced. It will be a
perfectly calm day, no wind or waves, and you'll see a seemingly stable iceberg start to go wobbly. All of a sudden, the
giant iceberg—sometimes weighing thousands of tons—will
flip over in an instant and settle into a completely new position. The warmer water melting the foundation of the iceberg
causes it to reach its tipping point. For me, it's the perfect
analogy for what's happening to our environment: it's reaching a tipping point where—all of a sudden—the changes will
become more drastic and occur almost instantly. It can happen at any time, and unless we quickly make some big
changes, our environment *will* roll over.

After a couple of weeks of research on the Petermann and
Humboldt glaciers, Arne checked the satellite photos of
the ice bridge and determined it was beginning to move. The
ice would take some time to reach us, but the clock was ticking. We had just a few more working days before we had to

clear out of the Nares Strait. We relocated back to the Kane Basin to begin research, lowering sensors into the water to take measurements of the conductivity (a measure of salinity), the temperature, and the depth (collectively, "CTD"). Some sensors also record current speed and direction.

The measurements give the scientists a better picture of the currents in the Nares Strait, and how they impact the health of the glaciers. It's been accepted fact for over a hundred years that the current in the Nares Strait runs south: it's the current that drives down all of the polar cap ice behind the ice bridge. What we discovered, however, was that in addition to the expected southerly current, there was a current flowing *north* toward the glaciers. This new current contained subtropical water that was 6 degrees Centigrade warmer than the water we measured at Petermann. It could be a major reason why the glaciers were melting so much faster than before.

With the sea ice moving down the strait, it was time for some serious ice breaking. Most of it was first-year sea ice—the easy stuff—and with 90 percent power we could break through its two feet of thickness. Certain parts were much tougher. Arne explained to me that sometimes the ice is under pressure, meaning that the tide or wind is pushing the ice together and/or against the ship. That pressure makes the ice harder to break. In one instance, a large iceberg had grounded on the bottom of the strait and the tide was pushing the sea ice against the iceberg. Every time the *Arctic Sunrise* made a crack in the ice, the pressure would close the crack up again. This meant that we had to ram the ice ahead of us, back the ship up again, and then ram it again to make any kind of progress. Ice breaking is time-consuming and it sucks down tons of fuel, which is why you try to avoid doing it as much as possible. It's also hard on the crew. Imagine trying to sleep down below while—inches from your head—the steel hull of the ship collides with the ice every minute or so. It feels like trying to sleep in a bathtub that's being dragged up the stairs. *Bang. Bang. Bang.* For hours on end. It's fun to do when you're at the helm, but it's hell down below.

"Arne! Look out for that rock!" Arne, on the helm, was startled as I pointed out the window of the bridge. He laughed when he saw that I was pointing at a boulder that was sitting on the ice a few hundred yards from the ship. It must have rolled off one of the cliffs during the winter and come to rest about a quarter-mile out. As the *Arctic Sunrise* slammed into the ice again and again, the ice eventually cracked and the boulder went down to the bottom. It had never been seen before and would never be seen again.

After several days of banging our heads against the seemingly endless ice, we decided we all could use a break, so we made a shore excursion to stretch our legs. It was the height of the Arctic summer, absolutely beautiful, with the ground covered in soft moss (typical of summer in the tundra) with an array of different-colored flowers. There was one flower, like a little ball of white cotton, that I remembered seeing in Amchitka, Alaska—at a latitude a thousand miles to the south. When you can say "Amchitka" and "a thousand miles south" in the same sentence, you know you are really up north!

The next few days were spent doing more CTD measurements. The CTD instruments, which weigh about sixty pounds, have to be lowered to depths of as much as 2,700 feet. We used winches to raise them back up to the ship. Sometimes we used the jet boat near the faces of the glaciers. This was hard going for the crews that had to raise the heavy sensors by hand. When the Humboldt was actively calving, we didn't dare let a boat get too close to the face, so we'd do "extreme CTD measurements" from the helicopter. We worked our way north along the face of the glacier until we got to Benton Bay on its far side. We took another break and allowed some of the crew to go ashore, where they made another unpleasant discovery.

Normally, a glacier slopes downward from the back to the front, with the lowest point being the end that meets the water. One of the team, however, noticed that the Humboldt had a reverse slope near its end: there was a dip in the glacier well behind the front edge. The scientists took some altitude readings to confirm it and to measure the amount of the dip. It was a very troubling sign for the glaciologists, as it means there is far more melting going on than previously known.

At one point, after seeing no other signs of civilization for weeks, I heard the sound of a passenger jet flying overhead. We had an aviation-band radio onboard, so for fun I called up to the pilot to say hello. I found out he was flying from Newark, New Jersey, to Singapore. He asked me what I was doing down there and when I told him "environmental research," he asked me, "Is Al Gore on board?" As you might expect, I didn't laugh. To me, global warming is not a laughing matter.

We continued the CTD measurements from the ship. It was a little monotonous but we did have one moment of real excitement. We spotted an iceberg with a "moulin," a giant, perfectly circular tunnel that is formed by a whirlpool of melting water and wind. It had made a hole clean through the iceberg. The snappers and shooters wanted to get some good photos of this so they and some of the crew got into the *Mermaid*–our jet boat. The ice here was broken up into big chunks floating close to one another, so the boat couldn't go all that fast as it picked its way through the ice. They hadn't gone much more than a hundred feet when someone spotted a polar bear headed their way. The polar bear, perfectly adapted to the conditions, was leaping from one piece of ice to the other with ease. The people in the *Mermaid*, however, were a slow-moving, international all-you-can-eat buffet.

Everyone on the *Arctic Sunrise* started shouting instructions or encouragement. The *Mermaid* was on the port side of the ship (where the pilot door is—the easiest way to get back aboard), while the bear was still on the starboard side. The bear's attention suddenly fixed on the *Arctic Sunrise* just in front of her. You could see the look of confusion on her face (from the huge size of her neck it was apparent that she was a "she") as she inspected the ship a mere thirty feet from where she was standing. She had probably never seen a ship this close before, and was probably deciding whether or not the *Arctic Sunrise* was edible. After a minute of deliberation, she lazily rolled over, scratched her back on the ice, and casually sauntered off. Phew. That incident made us a little more cautious about going out on the ice. I must say, though, it's a little nerve-racking to be walking around on the polar ice knowing that you'll be a delicious polar-bear snack if you don't watch your back. It reminded me of the *Far Side* cartoon with two polar bears sitting outside a smashed igloo. One—with his mouth full—says to the other, "I just love these things. Crunchy on the outside and a chewy center!" Some friends describe me as "crunchy," but I'm pretty sure I'm chewy through and through.

Back at the Petermann glacier, the anticipated separation was not following the script. Given the amount of time and effort we had expended to see it, we felt this was extremely inconsiderate. Time was running out. We had just a few more days before we had to head south, around the bottom of Greenland and then north along the island's east coast. We joked about trying mental telepathy to start the calving pro-

cess: *Calve, Petermann. Calve! Everyone concentrate now....*
Nothing doing. Jason was distraught, practically in tears. We
decided to leave some cameras on the glacier and arranged
for the Canadian Coast Guard to pick them up later. Hopefully, as the summer progressed, the cameras would capture
some action there.

It turned out that the Petermann didn't break up that summer,
but it did the following year (2010). Two years after we were there
(2011), I was flying back from Europe. I had a window seat and
when we flew over the northeastern corner of Newfoundland, I
recognized the chunk that had broken off of Petermann (it's
called Petermann 2010). There was no mistaking it. It's possible
we had tied up to that very piece of ice. The ten-mile-wide chunk
had floated south and grounded on Newfoundland. In 2012, a
piece almost as big (Petermann 2012) broke off as well.

With the polar cap ice marching down on us, we headed
south toward Sisimiut to provision for the run around Greenland and back north. We were headed for the northernmost
point on Greenland's eastern shore. We were going to be practically circumnavigating Greenland the "long way around,"
since going the short way—around the northern side—would
have been impossible with the sea ice. It had been seven weeks
since we had last been in a port, and no one had spent a night
onshore since we had left Amsterdam in mid-June.

As we were cutting through some amazing fjords in southern Greenland, we passed majestic, sheer stone cliffs towering almost a mile straight up in the air, with waterfalls flowing
straight down to the rocky shoreline. We passed two fishing vessels and a Danish navy ship. After the weeks of isolation in the Nares Strait, that felt like a traffic jam. But the

ships were not really a worry—the growlers and bergy-bits were.

"Growlers" are icebergs—weighing twenty or thirty tons—that are barely visible at the surface. "Bergy-bits" are even bigger icebergs that are a little more visible at the surface. Growlers don't show up on radar at all. Bergy-bits might or might not, depending on how high they are and their shape. In twenty-four-hour daylight both of these hazards are easy to avoid, but now that it was later in the summer and we were farther south, we were getting periods of real darkness. Running through the growlers and bergy-bits in the dark is like running through a minefield. Making matters worse, we were in warmer (relatively speaking) waters, which created fog: we were running through a minefield *blindfolded*! The ship's spotlight was worse than useless; the fog and the ship's bulwarks reflected the light right back at us, destroying our night vision. We were going to have to feel our way through, slowly and gently, to avoid pulling a *Titanic*.

Fortunately for me, I have been able to dispel the age-old myth that the captain goes down with the ship. It is the cook who goes down with the ship, as illustrated so well in another *Far Side* cartoon. It makes sense when you realize that, in a lifeboat, there won't be much food to cook and nothing to cook it on. Babu was, naturally, skeptical at first, but with a little convincing I think I was able to get him to believe it. (I'm being funny. Babu was one of the best cooks we've ever had. He put out a Thanksgiving-worthy spread just about every night.)

We stopped at several points along the way up the eastern coast for more CTD measurements. Fiamma Straneo, an oceanographer from the Woods Hole Oceanographic Institution, found that warmer, subtropical waters were reaching almost halfway up the coast, causing the glaciers in the area to move and melt at an increasing pace. More bad signs of global warming. Our ultimate destination on this side of Greenland was Nioghalvfjerdsbrae. Don't even bother trying to pronounce it. It means "79 North Glacier" in Danish. (Danish is considered one of the hardest languages for "foreigners" to pronounce, and there are many who say, "Danish is not a language. It's a throat disease.") 79 is a very important glacier as it extends all the way from the coast deep into the interior of Greenland.

It took two and a half days of constant ice breaking to get there. We used satellite-generated images to try to pick the easiest route through the ice, but they weren't always accurate. *Bang. Bang. Bang.* Progress was slow. It was not unusual to make only five miles of progress during an entire six-hour watch. You could easily walk faster than that (especially if you were being followed by a polar bear!). The *Arctic Sunrise* was cracking through ice that was six feet thick. Any thicker and we'd be testing the limits of the ship, and the limits of the crew.

Despite the torture of ice breaking, there were moments of incredible beauty that made up for it. Now, in mid-September, we were getting extended periods of darkness. Everyone's heard of the "Land of the Midnight Sun," but there is another rarely visible delight: the midday moon. The moon stays above the horizon all day, traveling in a complete circle just like the midnight sun. Unfortunately, we weren't in the right place at the right time to see it.

As a sailor who practices celestial navigation, I'm always interested in astronomy. My ultimate celestial "sight" (meaning a series of observations and calculations made with a sextant) is to sight the sun, moon, and Venus at the same time. For celestial geeks it's like having a very rare bird on your life list. Conditions have to be crystal clear, the time and place has to be just right, and you have to be damn good at celestial. Years before, my friend from the *Regina Maris*, Andy Chase, showed me how to do it.

The absolute hardest technique is a back sight. This you would use near a shoreline where you can't see the horizon (which is what all of your calculations would normally be based on). With a back sight, you have to do it over your shoulder in the opposite direction—like trying to use a mirror to shoot a rifle at a target behind you. I've never done a back sight because I don't use celestial navigation when I can see land. I don't want to have the ship hit something while I'm distracted with the sextant.

Another glaciologist, Gordon Hamilton from the University of Maine, went out on the helicopter to retrieve the data from the GPS sensors on the Kangerdlugssuaq Glacier. He had been taking measurements on this glacier since 2004. A year later (2005) he was sitting in the back of the chopper and calculating the rate at which the glacier had moved in the previous year. After reviewing the results, he thought he had made some kind of mathematical error, so he did it again. The results were the same. In that moment, Gordon became horrified by the sudden realization that the glacier's speed had increased 1,000 percent. It was an "oh shit" moment for everyone else too when he told us that story. It was incontrovertible proof of climate change. (The Kangerdlugssuaq Glacier has so much ice mass that if it melted completely, it would fill the Great Lakes in the United States four times over.) The results he found on this trip added to his concern.

We spent a few more days doing research at 79 North Glacier. The team lowered a CTD through a very deep rift in a floating glacial "tongue." To get there, the helicopter had to land inside the glacial rift. Then the team had to chain-saw a hole through which they were able to lower the sensor to a depth of nearly two thousand feet. The objective was to compare the findings with research performed by a Danish team in the mid-1990s. The results indicated a 35 percent increase in melting rates.

It was time to leave Greenland for the island of Svalbard to the east. The first part of our passage went smoothly, but then we hit the ice. And hit it again. And hit it again. Hundreds if not thousands of times. Some of it was really hard multiyear sea ice, some of it too thick to break. Sea ice there can reach a thickness of over 250 feet! Arne, as always, was up to the task, and we made it to Svalbard a day ahead of the schedule that we had originally laid out in Amsterdam five months before.

Svalbard is a really interesting archipelago under the jurisdiction of Norway. Longyearbyen, the administrative center, is the northernmost permanently populated village in the world (not counting research stations). The brightly painted houses on the hillsides makes the village look very European. It's not very big, but we were able to provision and pick up more av-gas for the helicopter. The next phase of our plan was to perform additional sea ice measurements, flying scientists around with the helicopter to where the sea ice was too thick for ice breaking. There was some risk involved. If the helicopter suffers a mechanical failure fifty miles away, there's no way for us to get to them or them to us. The scientists had a portable drill that used steam to quickly melt through very thick ice. The sensors were then dropped down the holes deep into the ice.

This continued for a few days, but then the weather started to change. A front came through, a sea swell started running, and my instincts, along with Arne's and the scientists', told us it was time to head home. We'd stop in Svalbard again, about thirty hours to the south, to provision, and then perform an action at the Norwegian coal mine there.

Every three or four days, a large bulk carrier full of coal departs Svalbard and heads toward Europe. Here, surrounded by evidence of global warming, one of the primary culprits—coal—continues to be mined. We brought the *Arctic Sunrise* right up to where the bulk carriers tie up and load at the dock. The miners were downright hospitable, and even offered us a tour of the mine! (Maybe they were just eager for some new faces.) Our plan was to shut down the conveyor belt with the emergency-stop button, have people chain themselves to it, put up some banners, and then take some pictures. Shutting this mine down for a day or two wasn't going to make much of a difference, but a new mine was being planned and we hoped that we could put a stop to that. The conveyor belt was automated so there was nobody around to stop us. It was like stealing candy from a baby.

As part of this action, a half dozen of us had our picture taken with our faces covered by photos of the faces of world leaders. Being American, I chose Barack Obama. We sent the photos out, and a couple of days later we heard that the campaigners back at Gp headquarters weren't happy because my hair was sticking out all around the mask! Like the public really would have believed Obama was there. In my defense, it had been five months since I had been to a barber. Besides, my body type is about as far from Obama's as can be.

After the coal mine action, it was time to head back to Norway. From there, we would return to Amsterdam. The North Atlantic can be a very nasty place that time of year but we got lucky with a good weather window on the way to Norway. Modern meteorology, satellite images, and broadband transmission have made storms much easier to avoid. Just twenty or thirty years earlier, passages like this one were far riskier and less pleasant. Still, unless you're in a very fast vessel, you can't avoid bad weather completely, and we had our fair share of it on the way from Norway back to Amsterdam.

There was a big welcoming committee when we got there and a big party on board the *Arctic Sunrise* that night. We had arrived home on schedule and without any major incidents. Not only had I seen some of the most spectacular scenery in my life, the crew and I were quite proud of all that we had accomplished.

Despite the length of time we had been at sea, and especially with the sleep deprivation we all suffered during icebreaking operations, the harmony of the crew never waned. It's been a long time since I've made a trip where internal crew conflict was a problem. As captain, crew morale is my responsibility, but I don't think our crew harmony has very much to do with me. My experience with Greenpeace crews is that the importance of what we are doing puts any crew issues in a different light. Interpersonal problems that might normally seem important are forgiven and forgotten. Between observing the destruction of the Amazon, and now seeing for ourselves the way glacial melting is accelerating, it is hard for any of us not to worry about the future. That keeps things in perspective.

The data from this expedition provided dramatic evidence that the warming of the oceans is an important driver of the climate changes occurring in Greenland and the Arctic. The combination of the warmer waters, and the increased sea level of the expanded/warmer water, is having an enormous impact in that area of the world, and that impact is already spreading around to the rest of the planet.

The speed and volume of the ice loss was beyond anything the scientists had imagined. To give you a sense of how much ice the glaciers are losing already, *just one glacier*—Helheim Glacier—in Greenland is losing twenty-five billion tons of ice a year! With the sensors we left behind, we'll be able to monitor the glaciers in real time and get a far more in-depth understanding of how fast they're moving and how much more ice they're losing. None of us are betting that it will slow down.

I've been all over the world (over four hundred thousand miles), but the scenery in Greenland really did it for me. Despite the discouraging measurements, I came away from the experience with renewed optimism, and more determination than ever to prevent such places from being destroyed in the name of progress. A few years later, this strong emotional connection to the Arctic led me into a direct conflict with the most powerful authoritarian regime in the world.

Mi. ⊢━━━━━━━⊣ 100

Novya Zemlya

Barents Sea

Greenpeace ship Arctic Sunrise
boarded near the Prirazlomnaya rig

ARCTIC CIRCLE

R U S S I A

RUSSIA

15

David vs. The Gazprom Goliath

SEPTEMBER 2013

PECHORA SEA (THE EASTERN PORTION OF THE BARENTS SEA), WESTERN RUSSIA—
APPROXIMATELY 125 MILES ABOVE THE ARCTIC CIRCLE

ARCTIC ANTI-DRILLING ACTION

Gazprom is one of the largest companies in the world, and the third most profitable. It produces 17 percent of the natural gas in the world, and a sizable share of the world's oil. It is also controlled by the Russian government. To give you an idea of how intertwined the two are, consider this: just over twenty years ago, the company was part of the Soviet state. It was "privatized" after glasnost, but is still under the ownership and control of the government. Gazprom is also far more than an oil company; it also owns two of the three largest broadcasting networks in the country.

Gazprom's president for much of the last decade was Dmitri Medvedev. Prior to joining Gazprom, Medvedev had served as Vladimir Putin's campaign manager. Putin's previous job was heading Russia's FSB—Russia's federal

counterintelligence and internal security service—and a suc-
cessor agency to the Soviet Union's KGB. If Medvedev's
name is familiar, it's because Medvedev's next job was president of Russia. This post was given to him by Putin with the
understanding that when Putin wanted it back in a few years,
Medvedev would hand the job back to his mentor. (Russia's
constitution prevents three consecutive terms in office, but
says nothing about puppet presidents.) In the meantime, while
Medvedev was Russia's president, Putin became the prime
minister.

To put this in perspective, imagine if the president of the
United States had been the head of the CIA before being
elected (as the first President Bush was). He then installs his
campaign manager as the head of an oil company the size of
Exxon and Shell *combined*, and which also owns ABC *and*
CBS at the same time. After two terms in office, this theo-
retical president arranges to make his puppet the president
of the country, and then four years later moves the puppet
out and restores himself to the presidency all over again, *all
while controlling the government, the media, and most of the natural resources and industry in America*. That's exactly what was
going on in Russia.

Now, imagine trying to stop this president's pet project—
the core of his power, influence, and the key to his future—by
bringing the rest of the world's attention to it. Oh, and the
project is heavily fortified and guarded, and you are completely unarmed. Would you take those odds? Well, we were
about to, because the Arctic is one of the most precious and
beautiful places in the world and the Russian government
doesn't care if they destroy it. None of us wanted that to
happen.

The Gazprom *Prirazlomnay* oil rig that we were headed to
was Russia's/Putin's first attempt to drill in the Arctic. It is

above the Arctic Circle and is subject to the heavy ice floes, weighing millions and millions of tons, which regularly sweep the surface of the sea. If anything goes wrong, there is no proven way to contain or clean up an Arctic oil spill. In these conditions, conditions where something is *mostly likely to go wrong*, there is virtually no way to get the resources, supplies, and equipment there to contain the environmental damage. Any malfunction of the rig could cause an environmental disaster that would make the BP *Deepwater Horizon* Gulf of Mexico blowout seem like a drop in the oil drum. Russia already had a dubious record of oil spills on land. Every year, *five hundred thousand tons* of oil spilled in northern Russia reaches the Arctic after being carried by rivers to the sea. And it's far easier to control spills on land than in the Arctic.

To the Russians' credit, they had engineered a new—but untested—type of drilling platform designed to resist the incalculable forces of the Arctic Sea ice. It is essentially a man-made island formed by sinking caissons filled with millions of tons of rock, surrounded with a smooth, heavy steel curtain wall a hundred feet high. The wall is engineered to withstand the ice by breaking it up and forcing it around the sides. Think of it as a giant icebreaker, but in this case the icebreaker remains stationary while the ice moves past it. The man-made island is sunk down to the seabed about a hundred feet underwater, while the drilling rig is almost 380 feet tall. It is, in any sense of the word, a fortress designed to stand against all floes and all foes—be they nature or man. The rig was definitely a Goliath, and we most certainly were David. Maybe it was symbolic, but all of our hopes relied—quite literally—on a slingshot. Several slingshots, to be precise.

I arrived in Kirkenes, Norway—about twenty miles from the Russian border—just a few days before the *Arctic Sunrise* was scheduled to depart for the action against Gazprom. The

Sunrise is not my favorite ship, but she's a certified icebreaker that is made to handle the worst the Arctic can throw at her. She was the right choice for the job. I met with the previous captain, Daniel Rizzotti; the ship's engineers; and other senior crew members to review her condition (standard operating procedure for captains assuming command of a ship), and met with Frank Hewetson—the action coordinator—to get briefed on the plan.

Greenpeace had performed a similar action against this same rig the summer before (I was on another action at the time). It had been fairly uneventful, as these things go. They had approached the rig unimpeded, hoisted up a number of climbers, and hung a banner denouncing the rig. The climbers were then blasted with cold pressurized seawater pumped from fire hoses, and then safely retrieved without too much difficulty.

The general action plan was much the same as the previous one, but with a couple of new wrinkles. The biggest difference was that Frank had brought the "pod" to protect our climbers from the fire hoses and to prevent them from being immediately arrested. The pod looked like a fiberglass septic tank, and was about the same size. Inside the pod were provisions for several days and communications equipment so that video, blogs, and "pod"-casts could be broadcast around the world. I've had experience with hoisting all kinds of things up to substantial heights using our outboard-powered RHIBs, but I was a little skeptical about being able to get this done given the circumstances.

The action would begin with the launching of five RHIBs from the *Sunrise* in close proximity to the rig. Gp's international lawyers had instructed us not to bring the *Sunrise* any closer than five hundred meters to the rig, unless the safety of the activists would be dramatically enhanced by our being that close in. As captain, I bear the responsibility of the safety of the crew and have the authority to call off any action that I feel is unduly dangerous. The mother ship—the *Arctic Sunrise*—would stay well outside this perimeter, and the five inflatables would approach the rig. There were three larger RHIBs and two smaller ones. The two smaller boats would create a distraction and act as a picket, while the three larger RHIBs would perform the actual action. One of the three larger RHIBs would carry the climbing team; one would carry Frank, the videographer, and the still photographer; and the other boat would tow the pod to the rig. This is where the slingshots would come into play.

The slingshots are about ten feet long and use surgical tubing as the elastic for the sling. They shoot small weights— each trailing a very light twine—up through part of the oil rig. The twine is then used to pull up much heavier ropes. The climbers would each go up on one of those ropes, and other ropes would be used to haul up the pod. Once the heavy ropes were attached to the pod, the other ends would be tied to the stern of a large RHIB equipped with powerful engines. The RHIB would then speed away from the rig, lifting the pod into position where the climbers could secure it. Once the pod was securely attached, the climbers would enter the pod through a hatch in its side and establish residence. Conceptually, it's quite simple. In practice, of course, it was far more complicated.

I was skeptical, but then I've been proven wrong many times when we've been successful with the odds stacked against us. I may have been a little pessimistic about our chances, but I wasn't particularly worried. It was, however, my first action since I had gotten married to Maggy a few months before, and so I had taken the time to familiarize her with my finances (such as they are), household routines, etc.

Maybe deep down inside I had "a bad feeling about this" (to quote Harrison Ford from both *Star Wars* and *Indiana Jones*) before I left. Maggy remembers me saying something like, "After ten years, maybe it's time to get arrested again." I also told her that I was afraid I was going to lose the tan I had developed from sailing all summer. Little did I know...

Once aboard the *Arctic Sunrise*, however, I was eager to get back into the action. The action team was practicing their slingshot aim, climbing techniques, etc. Sini Saarela, a young woman from Finland, was already an experienced climber and had climbed the Gazprom rig the year before. The rest were getting fairly proficient at it, which was encouraging, but practicing it on dry land or in a protected harbor is very different from being out on the open icy ocean with fire hoses shooting Arctic water at you. Still, we were as ready as we were going to be when we left Norway and headed north.

The passage north was unremarkable. The weather was fairly good, and Mother Nature entertained us with an incredible skyful of northern lights. I don't believe much in premonitions or omens, auspicious or otherwise, but it gave me a nice feeling. A reminder of what it is we're fighting for. I didn't know, of course, that I was about to spend a few months without seeing the sky at all.

Today's ships are equipped with an array of devices designed to let governments and rescue organizations track the movement of vessels far offshore. The equipment provides real-time position reports and also clearly identifies the name, type, and ownership of the vessel. The Russians were going to know well in advance where we were and where we were likely to go. A few months before, the *Arctic Sunrise* had been on a research cruise several hundred miles from the rig. They were boarded by the Russian Coast Guard and told, in no uncertain terms, to stay away from it. This time reports had confirmed that the Russian Coast Guard had put into port in Murmansk, but we were fairly sure they were monitoring us. They were going to know as soon as we left Norway. Still, we were planning to play it somewhat coy by seeming to head toward the gate (the main approach from the open ocean) near the Russian archipelago of Novaya Zemlya.

These islands were used as a nuclear testing site by the USSR, including the 1961 explosion of the Tsar Bomba, the largest, most powerful nuclear weapon ever detonated. Over Novaya Zemlya's history as a nuclear test site, it endured 224 nuclear detonations with a total explosive energy equivalent to 265 megatons of TNT. By way of comparison, consider this: *all of the explosives used in World War II* (including the two US atomic bombs dropped on Japan) amounted to only *two* megatons. *Noraya Zemlya had been hit with more than one hundred World War II's worth of explosives.* In 1988 and 1989, glasnost made the testing at Novaya Zemlya public knowledge, and in 1990 Greenpeace staged a protest there, so it wasn't *entirely* implausible that we would head that way.

While Novaya Zemlya is somewhat distant from the rig, we asked permission from the Russians to enter the gate. We were hoping that they would assume that's where we were headed and not come out of Murmansk to intercept us. There was a very slim chance they'd believe it, but stranger things have happened. This was not one of those times. Within twenty-four hours, we had company.

As soon as we left, the Russian Coast Guard cutter *Ladoga* mobilized to intercept us. It's an armed ship that is sort of a cross between a large tug and a small icebreaker. The *Ladoga* established a position a couple of miles from the *Arctic Sunrise* and shadowed us all the way to the rig. Two days later we arrived at our planned position just outside of the rig's perimeter. We still had several hours before daylight.

My preference was to launch the five RHIBs under cover of darkness, but Frank—as the action coordinator—made the call to wait until just before it got light. We turned in and tried to get some sleep. Tension mounts before any action, but we all felt a little more tense than usual since we were about to mess with the Russians.

It was still dark when we launched the boats. To stay in stealth mode and keep the launching from being noticed, we kept all the deck lights off and didn't use the radios. The five RHIBs were launched in quick succession, as was the pod, and all were making their way toward the rig before we saw the Russian cutter beginning to launch their first inflatable in response. We're well-practiced and experienced at doing these launches and can do them with impressive speed. The Russians, I guess, don't do it that often, so only one of their inflatables was onsite by the time three of our boats arrived at the base of the towering steel walls of the rig. The pod, however, was not as fortunate.

The towline for the pod had parted, leaving it adrift a few hundred yards inside the three-mile limit we had set for ourselves around the rig. Frank elected to leave the pod behind while the climbers scaled the rig and unfurled their banner. The Russian cutter headed for the pod. Who the hell knows what they thought it was, but they were at least going to investigate it and probably confiscate it. Up until now, I had been content to keep the *Arctic Sunrise* outside our self-imposed three-mile limit. My thinking was that if I didn't give the *Ladoga* a reason to engage with us closely, they would stay out of the fray too. But when I realized they might attempt to capture the pod, we throttled up to high speed and headed right toward the Russian tug and the pod. The Russian cutter's captain thought better of it and moved away from us and back toward the rig where the real action was taking place.

With the cutter out of the way, we recovered the pod and retreated back outside the three-mile perimeter. At the rig, however, things were getting very dicey very fast.

The slingshot team had done their thing, shooting the weights through a loop in a large mooring line that was attached under the deck of the rig approximately seventy feet above their heads. The first climber—the improbably named Marco Paolo Weber—was well on his way up, and Sini was just starting her ascent, when the fire hoses began cascading tons of freezing ocean on them both. Then the shooting started.

The Russian soldiers—fully armed and wearing balaclavas—began firing automatic weapons at the Greenpeace RHIBs, driving them back away from the rig. Bullets were hitting the water only a few feet away from our boats. They weren't necessarily trying to hit us, but they certainly were willing to risk it. Meanwhile, some of the other Russians were attempting to force our climbers down. In choppy seas, and with everyone's adrenaline pumping, it was definitely too close for comfort. On top of this, the Russians were brandishing guns directly at our activists while stabbing and slashing at our inflatable boats with military knives.

From the way the Russian Coast Guard team was equipped—with balaclavas, machine pistols, and large knives—it was clear they meant business. One of the Russians grabbed the rope that Sini was attached to and started swinging her out away from the rig and then back into it—slamming her body repeatedly against the steel-slabbed sides. Sini was taking a good beating while the rig crew was blasting her with the fire hoses. Marco came back down from the rig to help Sini, but both of them were quickly subdued and wrestled into one of the Russian RHIBs.

Our teams are trained to be completely passive in these circumstances, so everyone in our boats had their hands up in the air, making themselves as nonthreatening as possible. The Russians in the boats kept firing their pistols in the air while they repeatedly stabbed our boats. Because the flotation tubes of our RHIBs are chambered, it takes a number of holes in a boat to make it sink, but the number of holes was mounting fast.

Eventually, the Russian RHIBs headed back to the *Ladoga* carrying Sini and Marco—our two climbers. We had no idea what the Russians' intentions were, and they certainly weren't going to tell us. The entire action—from the time we had launched the RHIBs to the time they came limping back to the *Sunrise*—had taken just over two hours. Luckily nobody had been seriously injured in the action, although we couldn't be sure that Sini and Marco hadn't been hurt. We had suffered the usual bumps and bruises, but we were all very shaken by the Russians' unexpected use of force and the realization that two of our activists were now prisoners. From the standpoint of getting the kind of footage we were looking for, the action was a clear success. But with two of our team members being held prisoner, we couldn't head for home just yet.

The Russians approached the *Arctic Sunrise* in one of the RHIBs and demanded that we stop the ship. We knew if they boarded us, they would take control of the ship. After we refused, the cutter fired several groups of warning shots from their bow cannon. Four times over the course of a few hours, they fired three shots in rapid succession, telling us they would fire into the ship if we didn't stop. They even told us to move our crew toward the bow of the ship and away from the stern where they were going to aim. We told them, "Go ahead, but try not to hit the big round silver thing near the aft end of the ship. It's full of gasoline." Although that didn't stop them from continuing to fire the gun, they at least kept their aim ahead of the bow. They never tried to hit us, but mistakes can happen. It was still dangerous.

Eventually, they told us that they would discuss the return of our two climbers if we moved to a position roughly twenty miles away from the Gazprom rig. We followed their request, but after several radio conversations in which they kept telling us they were waiting for orders, we grew tired of the stalling and headed back in the direction of the rig. For the remainder of the day, things stayed fairly quiet. The Russians were hanging back, and so were we. I sent out a few e-mail updates and was feeling pretty upbeat. We had stood up to their threats, and felt like we had showed them up a bit. The *Sunrise* returned to a normal watch rotation and I got some decent sleep.

The next day was spent making lazy circles about three or four miles from the rig. The stab wounds to the RHIBs had been repaired, but with our plans exposed and half our climbing team being held by the Russians, we really couldn't accomplish very much. A group of us talked about it, and we decided that the following day we could launch the RHIBs again. We could at least get some more footage of the rig from a vantage point of several hundred yards away. The Russian ship maneuvered to stay in between the *Sunrise* and the rig, but toward the end of the day they stopped following us and seemed content to stand by a good distance way. We figured that the excitement was over. Once again, we figured wrong.

That evening, I decided to hit the elliptical machine and burn off a little stress. I was working up a good sweat when I heard the engines stop. That's never, ever a good thing, particularly when you're around a lot of pissed-off, well-armed Russians. Still, I didn't stop exercising; if I was needed, someone would let me know.

The mate on watch had seen a large Russian military

helicopter approaching at high speed and had stopped the *Arctic Sunrise*. (This was probably a mistake on his part, but it was what it was.) The next thing I knew, one of the crew burst into the gym to tell me what was going on. By the time we got up on deck we were faced with several commandos rappelling from the black chopper, with another dozen commandos or more hovering forty feet or so above the deck. The Russian commandos were in all black uniforms with no insignia. We were being boarded by Russian Special Forces. In international waters. The commandos announced they were taking control of the *Arctic Sunrise*; we were all being taken to Murmansk.

I was on the bridge when one of the commandos burst in. The Russians were pretty confident that we weren't going to resist. Since they had stormed the ship while I was working out, all I was wearing was gym shorts and a sweaty T-shirt. I politely asked their leader if I could change, and he was–surprisingly–OK with that. Back in my cabin, I used the opportunity to get a couple of e-mails out before the Russians could shut down our communications. I shot one off to Manuel Pinto (head of operations at Gp headquarters) and copied my wife: "Got boarded by Russian troops via helicopter at 18:30 local time. Everyone OK." Those words were the last thing she would hear from me for more than a month.

A few minutes later, to make sure we were completely incommunicado, the Russians proceeded to disable all of our communications equipment–radios, satellite systems, and anything else they found. Several of the crew had locked themselves in the radio room as the commandos were dropping onto the deck, to send out messages to everyone they could. The commandos headed for the radio room, broke down the door, and started throwing switches, yanking hard drives, and pulling wires out to kill the rest of our communications abilities as quickly as they could. To be fair, at least they weren't randomly vandalizing anything or doing "unnecessary" damage. They were clearly doing everything with a sense of purpose.

What the Russians didn't know was that as they were boarding the ship, we had hit the "pirate button," alerting several international authorities that we were under attack or being boarded. (This was an important piece of evidence for our legal defense months later, as it established our position in international waters when they boarded us.)

They brought the crew down to the mess, and began patting them down. All of the Russians were men, and when one of them began to search Ana Paula, she started to scream that they were molesting her. The Russians asked Katrina—a Russian and our ship's doctor—to perform the search, but she refused. After that, I don't think any of the women on the *Sunrise* were ever searched. They didn't seem to be looking for anything in particular; it was simply part of the routine. In general, the commandos were fairly respectful, not handling us roughly at all. Of course, as in all Gp actions, we stayed completely passive.

The commandos insisted on taking a number of cabins for themselves and the Russian ship's crew that would be put on the *Sunrise.* Our crew would be restricted to just two cabins. I wasn't happy with that arrangement at all and made my displeasure known. The Russian mate and I started to discuss the situation. It was strange, but it became a peer-to-peer negotiation between us. We eventually came to an agreement regarding the sharing of the cabins. Afterward, the Russians gathered up all of the liquor onboard and had a hell of a party. Having a bunch of drunk and well-armed foreign soldiers on your ship is more than a little unnerving.

After the commandos had secured the ship, a couple of

the Russian Coast Guard officers came aboard and asked me to motor the *Sunrise* to Murmansk. I refused. After all, we were being arrested and while we weren't going to *resist* them, we certainly weren't going to *assist* them. He understood and said they would tow us the several hundred miles to Murmansk. I explained we would have to secure the propeller and shaft to avoid them being damaged by free-wheeling while under tow. They readily agreed, and didn't seem to be too concerned with guarding our crew when they went below to secure the prop and shaft.

The tow to Murmansk took four days, and for all this time we had absolutely no idea what was going to happen when we got there. We were generally restricted to quarters, but were able to keep some systems operating (such as the generator), making meals in the galley, etc. I was allowed to stay in my cabin or visit the bridge, but since I was no longer in command I tended to stay away. Occasionally, however, I'd make a quick check to make sure everything was in order.

When we arrived in Murmansk, the *Ladoga* anchored in the port with the *Arctic Sunrise* lashed to her side. Later that same day an eighteen-member-strong international diplomatic delegation visited us on the the ship. One of the group, John Gimbel, was from the US Consulate in Saint Petersburg. He and I talked for a couple of hours. After describing to him the action and the subsequent events, I told him I didn't think it was going to be a big deal and that we'd probably be hit with fines of a few hundred dollars and let go in a few days. He was skeptical, but he didn't say I was wrong, either. He already knew, however, that the word going around onshore was that the Russians were going to throw the book at us and things were looking pretty dire. (Later, after we had been brought to the prison in Murmansk, we found out that the Russian prisoners knew we were in very serious trouble before we even arrived in the port. Everybody knew but us.)

After a few hours we were all brought ashore, under guard, to the investigator's office. The guards told us that we were only going to be away for a few hours, maybe overnight, and not to bring that much with us. I brought my toothbrush and my medication just in case (I have high blood pressure. I wonder why!?), but no clothes other than what I happened to be wearing. That night, however, the investigators told us that we were going to be charged with piracy, a charge that carries a sentence of ten to fifteen years or more. While the news of the piracy charges was a shock, we didn't really believe it would actually stick. It seemed ludicrous. We were certainly bummed, but still hopeful that Greenpeace would be able to secure our release in a few days.

The detention hearings began the next morning. We were all waiting together in a holding area when we heard that Putin had stated publicly that we were not pirates. That sounded pretty good and cheered us up a bit, but during the detention hearings we were all individually charged with piracy and our counsel (who had been arranged by Greenpeace) told us that we would be detained for at least sixty days.

Within a couple of days Greenpeace had gathered together thirty Russian lawyers—one for each of us. Many of the larger Russian law firms had refused to work with us. It was apparent they were afraid to go up against Gazprom and the state on our behalf, but Greenpeace was able to find enough brave (and/or dedicated, and/or dumb, and/or desperate) attorneys in short order.

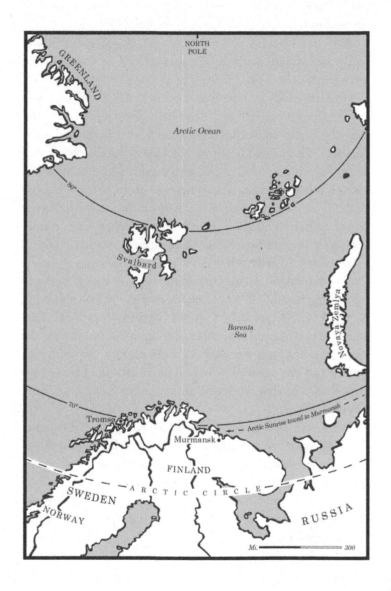

NORTH
POLE

GREENLAND

Arctic Ocean

80°

Svalbard

Novaya Zemlya

Barents
Sea

70°

Tromsø

Arctic Sunrise towed to Murmansk

Murmansk

FINLAND

SWEDEN

A R C T I C   C I R C L E

RUSSIA

NORWAY

Mi. ————————————— 300

16

"Don't Trust. Don't Fear. Don't Beg."

October 2013
Murmansk Detention Center SIZO-N1
125 miles north of the Arctic Circle

Prisoners in Russia have a saying that they live by: "Don't trust. Don't fear. Don't beg." Maybe it's a function of having grown up in the Soviet-era culture (and now in the Putin "democracy"), but it's deeply ingrained. In many respects, we were the bright spot in their lives. Prison-rights personnel, media, and reporters were all coming through the facility so the inmates were being treated better than they normally would be, and they enjoyed all of the attention and the break in the monotony of daily prison life.

The words "Russian prison" conjure dungeon-like images for most people, and I'm sure that in many cases that's accurate. Our group, on the other hand, was generally treated fairly well. It wasn't exactly the Ritz, but we weren't tortured or seriously mistreated. The hardest and most stressful part about the whole ordeal was the uncertainty of what was going to happen. The possibility of being sentenced to fifteen years in prison does tend to weigh on your mind.

* * *

The prosecutor/investigator, Sergey Torvinen, reminded me of a wolf. He would smile at me a lot, and seemed friendly, but the whole time we both knew it was his job to find a way to convict me and send me away for what would likely be the rest of my life. I remember when he had to tell me (weeks later) that the charges were going to be reduced to hooliganism. That just doesn't happen in Russia, and I knew that it was crushing him to have to tell me that.

During my stint in prison (both in Murmansk and later in Saint Petersburg), I kept a jailhouse diary, in part to keep me sane, but also to help me remember all of the little details and interesting anecdotes that I wanted to preserve for posterity. As you might imagine, in the prison there were many days where nothing noteworthy happened (in the very literal sense), but I did get to know all types of people, from a small-time pot dealer to one of Putin's top deputies with the improbable title of "Advisor to the President, Chairman of the Presidential Council for Civil Society and Human Rights." Talk about an oxymoron, but he really wasn't a bad guy—at least not to us.

I won't bore you with the day-to-day details because I was bored a lot of the time myself, but my jailhouse diary entries do capture some interesting moments and the wild and emotional roller coaster that we were all on.

The cell door slammed behind me and the echo clanged up and down the small hallway outside. The sound of the three dead bolts being thrown went right through me like a knife. In case they hadn't gotten their point across, the key was turned multiple times, loudly pushing around the tumblers. There was no getting out, and where would I go anyway?

In the cell with me was Dima Litvinov, our campaigner and chairman of the board of Greenpeace in Russia. We've known each other twenty years, and it was a real comfort to have him in the cell. We had been through a lot together, including—most recently—being strip searched, fingertip printed, fingerprinted, palm printed, and then having the soles of our feet printed.

The cell was about three meters by five meters, which is small—especially when you're a claustrophobic like I am. [I have been a claustrophobe for as long as I can remember. I have no idea why. There isn't any particular experience I can point to as the cause.] *If I am on an elevator and it stops for more than thirty seconds, I get a layer of perspiration on my forehead. At the end of the cell opposite the door there was a small, one-foot-square piece of opaque Plexiglas. We could tell if it was night or day, but that was it. They had taken my watch when I was processed into jail, so that the only way to know roughly what time it is is by how dark or light it is. I know from being in jail cells before that if I can see out of even a very small window, I can keep the claustrophobia in check. But I couldn't see out the window, and claustrophobia began to move in. I lay down on the bunk, and listened to my heart try to beat its way out of my chest.*

There was a small bench opposite the squat toilet—basically a hole in the floor.

I thought about pushing the guard's call button, throwing myself

*at his feet, and begging for a cell with a window. But I had the very
strong feeling that doing that would be as successful as trying to fly
out of here on a lead balloon. And I know if I do that, I will be in
worse shape than I am now. "Don't trust. Don't fear. Don't beg."
Right. So I lay in bed, listened to my heart, and tried to concentrate
on anything else.*

*The only thing that seems to help calm me down is making a
mental to-do list for my little sailboat at home. It is something I
have been trying to do for years, but never get around to. I guess I'll
have plenty of time to work on the list now, but who knows when,
or if, I'll ever see* Eyes of Fire—*my trusty little daysailer—again.*
["Eyes of Fire" is the name of the Cree woman who told the
legend of the "Warriors of the Rainbow," the inspiration for
naming our ships *Rainbow Warrior*.]

MURMANSK PRISON
FRIDAY, SEPTEMBER 27

*Initially, I was in the small cell with a friendly, middle-aged guy
who seems quite tickled to have an American cellmate. But later this
morning I was moved to a cell* [with a real window!] *that is larger,
with four bunks. It faces south. No TV, but at least I am alone with
some more space. In the afternoon I was taken for a chest X ray and
a blood test. They want to be sure that I don't get sick while I am
under their care. They don't want to be accused of harming us in
any way. I take it as a positive sign. This cell also has a real toilet.
Now we're talking!*

*This evening some Russian human rights people came to visit,
and I showed them that the water in the toilet has some kind of a
slick on the surface and told them that the water from the tap tastes
awful. God knows what's in it, so I asked them for some bottled
water and some fresh fruit too.*

But at least I have a larger cell and I'm by myself. That is huge in terms of the claustrophobia.

Today I was brought down to the Arctic Sunrise *to meet with the Russian investigator and an interpreter. Of course, nobody told me that was where we were going, so when we left the jail I didn't know to bring a jacket or anything. It was a nasty and cold day, but I was able to borrow a jacket* [from one of the Russian navy boats]. *From that experience I've learned that I shouldn't assume I am going to be told anything. I have to be prepared for just about anything at any time.* [I also learned pretty quickly to remember to go to the bathroom every time I was going to be taken out of my cell. I never knew how long it was going to be before my next chance.]

The Arctic Sunrise *was moored out in the harbor alongside the* Ladoga. *When we got aboard* Sunrise, *the investigator read out a long list of instructions for everyone. My instructions were different from the interpreter's, which were different from my lawyer's, which were different from the investigator's, the witnesses', and the experts'. Each one of us had to have our rights and responsibilities read to us individually. It was all very formal. You could tell everyone did things by the book. All during this time I was handcuffed, and handcuffed to a guard. It seemed that the handcuffs were a little bit of overkill, like they were afraid of me diving off the ship into the freezing water, then swimming about 3/4 of a mile to shore while wearing handcuffs, and then running 150 miles in freezing wet clothes to Norway without any money or being able to speak Russian. Still, they were taking no chances.*

We went up to the bridge, where they proceeded to rip out every hard drive they could find. They even took the monitor to the

ECDIS—the ship's electronic navigation and charting system. Every-one on board was hostile—looking at me like I was a dirty rotten scumbag who was going to jail for a long, long time. [The only exception was the government interpreter, who became my ray of sunshine for the next six weeks. She talked to me like a person, and tried to keep my spirits up. I really appreci-ated that.] *After lunch, they packed up all the equipment they had ripped out of the ship and we returned to the detention center.*

The guards in prison have been doing everything by the book too, but they are not giving me too hard a time. If they want to give you a hard time, it's pretty easy for them to do. One way is to limit your bathroom trips. If a guard is not happy, he can delay you for half an hour just to make a point. These guys never did that to me. One guard even gave me a closed-fist salute when no one was looking. It was like a pat on the back, and if he'd been caught doing that, it'd be a serious career-limiting move. That little gesture meant a lot to me.

MONDAY, SEPTEMBER 30

I noticed that above my cell door is a little calendar carved into the woodwork. There is a piece of string tied along the top of the num-bers with a little metal pointer you can slide along so as not to lose track of the date.

Today we went back to the Sunrise. *The first thing I heard is that Frank, our action coordinator, was going to be detained for two months for—get ready for it—"conspiring to harm the environment." Talk about ironic. That's right up there with the Seal Protection Act—an act passed by the Canadian government that made it illegal to get close to a seal unless you were licensed to club it* [as mentioned earlier]. *Kind of sounds Orwellian, doesn't it?! But the big thing is that the maximum sentence is three years, not ten to fifteen. Now we are getting somewhere.* [This seems to have been a completely bogus rumor, and not the first or last.]

On the way back, Alexander Mukhortov and I were put in a separate cabin on the ferry back to shore. [He preferred to be called Sasha. Sasha was hired by Greenpeace to be the ship's/owner's lawyer. Under maritime law the owner is represented even if they themselves are not incarcerated. Later, Sasha became my lawyer as well.] *Even though his English is very limited, just basic words, we found common ground in having second wives, daughters, etc. He told me that some heavy hitters are flying in from Moscow tomorrow to straighten the whole thing out. He is very optimistic. We shall see.*

WEDNESDAY, OCTOBER 2

This was a bad day. The investigator met us on the ship. The first thing he did was point out that there was a bag of "drugs" in Katya's backpack. Katya had picked a few wildflowers in Norway and was saving them to be dried and pressed. The investigator called it a "poppy plant" and confiscated it.

We then went down to my cabin, which was supposed to have been sealed as a "crime scene." The investigator removed the crime scene tape, which looked like it could be removed and put back pretty easily, while another investigator was filming him. The lead investigator was being a bit dramatic. He opened my desk drawer and found the key to the ship's safe. "Aha," he said. "I have found the key to the safe!" I know for a fact that I had hidden the key behind some binders on a high shelf before we were taken off the ship, and it would have taken someone a pretty good long time to find it. Despite the crime scene tape and the fact that no one is supposed to enter the cabin, this guy claims he just found the key in the drawer. He was

*clearly falsifying evidence, and that made me—understandably—
paranoid. God knows what else he was going to "find" in the safe.
He could have put anything in there.*

As it was, we had morphine and cash in the safe. The morphine is required by IMO regulations for all ships. (IMO
stands for the International Maritime Organization, which
is part of the United Nations.) Later on, to make us look as
bad as possible in front of the judge, the investigator used the
morphine as an excuse to claim he found drugs onboard. To
the Russian public (and our legal team), this indicated that
the investigators had a very weak case. Many felt that the
drugs were either planted by the authorities or simply non-
existent. They understood that these ploys are used with some
frequency when there is little actual evidence.

Thursday, October 3

*Half of us were dragged off to the investigator's office today. We are
now officially accused, not just suspected, and there was no reduc-
tion in the charges. The charges are quite humorous, or scary. They
actually say we are not environmentalists but only pretending to be.
How do they make this shit up?*

Friday, October 4

Vlad, my roommate [I had been moved to yet another cell,
where I would remain while I was in that prison] *made me
shoelaces today. They take your shoelaces, belt, and watch as soon as
you go to prison. Up until now I've been doing a real perp walk—*

holding my pants up—and I had no shoelaces. Vlad made a string
out of an old sweater and made me some shoelaces. It was a really
thoughtful present.

A couple of weeks later, I got an "e-mail" from our Dutch
chief engineer, Mannes Ubels. When I say "e-mail," what I
mean is a note carried on "The Road." The Road is a convo-
luted system of strings that the prisoners run outside the walls
of the prison from their windows. They use the strings to
carry messages contained in socks that are tied to the strings.
This is all done with the full knowledge of the prison guards.

Apparently, a few years before, a prison warden had let
the prison get completely away from him. Inmates were moving between cells at night and—incredibly—ripping up floors
so they could move between tiers of cells. The prisoners even
had big parties. When the word got out, the warden was replaced but the new warden went too far. There were riots
when he tried to ban The Road. So now everyone looks the
other way and the system is allowed to continue.

Mannes's note from The Road said that the Dutch consul
told him that we would all be staying there (in the Murmansk
prison), and the remaining eight crew members would be
transferred there as soon as there was room. The note also
gave me a full report of the condition of the *Arctic Sunrise.*
He had been brought out to the ship by the Russians to show
them how to take care of it while it was in their custody. It
was a very thorough and detailed report, which I appreci-
ated. He ended this dry report with a note that Po Paul—a
rather rotund member of our imprisoned crew—had lost so
much weight already that "he can now see his own penis."
Keeping a sense of humor was a great way of coping with the
stress.

Sleep deprivation and uncertainty about our situation added to the stress. Vlad–the local prisoner who was my cell-mate–was a chain-smoking insomniac who spent most nights cursing loudly while running new strings for The Road and passing along messages. We were meeting with our lawyers just about every day, but these meetings were anything but reassuring. My lawyer, Alexander "Sasha" Mukhortov, had no idea what was going to happen to us.

The next day Alexander and I met with the special prosecutor, who read to us a lengthy list of charges against me. As I listened to them I was thinking, *five years.* Then they got to the particulars and the translator said R20K (20,000 rubles) fine and no jail! This kind of fine was what we had been expecting based on our prior experience in other situations (and the prior action at the rig the year before), and it beat the hell out of facing a sentence of ten to fifteen years! I walked out feeling like a million bucks.

A short while later, however, we found out this was merely the fine for entering the exclusion zone for the oil rig. The piracy charges were still in force and I was still facing living most of the rest of my life in a gulag. It was just the beginning of the wild emotional ride we would experience over the months to come.

Greenpeace's lawyers put together an offer to post bail for us, and the Dutch government pledged that they would be responsible for our appearance in court if bail were to be granted. Each of us had to have our own separate bail hearing. By the time my turn came (I was pretty close to last), I had heard through the grapevine that none of the other crew had been granted bail.

When my turn came, I was put in a cage in the courtroom. There's nothing like being put in a cage to make you look guilty. The translator had to whisper to me through the bars, and what she was telling me was horrific. The prosecutor was claiming that Greenpeace was an organized crime group and that we attacked the rig with weapons for our own personal gain. This was all about making the case for being charged with piracy.

Once or twice during the day I was able to say that in my forty years of experience I have never been accused of anything like this. We denied the charges and refuted the facts, but at the end of the day, the judge didn't give a rat's ass for the fine arguments of my lawyers or my statement. The judge gave a long statement ending with "Bail denied!" and popped out of court so fast it was like she had magically disappeared. It was clear that everyone was following marching orders from a much higher level.

To make matters even worse, I found out from a US consul that the US government had just shut down over the debt ceiling debate. This was sure to slow down any efforts the US State Department would be making to help us. (In truth, the State Department ended up doing very little to secure our release.)

WEDNESDAY, OCTOBER 16

Today I got my first phone call, but Maggy wasn't home. It was between 8 and 9 A.M. island (Islesboro, Maine) time. I am afraid my voice, which was strong at the beginning, broke at the end of the message. About the last thing I wanted to do was cause her more worry, but it was too late. It upset me.

We would occasionally get care packages from Greenpeace, friends, and family. Usually we would get fruit or other foods, items of clothing, miscellaneous things—like a pair of earplugs—to make prison life a little more tolerable, and lots of books. I received several Harry Potter books, which I enjoyed immensely. Less enjoyable was a Russian-English dictionary/phrasebook. I couldn't help but wonder if someone was trying to tell me I was going to be in Russia for a very long time. I shuddered just thinking about it.

FRIDAY, OCTOBER 18

The ride back to the cell was another three-hour ordeal. Those trips are exhausting. There always seems to be a one- to two-hour wait in the transfer cells when we get home. I got back to the cell just before the 8 P.M. inspection. I stepped outside the cell, put my hands on the wall, spread my legs and got patted down. When the guard was done, I put my hands behind my back, as we are supposed to, and just stared at the ground. One of the officers in the inspection team stepped up to me, put his hand on my shoulder and said, "Are you OK, Captain?" Just when you lose hope, somebody throws you a life ring. I don't mean to say I was losing hope, but it was the end of a long, bad day. I smiled at the guard, and said "spacibo" ["thank you" in Russian]. It was a really nice thing for him to do. I went to bed much more hopeful than I would have been otherwise.

We had been incarcerated and investigated for a month when suddenly all of the Russian investigators were removed from our case. We didn't have a clear idea as to why they had been changed, but it just added to all of the uncertainty. Maybe one of the higher-ups thought they were being too soft on us? Were there new marching orders for them? The old saying about "the devil you know versus the one you don't" seemed appropriate.

The new team of investigators took us back to the *Arctic*

Sunrise several times to take a look at things for themselves. They removed more equipment and took even more pictures. To some of us, it appeared that they were trying to prove that they were even more thorough than the original bunch. They seemed a little nicer (although later that turned out not to be the case), and they even let me walk around the ship without handcuffs. What freedom! Luxury!

After several attempts to reach my wife, I finally was able to connect with her at my parents' house. My father, Roger, is in his nineties, and my stepmother, Joan, is in her eighties, so I had to face the prospect of never seeing them alive again. It felt good to hear my wife's voice, and I tried my best to sound positive and upbeat but wasn't sure I succeeded.

A few days later one my guards got hugely upset when I threw out a crust of bread. Since he didn't speak English and I don't speak Russian I had no idea what the big deal was. Finally a lady from Russian human rights told me that this anger went all the way back to World War II when 1.5 million Russians died of starvation and disease during Hitler's siege of Leningrad (now Saint Petersburg). To this day, many Russians still abhor the wasting of any food. Even if it is not edible, they'll feed it to pigs so absolutely nothing goes to waste. We can all learn a lesson from that. The growing of food (both crops and livestock) is a significant contributor to environmental devastation (it's one of the reasons I'm a fish-eating vegetarian), and wasting food just adds to the total damage.

WEDNESDAY, OCTOBER 23

One bit of very, very good news is the "marijuana" in Dr. Katya's bag was dried flowers she was doing artwork with. I guess

Hatchet-Face [the lead investigator] *never saw pot before. I suppose he had a thrill announcing he had found drugs on the boat. I am hugely relieved. That was a bad moment.*

The investigators had been touting the finding of the "drugs" for some time, but when they had to do an about-face and admit that they had misidentified (or misrepresented) the dried flowers, it was hugely embarrassing for them.

what to do when your
husband is in a
Russian prison —

1. pinch yourself — this
   is real — it only feels
   surreal

   You now have 2 lives
   to lead

   You are the
   captains wife
   which, in this
   circumstance
   carries a responsib.
   thought you were

strong? well, its not
enough. you dig.
deeper. And deeper still
and learn to be thankful
that he is alive,
that he is not being
mistreated.

17

One Happy Hooligan

Thursday, October 24

Red letter day, I guess. Maybe. My guard met me on the way out. Also there were a bunch of toughs, all cuffed behind. They went to another paddy wagon. We went to the investigator's office building. Sat around in the nice van (with windows) and then Olysha showed up. First thing she said was, "You are not a 'pirate' anymore." I would have kissed her, but the last thing I want to do is piss her off. Turns out we are now "hooligans." The difference? Zero to seven years versus ten to fifteen years. Big emphasis on the zero. *But the biggest difference is that Sasha* [the lawyer] *thinks we will be released tomorrow. "I am sure of it," he said. I do not know what the definition of "hooligan" is, but I would bet it has property damage in it, so they will have a hard time proving that one too. But the big thing is that he says we will be out tomorrow. I am ready.*

―――――

I have never wanted to leave this place more. Sasha [My cell mate, not my lawyer. "Sasha" is a very popular nickname in Russia.] *kept me up all night again, but I still got up at 5:10, ready to go. But I am not going anywhere. At ten, the guards came to get me for exercise. While I was walking the cage, I imagined myself giving a talk at Putney (my high school) or someplace else. "You snooze, you lose." It was a good speech, and put me in a much better frame of mind.* [Interestingly, the following summer I would make a commencement address at Putney titled "Oh, the Places You'll Go," inspired by the Dr. Seuss book.]

The IMO court will decide the case by mid-November. As Russia is not sending any lawyers, the IMO are expected to rule in our favor. I have no faith that the legal team will be able to put a case together for the IMO. Then I hear that they are trying to take the case to the International Court of Arbitration in Geneva, a process I know is likely to take two years.

Dima [another lawyer, not the Russian Gp Dima] *said the prosecutor was not sure how he could charge us with hooliganism, as we were never near the rig. So tonight I am not expecting to get released anytime soon. But I am still optimistic about getting out at the end of this detention period, in another month.*

Sasha [the lawyer] *said I look like Robinson Crusoe. It's only been three days since I shaved my face, but my hair is getting pretty long. I could use a haircut, but the only haircuts I have seen around here are done with clippers.*

Lazy day. Heard some crew talking at exercise, saying the prosecutor is trying to split us apart into activists and non-activists. This is what Sasha [the lawyer] *was worried about. I was so down during exercise I did not call out or talk to anyone. Not for the first time.*

SUNDAY, OCTOBER 27

On the building across the yard, there is a porch. The porch has a lightbulb on the wall inside the overhang. There are many large icicles hanging down. When I looked at it last night, I thought, Oh, someone has put up a row of icicle lights. *Then I realized,* No, it's the real thing! *It was so beautiful. It must have been just at the freezing point, because it seemed like there was some water running down the icicles, making them twinkle. So cool.*

I put in a complaint about Sasha [the cellmate] *late in the afternoon. Complaints and requests get picked up Sunday evening. While I was napping, the little bugger read my note, and now he is not happy about it. I did not realize his English was so good. Well, I am sorry, but not that sorry. Later that night I got a note* [via The Road] *from Roman* [Dolgov, a Russian crew member and fellow prisoner] *saying we had to stop complaining about things at the prison, because we are going to turn the rest of the population against us. Oh well . . .*

After several more legal proceedings, statements, and appearances, we were officially charged with hooliganism. Hooliganism is becoming a catchall charge in Russia for anyone who pisses them off. Eighteen months before the arrest of the Arctic 30 (as we were now called), the girl band Pussy Riot had been arrested and charged as hooligans. Regarding the charge of piracy, we were in a strange situation. From what our lawyers were telling us, the Russians were having trouble figuring out a legal way to *drop* the piracy charges. That tells you how often people are found not guilty in their system.

Meanwhile, the Russian prosecutors were trying to split us up and turn us against each other. They kept trying to convince one of the crew to sign statements against the rest of us in return for being released. He was resisting, but he was slowly getting worn down. He told us that he was done with Gp and wanted to see his family again. For my part, I was still committed to Greenpeace. Just as I had felt after the bombing of the *Rainbow Warrior* in 1985, the fact that we were going through this was proof that we were having our intended impact.

TUESDAY, OCTOBER 29

So at inspection this morning, the angry crust-of-bread guy walks in. I check him out, and he has three big stars on his shoulders. He looks right at me, and says in a very challenging voice something in Russian. Someone else translates: "Do you have problems?" So I say right away, "No, no problems!" He puffed once or twice, looked around, and stamped out. So I reckon he is the big boss. I think if I had asked for a single last night, I would be in the isolation cell, in the basement, right now.

Exercise time today was a horrible joke. It's raining out, and everything is melting. The exercise cell was either under a couple inches of water, or frozen ice. There was one three-foot spot along the far wall where I could get out of the rain. Mostly, I just stood in that spot, and wondered how the hell I had gotten here. So much for exercise.

I got a care package today and I found two big pictures of Maggy (one with me in it), and I went right over the moon. Now the pictures are right over my bed, where I can look at them all day. I am one happy boy! But . . . Always in my mind when I look around this cell is: They have not dropped the piracy charge. The hooligan charge carries up to seven years. And they will most likely do another sixty-

day detention. This is not over by a long shot. Yes, I am getting used to it, but I am not liking it.

The prosecutors were still working on splitting us apart, trying to get one of us to "turn." Dima Litvinov, the GPer descended from a family of Russian dissidents, had been placed in "the cooler" (isolation cell) for a couple of days to encourage him to sign a statement against us, but he didn't cave. My lawyer suspected that because I was the captain they would try to add to the charges against me to try to make an example of me. He felt, however, I would probably be released with everyone else, but he was making no forecasts as to when that would happen. Greenpeace, and its growing team of lawyers, was of the opinion that we would be released sometime before the Winter Olympics in Sochi, Russia. They felt that Putin wouldn't want the negative publicity to overshadow the Games. But that was still a few months away, and it gets mighty cold in Murmansk in the winter. It's well above the Arctic Circle and the record low for November is minus-23 degrees Fahrenheit. Even more depressing, in another month the sun would go down and not come back up for a few months. That certainly wasn't going to help my claustrophobia or my mood.

THURSDAY, OCTOBER 31

When we got back [from a meeting with the investigators] *I was put in a holding cell. That's no drama at this point, but after ten minutes, two more guys came in. Fortunately, they did not have cigarettes. One of them spoke pretty good English. Said he was a very small-time drug dealer; just sold to his friends. He was twenty-four and got ten years. Then five more guys came in to this little holding cell, which is not meant for more than three people, really. Then of course they all started smoking, and I started freaking. All the guys knew who I was: Peter Willcox, captain of the* Rainbow Warrior. *I was kind of surprised by this. But I guess everyone in Murmansk knows we are here.*

FRIDAY, NOVEMBER 1

Today I got taken to a room up on the fourth floor, which was some kind of a meeting room. Two guys—one in a suit, one in a plain shirt—said they were from "Special Services" or something like that. The suit started to talk, but the other guy was such a shitty translator it was really hard to figure out what they were trying to say. They made the point that I was responsible for the crew being here. I did not like it, but agreed anyway. They then spent a long time saying if I made a statement, things would be better and we would go home. . . . In the end, they might have thought they convinced me, but if they think I am going to make a statement without my lawyer, they are smoking crack.

Later, when talking with some of the other Arctic 30—especially those who were Russian—the general consensus was that the two guys were FSB, members of the Russian government's internal security service. They seem to all have the same haircuts, and it's a dead giveaway.

Rumors were circulating that we would be transferred to Saint Petersburg in the next few days. I had mixed feelings about this. On the one hand, we were moving south. And while Saint Petersburg's winter weather was better than Murmansk's, you wouldn't confuse it with the weather in Saint Petersburg, Florida. On the other hand, Saint Petersburg was also where the investigators and prosecutors were headquartered. And we would be much farther from my ship. The human rights lady told me she wasn't sure how we would be transported—it could be by prison train or some kind of bus. Once again, the uncertainty of when, where, and why started gnawing at me. I had no facts, and even worse, no control over my future.

THURSDAY, NOVEMBER 7

Went to the boat today. A generator is still running. The investigator seized five out of six RHIBs ["seizing" is the legal term for arresting the boats, even if they don't take possession of them. The *Arctic Sunrise* had been seized earlier. *For some reason he did not seize the* Avon [another RHIB] *on the starboard rail. It would have been a lot worse if they had actually taken the boats off the ship. But they left them all on board. Oh, today I had to wait forty-five minutes or more in a holding cell to get out. Really do not like those holding cells. The balaclavas were pretty nice today. Just heard "Capitan de Greenpeace" on the radio news. Not a clue. Now I am shitting again.*

FRIDAY, NOVEMBER 8

Got my copy of the Islesboro Island News [my wife's newspaper] *today. It is such a gift. Naturally I started with an editorial Maggy had written about me. It chokes me up every time. I get about four good sobs in, and then my big-boys-don't-cry reflex action kicks in and everything stops. I wish I could cry. My daughters say it always makes them feel better.*

Quiet day. Exercise pit 7. [This was the good pit because you could actually see a sliver of the sky!] *Then around 4:30 P.M., the jail rights lady came for a visit. She had a one-page typed paper on how to survive the move to Saint Pete. She said 90 or 95 percent chance we will go in plane or passenger train. But if we go by prisoner train, then we are fucked. The prisoner train takes two to three days. There are cells with four bunks in them, but they often put twenty prisoners in them. And they don't let you out to go to the bathroom. I am praying. . . .*

Spent the day (part of it) reading the I. I. News. *I am so proud when I read "Maggy Willcox, Editor." And I miss her so much. Better stop. I am losing it again.*

More people coming in the cell telling us to be ready for the big move, and to dress warmly. I still don't believe they are going to fuck us with a prison train, but ya never know. After all the non–paddy wagon rides of the last two to three weeks, I do not see them going backward.

Was told we would be woken up at 4:30 for a 5 A.M. departure. I hope I do not miss the old place when I see what waits for us in Saint Pete!

Being moved down to Saint Petersburg was a little nerve-racking. After several weeks in Murmansk I was fairly well settled into a routine that was at least familiar. I had heard that the prison in Saint Petersburg was the oldest in Europe, and that certainly sounded like it wasn't going to be any nicer than where I was. Elena, our prison/human rights representative in Murmansk, was the one who told me about the transfer. Even my lawyer didn't know, and the prison staff in Murmansk didn't know. I had just told Maggy that I was at least comfortable where I was, but right after that she had found out in a November 1 call from John Gimbel, who had "heard from Moscow," that we were being moved. It broke her heart that I had no idea what was coming. Of course, winter was approaching and the Murmansk prison might have been an entirely different world at minus-30 degrees. John had been in communication with Maggy on an almost daily basis and seemed to have his finger on the pulse. When he had told her that the charges were being reduced to hooliganism, he advised Maggy not to get too hopeful. He was very good at not letting her get too optimistic or too pessimistic.

Elena had explained to me that there were three options for the thirty-six-hour transfer down to Saint Petersburg. The best was a fairly standard bus ride, which would be great. The second-best option was a passenger train car—the most likely. The worst was a prison train—not heated, twenty people in a six-man cell, no toilet. It'd be pretty rough. She felt that we were past that point as we had been treated fairly well, all things considered.

Our group was loaded into two buses. The windows had been covered so we couldn't see out of them. The buses stopped and we stepped right into option number three—the worst option, the prison train. My heart sank. As I looked around, however, I could see that this was a brand-new prison train car, and it didn't look nearly as bad as Elena had led us to believe. This was, at least, somewhat encouraging.

The prison train was the first time the Arctic 30 had all been together since getting off the ship. I was in a cell next to the women, and I enjoyed listening to their chatter and laughter combined with the rhythmic sounds of the tracks beneath us. When someone needed to go to the bathroom, as they walked through the center aisle between the cells, everyone would high-five them through the bars along the way. It made all of us feel good.

Thirty-six hours later we arrived in Saint Petersburg.

Mi. ━━━━━━━━━━━━━ 200
▭▭▭▭ Murmansk - St. Petersburg train

Barents
Sea

• Murmansk

FINLAND

RUSSIA

Helsinki
St. Petersburg •

ESTONIA

18

Igor Kills Me Twice

The prison railcar taking us from Murmansk to Saint Petersburg had been hitched to a regular passenger train, and after the regular passengers were let off, the train was backed into a separate siding. They clearly didn't want to give us any additional visibility or coverage. We were split into three groups, loaded into three prison buses, and brought to three different prisons. After being all together on the train, the separation added to the anxiety of facing the unknown.

I was sent to Kresty Prison—officially the "Investigative Isolator Number One of the Administration of the Federal Service for the Execution of Punishments for the City of Saint Petersburg." Built in the late 1800s, it is the oldest prison in Europe and still the largest. The history of the prison includes many famous political prisoners, including Leon Trotsky. The Kresty is so famous it even has its own Facebook

page with—believe it or not—twenty-one likes. I am not one
of them.

Our group exited the bus and found ourselves in a small
courtyard inside the prison walls. We couldn't see anything
of the outside. We were brought down to the basement, strip-
searched, officially processed into the prison, fingerprinted,
etc., and then brought to our cells. My cell had been painted
so recently the paint was still wet; the fumes made my eyes
hurt. Even the windows had just been replaced with new
double-pane windows. The whole frickin' cell had been re-
furbished! The Russians were clearly aware of the media coverage we were getting, so they wanted to look as good as
possible. In hindsight, it seems that everyone knew we were
going to be let go; they wanted to give us as few reasons to
complain as they could. Dima, the Russian crew member,
told me later that he was not nearly as lucky: his cell made
Murmansk look like a palace. Being Russian, and the son of
a Russian dissident, had given our hosts a reason to single
him out for harsher treatment.

Tuesday, November 12

*Got to the Saint Pete prison around noon, and I was "injected, in-
spected, detected, infected, neglected, and selected"* [a nod to Arlo
Guthrie, whom I had met very briefly through the *Clearwater*
and Pete Seeger] *and put away. The cell is about half the size and
I have a roommate. So it sucks. The view is a bit of a large canal*
[the Neva River] *out to the left and a Russian Orthodox church to
the right.*

*I am not doing very well. Is this shit ever going to end? I would
like to see my lawyer or consul John Gimbel. Gimbel knows my blood
pressure drugs are running out. . . . My roomie Igor is twice my size*

but very nice. He has been here eighteen months. I do not know what for. He is at least very hygienic. We do not talk much. All in all, I would much rather be back in Murmansk.

WEDNESDAY, NOVEMBER 13

Got a copy of the prison rules in English. Tried to read them but quit when I got to the part about how the family of the inmate can recover his body. The prosecutor [new for Saint Petersburg] *stopped by after dinner. They all had a good laugh when I said Igor "killed me twice" at chess today (they saw the board out). I almost asked him what he was going to do with us. But I chickened out.*

Fairly soon after my arrival at the Saint Petersburg prison, I was visited by a group of three very imposing men—with big brass attitude—and lots of stars on their shoulders. They were the entourage for the fourth man who handed me a business card that read "Dr. Mikhail Fedotov. Advisor to the President, Chairman of the Council of the President of the Russian Federation on the Development of Civil Society and Human Rights." Imagine that—Putin's human rights guy . . . what a contradiction! He asked me how I was. Anytime I had been asked that question, I was always careful to respond, "You tell me!" Fedotov replied, "Your problems are almost over." This is a man who speaks for the president! That made me feel pretty damned good.

My Russian roommate, however, was in shock. He thought "your problems are almost over" could only mean one of two things: 1) They were setting me up to get taken out and shot, or 2) I was going to be let go. Given that 99 percent of prisoners in Russia are found guilty, he was betting on number one, "shot." As for his fate, he was about to be convicted for selling pot and sentenced to twenty-five years in Siberia. He enjoyed being in the cell with me because he knew we weren't going to get picked on for keeping the TV on too late at night. I was probably the best thing that was going to happen to him for the rest of his life. That helped me keep things in perspective.

Our future seemed to be getting a little clearer. In a week or so, the trial would begin in Saint Petersburg. The legal teams were hopeful that we would be exonerated, but given the general reputation of the Russian justice system, and the specifics of our situation, no one was going to be caught making any hard and fast predictions.

SATURDAY, NOVEMBER 16

So now I am on pins and needles waiting to see if John Gimbel says the same thing. But the fear is gone. Temporarily? I just do not feel it anymore, and I wonder if that is a good thing. I have decided it's fine. It can't be good to live with the constant anxiety and stress. If Gimbel has bad news on Monday, I will just go back down the tubes at that time. This whole thing would have been a relative walk in the park if they had said at the beginning, "Two months and then you go." But I am sure that they know that.

So about two hours ago I pounded on Dima [Litvinov]'s wall to find out how to say "private chess lessons." But before I could ask him, he told me that the hearings next week were not the trial, but a hearing about three-month extensions for detention. So my heart did a nosedive, and I crawled up on my bunk and stared at the ceiling, which is only three feet away. Totally bummed. Then, ten minutes ago, he told me that he had just been to the head of the prison. The guy told him that they are going to start releasing us next week. A few at a time. Fuck me! I am mush.

MONDAY, NOVEMBER 18

Got up this morning and saw a beautiful full moon over the church. My cell in Murmansk faced north, so I never saw either the sun or the moon. I have now decided to take the heavenly observations of the last two days as a good sign. Not that I have always read the signs correctly. Note the rainbows in New Zealand in 1985 [just before the bombing]. *But I am taking this as a good sign. Now we will see what happens.*

It turned out that we were all going to go through bail hearings. It seemed that Dima's information from the head of the prison was going to come true: we were going to get out! The next day, however, I saw a clip of the bail hearings for some of the crew on TV; they were looking very dejected. I didn't understand the Russian newscasters, but the crew certainly didn't look like they were being let out. That really threw me for a loop. I started preparing myself for another three months of prison, but I tried to remain calm and tell myself—as I always do—"it is what it is."

Later that night, I was able to talk to Dima over the wall of the exercise yard. Dima's cell had a TV, and of course, being Russian, he could understand the newscast. That's when I was surprised to hear that we were all getting bail. Wow, talk about a head spin! Still, I wondered why they had looked dejected. I found out the next day when it was my turn before the judge.

I was taken from the jail and put into a bare isolation cell in the courthouse basement. From there, I was brought up to the courtroom itself for the hearing. I was handcuffed behind my back, accompanied by four guards, and placed in a cage before the judge. Through the bars, I could see many

Greenpeacers in the courtroom, including action coordinator Al Baker. Al kept making little bird-flying-away pantomimes with his hands. That made me feel pretty good. There was still a risk, however, that as the captain I would be treated more harshly than the rest of the crew.

Before the judge started reading, John Gimbel whispered over to me that "Maggy is watching this on the live feed and she says you look good." That was the second time John told me something in court that just lifted me right out of there. I spent the rest of the hearing with my left hand gripped around one of the bars so that my wedding-ring tattoo would be prominently displayed. I hoped Maggy could see it.

My heart began to sink as my translator began translating the judge telling the court all of the reasons why I should not be granted bail. It seemed to go on forever, but I was watching the clock and it went on for a full eight minutes. She had a lot of reasons to keep me in jail.

I had an additional lawyer, along with Alexander. He was an older guy specializing in criminal law. He did most of the talking. I quite liked him. At one point the prosecutor said if I was released, I might flee the country. So the new lawyer questioned me:

"Do you have your passport?"

"No. I have no idea where it is."

"Do you have any identification at all?"

"No, my wallets were taken away in Murmansk."

"Do you have any bank cards?"

"No, I have nothing at all."

He then looked at the prosecutor. Point made.

After summarizing the lengthy list of reasons why I should be kept in jail, the judge suddenly switched gears and started talking about all the reasons why I *should* be granted bail. Another head spin! It finally dawned on me that she had merely been outlining the prosecutor's case, and that was why the crew had looked so dejected on the TV the day before. I'm sure I was looking pretty dejected after that too. When she began reviewing the reasons for granting bail my hopes began springing up again. After a few minutes, both of my lawyers started giving me the thumbs-up. The judge paused to render her decision. . . .

"Bail is granted."

The cramped courtroom was instantly filled with the sounds and flashes of cameras. Wow. This was a perfect analogy for the whole two months I had been in prison. All that time I had no idea what was coming, what was going to happen next. I can't say I was elated, though. Being brought right back to the detention cell didn't leave me in a celebratory mood. The guards had already heard about the decision. They were exceptionally surprised that I got bail because that almost never happens in Russia. They treated us like VIPs–very important prisoners–until we were allowed to leave a couple of days later.

As we were processed out for bail, I got my passport back, my personal items, and even the old Casio digital watch that I've worn since 1984. I walked down a long hallway with a thick steel door at the end. It was a side exit of the prison. As I got closer to the door I could hear some activity on the "freedom" side.

When the door swung open, I was immediately faced with a throng of media and supporters. A young Danish lady, Birgitte Lesanner, who had been sent by Greenpeace to escort me from the prison to our hotel, told me I didn't have to talk to anyone if I didn't want to. "Hey," I replied, "I've been in prison for two months. I *want* to talk!" She let me make a few statements before politely reminding me that while I had been granted bail, I was still under indictment. Anything I said could still be used against me. That shut me up pretty fast, but not immediately.

We got in the car, and my lawyer, Alexander, handed me a flask full of brandy. I took a couple of good, celebratory belts of it as we headed off for the hotel. I never looked back.

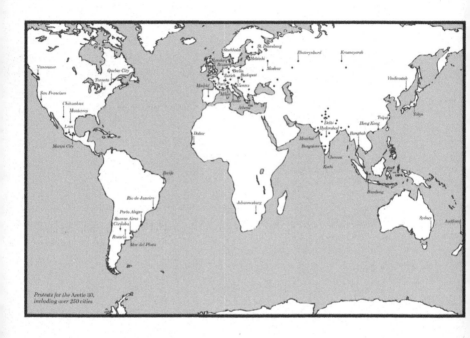

Vancouver
Quebec City
Toronto
San Francisco
Chihuahua
Monterrey
León
Mexico City

Stockholm
St. Petersburg
London
Brussels
Helsinki
Moscow
Berlin
Paris
Budapest
Zurich
Vienna
Madrid
Milan
Rome
Athens
Dakar

Ekaterinburg
Krasnoyarsk
Vladivostok

Trieste
Delhi
Tokyo
Hyderabad
Mumbai
Hong Kong
Bangalore
Bangkok
Chennai
Kochi

Seville
Rio de Janeiro
Porto Alegre
Buenos Aires
Cordoba
Rosario
Mar del Plata

Johannesburg

Bandung
Sydney
Auckland

Protests for the Arctic 30,
including over 250 cities

19

Twelve Nobel Prize Winners, a Beatle, and the Pope Can't All Be Wrong

Maggy had been watching a live Greenpeace feed in our home in Maine, anxiously awaiting the moment when my head would pop out from behind the huge prison door. Just before I walked out, the video feed was lost and she missed the big moment. She didn't know I was out until I called her from the car to tell her I was drinking Alexander's brandy.

While I was relieved to be out of jail, during the car ride from Kresty Prison to the hotel my joy was tempered by worrying about the reception I would receive there from the Arctic 30 who had been released before me. Would they blame me for their incarceration? I had certainly made decisions that contributed to our arrest and the arrest of the ship, but then again, not one of us had anticipated the muscular response from the Russians. As I exited the car and walked into the lobby of the hotel, my concern grew. Would they vent their anger at me, or would I just get the cold shoulder?

The first people I saw were my shipmates Sini, Camila Speziale, and Alexandra "Alex" Harris. They saw me in the same instant and immediately moved toward me with their arms raised. I realized the three were all opening their arms to me. Seconds later we were in a group hug. Their shoulders were anything but cold. It was the best I had felt in a very long time.

The hotel had been selected by the police so they could keep an eye on us while we were out on bail. We assumed the hotel was bugged, and there was an undercover cop in a van parked across the street from the hotel. While we wanted to give him the finger, we would flash him the peace sign instead. That probably pissed him off even more. Having him there was their way of keeping us under pressure. The peace sign was *our* way of saying, "We don't give a shit."

Although we were out on bail, we were still under indictment and not allowed to leave the city. It was kind of like being in purgatory, but after being in prison it was still a major improvement in living arrangements. I was able to see my wife, my daughters, Skype with friends, and—of course—be interviewed by newspapers, Web sites, and TV and radio broadcasters all over the world.

At this same time, Putin was preparing a mass amnesty bill. Officially, the amnesty bill was to commemorate the twentieth anniversary of the Russian constitution. The reality was the bill was an attempt to polish up Russia's record on human rights just weeks before the start of their Winter Olympics. Our lawyers were hoping that the Arctic 30 would be included in the bill, but no one knew for sure who was included or not. The more publicity we got, the better the chance we'd make it into the bill, so we focused on that.

In prison we had been cut off from the outside world. We were pretty much in the dark (literally, in some cases) and just trying to keep our spirits up. There were a few TVs in prison, but since the government controls the media we didn't see any news covering the efforts to put pressure on Putin to release us. We got some reports via our lawyers, Greenpeace, letters and, eventually, phone calls with loved ones, but that was just the tip of the iceberg.

Every written word we received in the prison was read by the Russians and translated into Russian before we got them. Everything we received had typed notes with Russian translations that were taped or stapled to the originals, including the "Free the Arctic 30" greeting cards made by eight-year-old children in Africa. I still have a stack of them with all of the Russian translations.

Now that we were on the outside, it was just becoming apparent to me (and to the rest of the Arctic 30) just how much publicity we were getting. It's an amazing feeling to realize that hundreds of "Free the Arctic 30" protests demanding your release have taken place in dozens of countries around the world. Words can't describe it, so I won't try. The bottom line is that the international reaction makes me believe that what Greenpeace is doing is deeply appreciated and important.

Thousands of people had protested in front of numerous Russian embassies. Letters from statesmen, world leaders, religious leaders, celebrities, actors, and media figures from every corner of the globe joined in the effort to release us. It's an impressive list, and it's not just the *length* of the list that's amazing, it's the *breadth* of it: twelve Nobel Prize winners. Paul McCartney. The Pope. Madonna. (It's not too often that the pope and Madonna are in agreement on anything!) Angela Merkel, François Hollande, and David Cameron. Desmond Tutu. Even the V.P. of Iran, Dr. Masoumeh Ehtekar (she's also the head of Iran's EPA) supported us. The list goes on and on.

One protest letter that was especially important to me was written to Putin by Pete Seeger, the family friend, folksinger,

> TOSHI & PETER SEEGER
> BOX 431, BEACON, N.Y. 12508
>
> Nov. 19, 2013
>
> To President Putin
> Moscow, Russia
>
> Dear President Putin -
>
> I am an American singer of songs, and have given performances in Moscow (Tchaikovsky Hall) when I was young (I am 94 now).
>
> I am one of thousands now who believe you should let Capt. Peter Wilcox out of jail to explain why they climbed an offshore oil rig.
>
> Thank you very much for reading this letter. I'm sure you'll make the right decision.
>
> The people of the world are watching.
>
> Sincerely
> Pete Seeger

This is the note that Pete sent to Putin. It's fair to say that it was probably one of the last things he ever wrote.

and my boss on the *Clearwater* so many years before. It was Pete who put me on the path I was still following years later. Pete passed away at age ninety-four just a few weeks after I got back to Maine, so I never saw him again.

When you're in prison you have a lot of free time on your hands. Often you find yourself thinking about happier times and places and people that you miss. A lot of those times were with Pete, singing and sailing and saving the river.

It was hard on Maggy to have me imprisoned in a hostile country, particularly since it happened such a short time after we were married. And a good chunk of that time I had been at sea on other actions. For her part, she always put up a brave front, and never stopped fighting for our release. She helped organize rallies from Maine to Connecticut, wrote letters and editorials, and urged governors and senators to write Putin. Maggy was a real emotional anchor for me during this stormy period of false dawns and dark threats. She's an amazing woman and I'm lucky to have finally landed her.

All of us in Saint Petersburg (the Arctic 30, family, friends, lawyers, diplomats, and supporters) were holding our breath until the amnesty bill was passed. When it passed, it released close to twenty-five thousand prisoners—some petty criminals, some political prisoners, all kinds of people—but *not us.* The bill did not include "hooligans"—our "category of criminal." It was, yet again, another shock and disappointment. Still, there was *some* hope. A few days later, the Duma (the Russian legislature) passed an amendment to the bill that included those charged with hooliganism—that meant us, and Pussy Riot, among others. We were greatly relieved, of course. We were close to home free. ("Home" and "free," two words that will always mean a little more to me now.) Still, we had to wait for the inevitable paperwork to get processed, etc. Who knew how long that was going to take? It looked like "I'll be Home for Christmas" wasn't in the cards, but we were hoping to be back in time for New Year's.

There is a video called "Thank You" that Greenpeace put together after we were released. It shows highlights of the protests all around the world, and then we—the Arctic 30—thank all of the people who took action to secure our release. (You can watch it yourself. Search YouTube for "Arctic 30 thank you for your support." I think I speak for all of us when I say that if it were not for all of their support, we might still be languishing in a Russian prison somewhere. Thank you. Thank you. Spacibo. Spacibo.

A few days after our amnesty was granted, Maggy and I were driven by a volunteer Aleksandr "Sasha" Kharitonov (yet another Sasha) to the airport. He's an engineer on the *Esperanza* (the Gp ship) and had specifically asked to be our driver. He had been exceptionally helpful to Maggy and me while we were at the hotel waiting for my release. When we finally got our tickets and papers, Maggy and I made our good-byes and hopped into Sasha's car to be driven to the airport. Just in case I was detained or delayed, I told Maggy to go through Immigration and Security before I did. I also gave her a phone number to call in case something happened. After over thirty years of doing this kind of stuff, you learn how to anticipate what might go wrong. Being just a little paranoid is often helpful: a lesson that had been reinforced during the prior three months! Maggy was allowed through without a hitch. She then had to watch helplessly as I was stopped by the officials. She feared the worst, that she was going to be forced to leave the country while I would have to stay behind.

What was actually happening was that the immigration officer did not see an entry stamp in my passport. It was a typical bureaucratic glitch. The Russian Coast Guard had brought me into the country as a prisoner, and therefore the immigration office didn't have any paperwork showing how I entered the country. Immigration needed to match an official entry form to my exit visa: without an entry stamp, they couldn't give me an exit stamp. Officially, I had not "entered," and therefore I couldn't leave without having "officially arrived." It was a classic bureaucratic, Catch 22–like situation. A senior officer came by a few minutes later. He took one look at me and my passport and ordered the others to immediately process me *into* the county and then *out.* I quickly filled out an arrival card (they didn't have to ask me twice), my passport was stamped, and I was through. That made Maggy happy, me happy, and I'm sure the border officials were just as happy to have us gone.

I walked over to Maggy and took my phone back. As we walked up the stairs to the departure lounge to await our flight, the phone rang. It was a "babysitter" from Greenpeace congratulating me for making it through. They had put an observer in the immigration area to make sure we got out. I was impressed with both their care and thoroughness. While I was often uninformed and/or confused about what was going on throughout this ordeal, I always knew that Greenpeace was going to do everything they possibly could to help us out.

Many hours later (it seemed to be forever), we arrived in Boston's Logan Airport, tired from the long flight. But after being in a Russian prison for a few months, the cramped quarters and bad airline food seemed like first class to me. (Not that I've ever been in first class!) We spent the night in Boston, flew to Maine the next morning, and then took the ferry from the mainland to our home on Islesboro Island.

Arriving at the house, we were greeted by the reality of having to shovel through four feet of snow just to make our way to the front door. It was the dead of winter in Islesboro, and since Maggy had been with me in Saint Petersburg, our driveway hadn't been plowed in weeks. Shoveling deep snow-drifts in your driveway doesn't seem all that bad considering I could easily have been breaking rocks in Siberia. I guess that's the bright side of having been in a Russian prison: the grass is always greener on the outside.

Not too long after we reached the front door, Maggy and

I were sitting by a roaring fire. That's when I really felt I was home. It was a nice, warm feeling. A great feeling. But I knew it wouldn't be very long before the sea—less than a mile from our fireplace—would call me back. There's a long-standing maritime tradition to come to the aid of anyone at sea who is in peril. So when the ocean itself is in trouble, I can't refuse the call.

Epilogue

Put your good where it will do the most.

—*Ken Kesey*

You may have heard the expression "You're either on the bus or off the bus" (Ken Kesey, as quoted by author Tom Wolfe in *The Electric Kool-Aid Acid Test*). For the last forty years I have wanted to be on the bus. That the bus has been a series of ships and boats working toward any one of the social issues affecting us is just a by-product of the way I was brought up in the family that I was brought up in.

Another expression is "We're all in the same boat." That's us. That's Earth. Everyone's in the same ecological boat, and we're sinking our own planet-boat by drilling holes in it while ignoring the fact that it's causing the water to rise faster and faster. Whether you believe in global warming or climate change or whatever, pollution is pollution is pollution. I have a lovable, slightly dimwitted, little mutt named Deacon. Even *he* won't shit in the house. But we so-called *sapiens* do it all the time. In what world is dumping dioxin into our own food chain in the ocean a good idea? Sadly, the answer is "this one." Some people think I'm stupid for standing in front of a harpoon gun, but the human race is standing in front of its own harpoon gun while pulling the trigger at the same time. Sometime soon, the cannon that we're pointing at ourselves is going to go off. *That's* stupid. Trying to stop it from going off *isn't.*

Greed is always a powerful motivator for our species. Now we are letting our greed dictate how we live on our little planet, a planet that seems to get a bit smaller every day as our population grows. It is too familiar a story. It was cheaper to dump nuclear waste in the ocean—out of sight, out of mind. It was easier to use the Marshallese as guinea pigs in nuclear experiments than it was to build their country as the US promised to do. It's cheaper to dump your toxic waste in another country than it is to recycle it at home. The list goes on and on.

Will the battle against our own shortsightedness ever be won? I've never been much of a dreamer. The only reoccurring dream I have is that I've been reincarnated from some kind of pirate. He must have been hung for his crimes, because to this day I can't stand to feel anything tight around my neck. I even cut open the necks of my T-shirts and sweatshirts. (And you can forget about neckties. Not even for my own wedding!) I don't fantasize there will be this sudden, massive moment of global self-awareness. Yeah, right, *that'll* happen.

I have a rusty old Toyota with about 280,000 miles on it. (About two-thirds of the number of miles I've sailed around the Earth.) I've never made a lot of money. I live pretty much the way I did when I first started working on the *Clearwater* forty years ago. Most people feel that I've made great sacrifices to do what I do, but I don't see it that way at all. Life has been very rewarding for me. I have no regrets. (Well, maybe wishing I'd seen my daughters a little more, but I've been away working to defend the environment that they'll be living in after I'm gone, so I'm good with that.)

Despite all of the horrendous things I've seen, I still have a pretty upbeat attitude. It's probably because I'm constantly surrounded by people who give me hope. The crews of the ships I've sailed on. Greenpeacers. All the locals and volunteers I've met who are willing to do something to make a difference in their own little corners of the world. Amazonians. Inuits. Pacific islanders. The fact that I get to sail all around the world to help save the boat we're all in together is a pretty cool way to be living life. What more could I wish for?

I guess I could wish for more people to do something, even if it's something small, to protect and defend our environment. And if the environment isn't your thing, then do something good for something that you *do* care about; maybe a social issue like caring for the elderly, or helping to fight a disease like malaria or cancer. Not only will it help make the world a better place, it'll make a difference in your own life. Any small gesture you make, or any small difference you make, will make a *big* difference in you. It's not about giving something up and feeling noble about it; it's really about feeling good about yourself and your contribution to the community.

I grew up in a real community, and I sometimes think we've lost that sense of being a part of a whole. There's no denying that we are, but we also get so caught up in our own lives that we miss the bigger picture. We are literally losing the forest for the trees.

I like to take things one step at a time. Start with doing

one small thing on one day. If it makes you feel good, do it again. Pretty soon you might find it's a habit—like yoga or going to the gym—that makes you happier and healthier. Take it from me. It's not really a sacrifice. It's a reward.

Acknowledgements

So we shall let the reader answer this question for himself: Who is the happier man? He who has braved the storm of life and lived, or he who has stayed securely ashore and merely existed?

—Hunter S. Thompson

How can you thank everyone for an entire lifetime of incredible experiences? I was extremely fortunate to get involved with Greenpeace all those years ago. And I still feel that way. I tried making a comprehensive list of my Greenpeace colleagues and crew. It got way too long; but the support and camaraderie from all of you has kept me fighting for the environment and human rights after more than thirty-five years. I am lucky enough to have friends in Auckland; Moscow; Buenos Aires; Waiheke, N.Z.; San Francisco; Amsterdam; Manaus, Brazil, and a few hundred other places in every corner of the globe. (I am very grateful for the existence of Facebook!) I have been inspired by so many of you. If I have returned the favor by providing even a small fraction of the inspiration that I've received, I consider that to be my proudest professional achievement.

I would like to thank my parents—all four of them. Roger and Elsie Willcox, my official parents (they adopted me at the age of three months), started me off in the right direction. Both were people fully committed to peaceful ideals, and Dad still is. (Elsie died in 1973.) Joan Willcox, my stepmother for the last thirty-five years, is also close to me. And my bio-mom, Eleanor Sharpe Fraleigh (who I met about twelve years ago), is also a good friend. My daughters, Anita and Natasha, have more grandmothers than they know what to do with. And that's not a bad thing. Thanks to Eleanor, I now have three biological half-sisters and a half-brother to go along with my "real" brother and sister, plus two stepsisters and a step-brother.

North Country School in Lake Placid, N.Y., in the Adirondack Mountains, was the first—and really *only* place—where I had any academic success. It was also the best thing that happened during my childhood. It's a magical place. Later, Putney School was another very positive influence. Thank you to all the faculty and friends that I met in both schools, especially for the patience.

I met folk singer/activist Pete Seeger and his wife, Toshi, sometime during my childhood. Pete claimed it was when I was still in diapers, and he's probably right. Getting to know them right out of high school when I was a mate on the Hudson River sloop *Clearwater* made a big impression on me. Two people so committed to each other and what they were trying to do was a great template for a well-lived life. They had more energy and accomplished so much more than a teenager could believe. When I became the boat's captain a few years later, Pete was trying to step back from being on the *Clearwater* quite so much. He wanted the focus to be on the Clearwater Foundation and the need to clean up the Hudson River. As a result, I did not go up their hill a quarter as much as I should have. And it was my loss completely. I know they are another huge part of why I am still doing what I am doing.

At some point in my youth, our family motto became "When all else fails, go sailing!" There is no better way to learn how to sail than to go racing. I have been big-boat racing since I was ten or eleven, when my father would bring me along on races. Morty Engle, Jack Sutphen, Jonathan Asch, Andrew Weiss, and the whole *Christopher Dragon* crew taught me so much over the years. My father—at age ninety-five!—still goes out racing on his little dinghy in New York in the winter time. As he demonstrates, sailing is a sport for life. Plus it's a lot of fun.

I have been lucky to have had several best friends: Jon Asch, Andy Chase, Jack Steel, and Ross Williams. We stay in touch. And no matter how many years it's been since we've seen each other, it's always easy to pick up where we left off. Sailing is how we all met, but friendship keeps us together.

The main reason I am still defending the environment is that I am trying to ensure that there will still be a liveable planet for my daughters, Anita and Natasha. (And now Maggy's son—my stepson—Sky Purdy.) It's an infinitely richer life for me with them in it. My daughters are both sailors. As I write, Anita is in India doing research for her master's degree thesis, "Casual Recycling of Electronic Waste." Natasha is studying marine biology at the University of Rhode Island. And she's on the sailing team, which makes her father very happy. Sky and his wife Marianne are both serious outdoor types in Denali, Alaska, as I write.

A big thanks to my sister, Bani, for helping me so much with the "Maggots" (my term of endearment for Anita and Natasha—it's strange, I know, but they don't seem to mind) during the eight years we lived in Norwalk. Bani and her husband, Patrick, live in the house my dad built, just a hundred yards through the woods from our family's house in Norwalk. It sometimes seemed like the girls were there more than at home.

When the Arctic 30 and I were released from prison in Russia, two of the first people Maggy and I went to visit were our friends Ron and Marty Weiss. "Free the Arctic 30" protests all around the world had generated huge amounts of publicity. Ron, a marketing guy, let me know that the potential for a book would soon "sink like a stone in the Atlantic Ocean." He advised that I strike while the iron is hot and volunteered to get the ball rolling. My agent, John Silbersack (another sailor) at Trident Media, had been working for a while to sell the book, but we could never find the right writer. After reading Ron's sample rewrite, John got enthusiastic and convinced Ron to complete the job. A few months later we had a deal with Thomas Dunne Books and St. Martin's Press. Our editor there, Marcia Markland, has been very supportive and wonderful to work with. Huge thanks to all of you.

My wife Maggy and I dated in the late 1970s when we both worked on the *Clearwater.* We stayed in touch. Finally, in 2011, we were both single at the same time and we were married a mere six months before I was taken prisoner in Russia; hardly a honeymoon. Maggy has made a wonderful home for us on Islesboro Island in Maine. Having a loving wife waiting for me makes going to sea harder and harder, but I know I am truly most fortunate.

Last, I would like to sincerely thank Russian president Vladimir Putin. Without your "two-month, all-expenses-paid vacation in Russia," this book never would have happened. President Putin once said in an interview that when's he's done running Russia, he would like to be an inflatable boat driver fighting for the environment. President Putin, when the time comes, let me know and I promise I'll have a boat all warmed up and ready for you.

Index

www.sandstonepress.com

![f] facebook.com/SandstonePress/

![twitter] @SandstonePress